The Oracles of the Ancient World

The Oracles
of the
Ancient World

Trevor Curnow

Duckworth

First published in 2004 by
Gerald Duckworth & Co. Ltd.
90-93 Cowcross Street, London EC1M 6BF
Tel: 020 7490 7300
Fax: 020 7490 0080
inquiries@duckworth-publishers.co.uk
www.ducknet.co.uk

A catalogue record for this book is available
from the British Library

ISBN 0 7156 3194 2

Typeset by Ray Davies
Printed and bound in Great Britain by
Biddles Ltd, *www.biddles.co.uk*

Contents

This book is dedicated to

the memory of my parents

Archie Curnow (1910-1999)

Marion Curnow (1916-2001)

Acknowledgements

Many people have contributed to the writing of this book in a variety of ways, and it is a pleasure to acknowledge them here. Deborah Blake of Duckworth showed faith in the book when it was at a very rudimentary stage and helped to guide it to its completion. She is also responsible for the excellent maps. Maria Chippendale of the Division of Religion and Philosophy at St Martin's College, Lancaster, allowed me to 'consumer test' several parts of the book on her and provided invaluable moral support when occasion demanded. The college itself also contributed by providing some funding for fieldwork and a period of sabbatical leave in which to spend it. Dr H.R. Goette of the German Archaeological Institute in Athens gave me access to the Institute's wonderful photographic archive. The illustrations of Delos and Kos are from there (all the other photographs in the book are my own). Dr John R. Hale of the University of Louisville was generous in supplying materials relating to his research at Delphi. Danielle Kemp helped with the selection of photographs. Dr K.P. Kuhlmann of the German Archaeological Institute in Cairo, and Director of German Excavations at Siwa Oasis, found time to meet me at very short notice and bring me up to date with developments at Siwa. Professor Jennifer K. Berenson Maclean of Roanoke College arranged for me to see some pre-publication extracts from a new translation of Philostratus' *Heroikos* relating to the oracle of Protesilaus at Elaius. Professor Bruce MacLennan of the University of Tennessee, Knoxville, provided invaluable help on dice and letter oracles. Dr Daniel Ogden of the University of Wales Swansea drew my attention to important research on the Nekromanteion at Ephyra that I had completely overlooked. I first heard about the Asclepeion in Jerusalem from Dr Philip Shand. Professor T.G. Wilfong of the University of Michigan responded in fulsome fashion to my enquiries concerning Karanis. Dr David Woods of University College Cork helped to fill in some of the gaps in my knowledge of Byzantium. Paula Wakefield was a source of encouragement and shared a memorable visit to Karanis. Finally, of all the places I stayed in on my travels connected with this book, the Manolya Pansiyon in Bergama and La Belle Hélène in Mikines stand out as providing levels of hospitality way above and beyond the call of duty. Thanks to all.

Lancaster   T.C.

October 2003

Conventions

A number of conventions have been used throughout this book, and an understanding of them should both help the maximum benefit to be derived from it and minimise unnecessary confusion. They relate to cross-referencing, spelling and references.

Oracular sites are written in bold capitals, for example **DELPHI**, the first time they appear either in the introduction or in any individual gazetteer entry. On the same principle, items dealt with in the glossary appear in ordinary bold, for example **Pythia**.

The transliteration of place and personal names is ridiculously problematic. Arabic, Greek and Latin all pose their own difficulties, and this book deals with all of them. The difficulty is compounded by the fact that some places in Egypt, for example, have at one time or another had names in all three languages! To list every possible option would be remarkably tedious, and take up space better devoted to other things. Consequently, I have had to develop or adopt a number of principles in the hope of simplifying matters without distorting them. They may not all be equally clear, defensible or consistently applied, but I have at least tried to inject some method into the madness.

As a general principle, oracular sites are listed under their ancient names rather than their modern ones (where the two differ). Modern names are preferred only where the ancient one is unknown. However, with the conquests first of Alexander the Great and then of the Romans, many existing places came to acquire either a new Greek name or a new Latin name or both. Sometimes they resembled the earlier names, sometimes they could be quite different. Fortunately (as far as this book is concerned), the most commonly encountered examples concern Latin alternatives to Greek originals, and here some simple principles of transformation were routinely followed. So Greek place names ending in '-on' ended in '-um' in their Latin forms (so Pergamon became Pergamum), while '-os' became '-us' (so Termessos became Termessus). In such cases, I have generally favoured the Greek originals, although there are a few exceptions, such as Ephesus, where the Latin alternative seems, for whatever reason, to have become so firmly established as the norm that to use an alternative would appear perverse. In any event, the similarities between the two versions of such names are unlikely to lead to any serious confusion. With personal names, I have opted for the '-us' ending throughout (e.g. Menelaus rather than Menelaos) as this is the form most commonly encountered.

Another complication arises with the Greek letter kappa. Although the Romans had a letter 'k' they became increasingly reluctant to use it, preferring instead their own 'c'. Here I have taken a mixed approach. Sites within Greece beginning with kappa (such as Kassopi) are listed under 'K', which reflects their spelling on contemporary Greek maps. Those outside Greece are listed under either 'K' or 'C', depending on which form is more commonly encountered in the literature and on maps (so Cyrene not Kyrene). Whatever loss there is in consistency should be offset by the practical advantages in actually tracking the places down. Cross-references have been provided where confusion is most likely to occur. In the case of personal names I have used 'c' throughout (so Sophocles rather than Sophokles), again on the principle of familiarity.

The Greek letter phi also poses problems, as it is sometimes transliterated as 'ph' and sometimes as 'f'. Here I have always used 'ph' for the ancient names of both people and places (e.g. Phigalia), but 'f' appears in modern names (e.g. Figalia) when this seems to be the presently preferred form. However, it should be pointed out that not even the best Greek maps achieve consistency with regard to phi.

In the case of Egypt, I have generally opted for Graeco-Roman names rather than ancient Egyptian names, where alternatives exist, as these tend to be more easily recognisable (so Heracleopolis Magna rather than Henen-nesut). With regard to Arabic names, I have always used 'el' rather than 'al' for the definite article. My general aim has been to try to use what seems to be the most common transliteration in each case, while having to make some adjustments in the cause of consistency. I have therefore used 'kom' rather than 'qom' throughout, for example, even though the latter is certainly sometimes encountered. A little persistence should be enough to overcome any initial confusion.

Different problems arise with Turkish. Although it uses the Roman alphabet, it has proved technically impossible to reproduce all of its diacritical marks. So 's' is sometimes to be pronounced 'sh', and 'g' is sometimes silent. Rather than trying to represent the differences phonetically, I have reluctantly chosen to ignore them. This makes it rather easier to find names on maps, but rather more difficult to pronounce them properly.

All of the above rules have been tempered in the direction of common sense in those very few cases where an anglicised version of a place name is so widely used as to be clearly the standard. So there is no mention of Korinthos or Corinthus but only of Corinth.

Everything that has been said here may give the impression that things are more complicated than they really are. In practice, anyone who looks for a particular site in the book should be able to locate it with little or no difficulty as long as it is here. Purists may find some of my conventions less than ideal, but they have been designed to make life as easy as possible for the average reader. If any offence is caused, I hope that at least the reasons for it are understood.

My system of referencing is also intended to compromise consistency for the sake of helpfulness. Modern texts are cited in the form of author and date, followed by page number if appropriate, for example, Aune 1983, p. 20. Full details of the texts are to be found in the bibliography. Ancient texts are cited according to their traditional divisions. In the case of Herodotus, for example, this is by book and page number (so III.21), whereas for Pausanias it is by book, section and sub-section (so IV.13.6). The aim is to make it possible to track down the relevant passage in the original text and in any translation. The translations I have actually used appear in the bibliography. Readers should be aware that there is a slight difference in the numbering of sub-sections between the Frazer and Levi translations of Pausanias. Here I have opted for the Levi system.

It should also be pointed out that it was decided at an early stage of the project that for various reasons it would not be possible to include a full scholarly apparatus in the book. References are therefore relatively thin on the ground. Academics may find this frustrating, but in most cases the bibliography should indicate the obvious sources for materials. If it doesn't, Google may be able to track them down.

The only abbreviations I have used are, I think, self-evident.

Plates

30. Pagasai.
31. Patrai. Entrance of shrine.
32. Perachora. Temple of Hera Akraia.
33. Phlious. Church of Zoodochos Pigi.
34. Piraeus. Temple of Asclepius.
35. Mount Ptoon.
36. Sikyon. Fountain.
37. Skotussa.
38. Sparta. Theatre.
39. Thebes (Greece). Ismenion.
40. Therapne. Shrine of Menelaus and Helen.
41. Thermos. Temple of Apollo Lyseios.
42. Titane. Inscribed stone from the Asclepeion, built into the church wall.
43. Avernus. 'Temple of Apollo'.
44. Cumae. Entrance to the Sibyl's cave.
45. Baiae.
46. Pompeii. Temple of Isis: purgatorium.
47. Puteoli. 'Temple of Sarapis'.
48. Adada. Temple of Zeus Sarapis.
49. Claros. Temple of Apollo: underground chamber.
50. Cyaneae.
51. Didyma. Temple of Apollo.
52. Ephesus. Prytaneion.
53. Hierapolis. Temple of Apollo.
54. Limyra.
55. Magnesia on the Maeander.
56. Olympus. Oracle tomb.
57. Patara. Temple.
58. Pergamon. The sacred way.
59. Pergamon. Temple of Sarapis.
60. Priene. Sanctuary of the Egyptian Gods.
61. Sura. Temple and spring.
62. Termessos. Ruins of the city gate.
63. Smyrna. Temple of Athena.

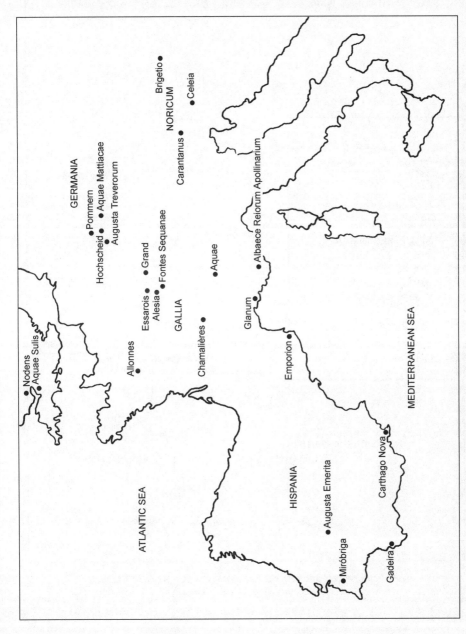

1. Oracle sites in Spain, Portugal, France, United Kingdom, Germany, Austria, Slovenia and Hungary.

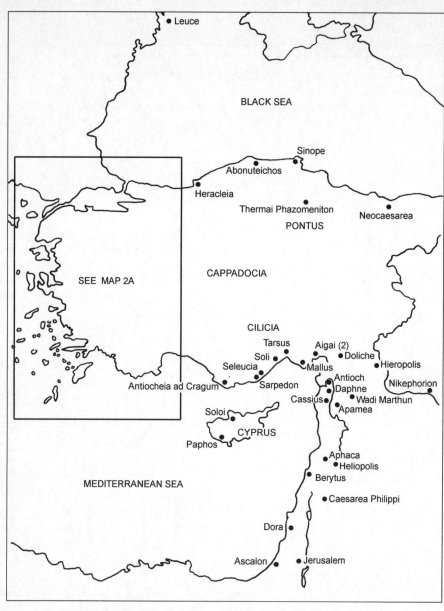

2. Oracle sites in Turkey, Syria, Lebanon, Israel, Cyprus and Ukraine.
For detail see 2A (on facing page).

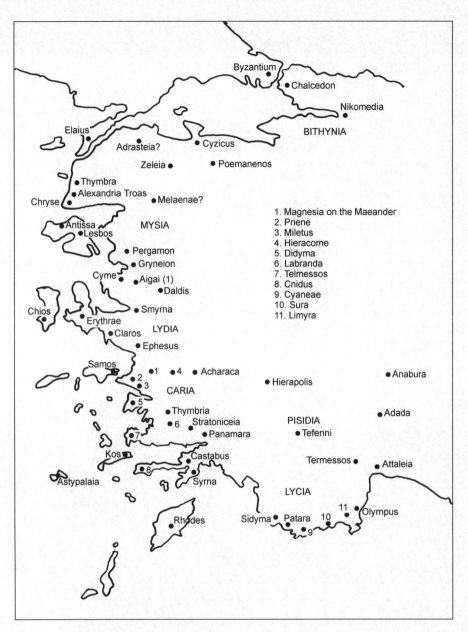

2A. Detail of Map 2: oracle sites in western Turkey and the Dodecanese.

Byzantium
Chalcedon
Nikomedia
BITHYNIA
Elaius
Adrasteia?
Cyzicus
Zeleia
Poemanenos
Thymbra
Alexandria Troas
Chryse
Melaenae?
Antissa
Lesbos
MYSIA
Pergamon
Gryneion
Cyme
Aigai (1)
Daldis
Chios
Smyrna
Erythrae
Claros
LYDIA
Ephesus
Samos
1
4
Acharaca
2
3
Hierapolis
CARIA
5
Anabura
Thymbria
6
Stratoniceia
PISIDIA
Adada
7
Panamara
Tefenni
Kos
Castabus
Termessos
Attaleia
8
Astypalaia
Syrna
LYCIA
11
Rhodes
Sidyma
Patara
10
Olympus
9

1. Magnesia on the Maeander
2. Priene
3. Miletus
4. Hieracome
5. Didyma
6. Labranda
7. Telmessos
8. Cnidus
9. Cyaneae
10. Sura
11. Limyra

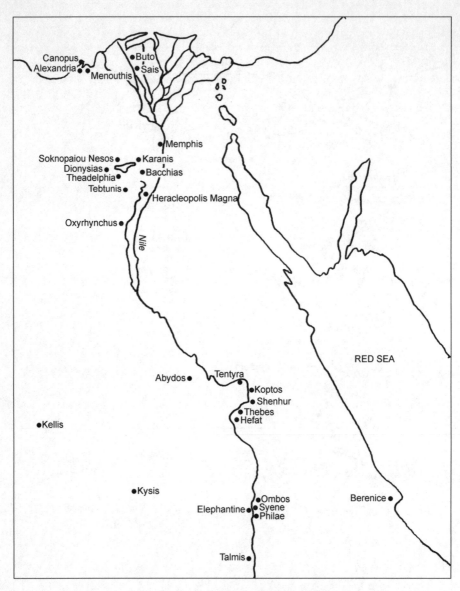

3. Oracle sites in Egypt; see also Maps 6 & 8.

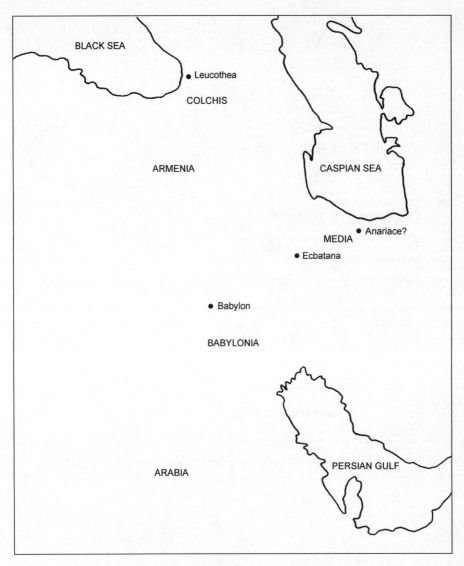

4. Oracle sites in Georgia, Iran and Iraq.

5. Oracle sites in Albania, Bulgaria and Romania.

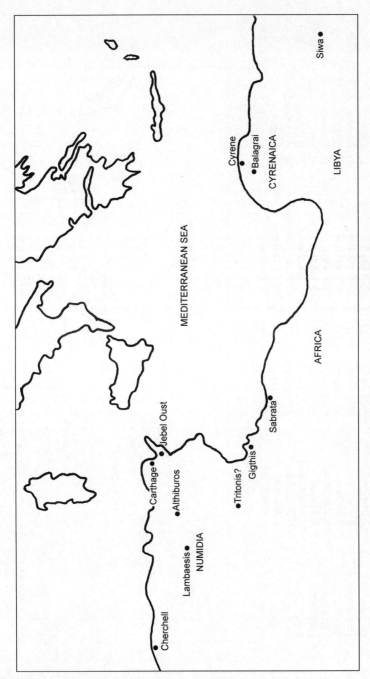

6. Oracle sites in Algeria, Tunisia and Libya (including Siwa in Egypt).

7. Oracle sites in Greece.

1. Skotussa
2. Delphi
3. Amphikleia
4. Tithorea
5. Panopeus
6. Lebadeia
7. Koronia
8. Orchomenos
9. Tegyra
10. Hyettos

11. Onchestos
12. Thespiai
13. Thebes
14. Eutresis
15. Kithaeron
16. Oropos
17. Rhamnous
18. Marathon
19. Megara
20. Pharai (1)

21. Patrai
22. Bura
23. Aegira
24. Lousoi
25. Pheneos
26. Pellene
27. Sikyon
28. Perachora
29. Corinth
30. Titane

31. Kenchreiai
32. Asine
33. Epidauros
34. Hermione
35. Halieis
36. Lykaion
37. Mantineia
38. Achladokampos
39. Megalopolis
40. Pamisos

41. Pharai (2)
42. Abia
43. Gerenia
44. Leuktra
45. Thalamae
46. Las
47. Gythion
48. Hyperteleaton
49. Asopos

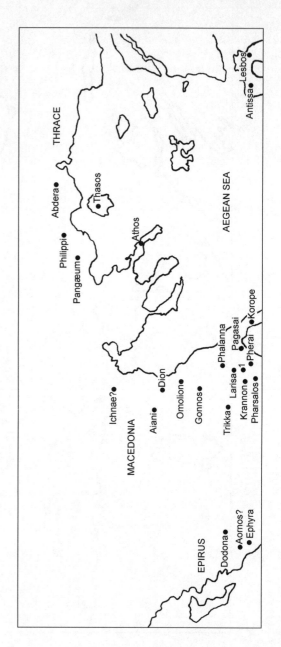

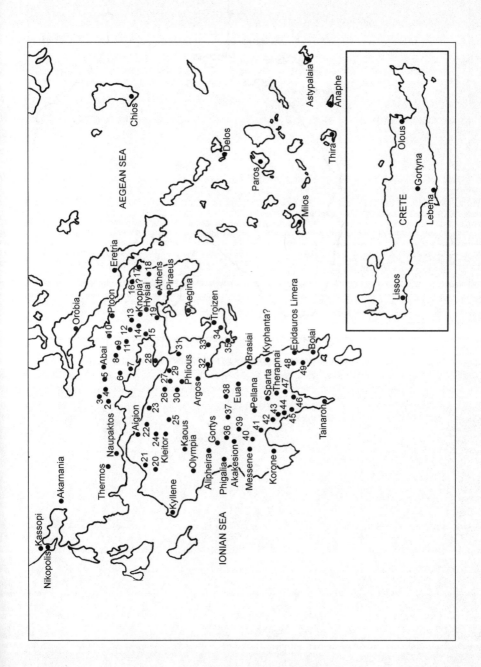

AEGEAN SEA

Chios

Delos

Paros

Milos

Astypalaia
Anaphe
Thira

CRETE
Olous
Gortyna
Lebena
Lissos

Orobia
Eretria
Ptoon
Abai
16 Knopia?1
13 Hysiai 18
12 10 Athens
14 19 Piraeus
9 15
8 7 28 Aegina
11 6 29 31 Troizen
5 27 32 33 34
4 26 30 Phlious 35
3 2 Naupaktos 23 Argos Brasiai
Thermos 22 25 36 37 38 Eua Kyphanta?
Aigion 24 39 Pellana Sparta 48
21 20 Kaous 40 43 Therapnai 47 Epidauros Limera
Akarnania 44 45 46 49 Bojai
Kassopi Kleitor 41 42 Korone Tainaron
Nikopolis Olympia Phigalia Messene
Alipheira Akakesion
Gortys
Kyllene

IONIAN SEA

XXV

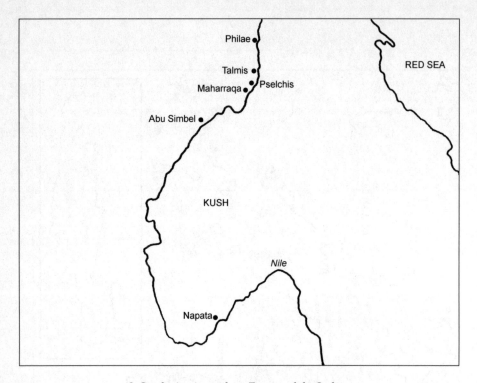

8. Oracle sites in southern Egypt and the Sudan.

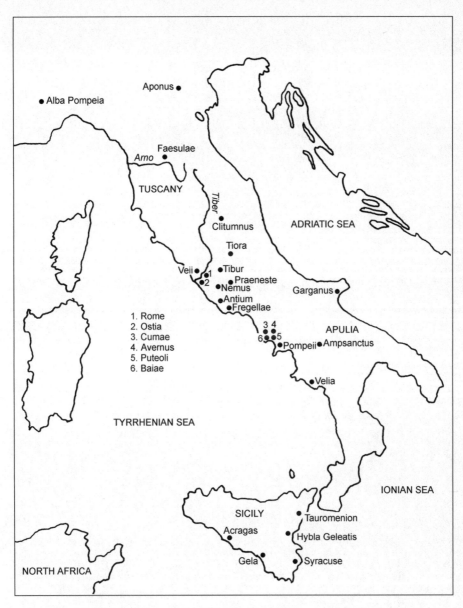

9. Oracle sites in Italy.

xxvii

Introduction

I first became interested in the subject of oracles many years ago when I was engaged in research on the subject of wisdom in the ancient world.[1] Two things in particular quickly became apparent: first, that oracles were regarded as an important source of wisdom in the ancient world; secondly, that there were far more of them than I (or, I suspect, most people) had realised. At the time, however, my focus was on the content rather than the sources of wisdom, and so I had to put the subject of oracles to one side while I concentrated on other matters. However, I made a mental note that, when time permitted, I would return to the subject in order to investigate it at greater depth. This I have subsequently been able to do. Over the past few years I have sought to collect information on all the oracles I could, and visit as many of the locations as possible. The outcome is this book, with information on around 300 oracular sites, of which I have visited about a third (principally in Egypt, Greece and Turkey). Details on the sites will be found listed country by country in the gazetteer section, with supplementary information provided in the glossary. The aim of this introduction is to provide some general background to the topic against which the details can be better understood.

What is an oracle?

As with many simple questions, this one has no simple answer. Indeed, it is the variety rather than the uniformity that stands out. More than once I have had to reconsider my views on the subject, and that will doubtless happen again. However, in order to be able to decide what to include and what to leave out, I have had to come up with at least a working definition of an oracle, even if it is neither a final nor an authoritative one. For the purposes of this book, therefore, I regard an oracle as a place where people go to make a special kind of contact with the supernatural. Having given this definition, I will try to explain what it means.

By an emphasis on place, I distinguish oracles from prophets. Taking the prophets of the Old Testament as reasonably typical, prophets may be

---

[1]The results of this research can be found in Curnow 1999, pp. 11-80.

1

thought of as people who claim to receive messages of a divine origin. In this respect, their resemblance to oracles is quite substantial. However, Old Testament prophets were individuals who could, and usually did, move from place to place, and who, in due course, died.[2] Oracles, on the other hand, were institutions rather than people. Some, such as **DELPHI**, certainly made use of people as mouthpieces for the god. However, when one **Pythia** died, she was replaced by another. At **CLAROS**, people performed this function for only a year each. Yet at both places the oracle itself continued to operate for centuries. Some oracles, such as the **dice** one at **TERMESSOS**, dispensed with human intermediaries altogether. The principal exceptions to this emphasis on place were those few oracles that revolved around a **Sibyl**. However, even these were less exceptional than might at first appear. Each Sybil was clearly identified with a particular place, and the Sybils' legendary long life-spans conferred on their oracles a special kind of durability. So this book is above all about places.

In order to understand the special kind of contact individuals sought at oracular sites, it is necessary to understand a little about how religion generally worked in the ancient world. While there were obviously variations in practice between different cultures, much of ancient religion centred on the ritual of sacrifice. Gods could be very fickle individuals, and the point of sacrifices was, crudely, to keep them sweet.[3] Whether or not a sacrifice had achieved its desired end would be assessed with reference to subsequent events. Most religious practice was therefore essentially a one-way affair: once the sacrifice had been made, there was nothing to do but wait. Oracles differed in that they constituted a two-way religious phenomenon. Although sacrifice usually played a part in the process, it was also expected that there would be an immediate (or at least prompt) response. Consequently, oracles offered a very special kind of contact with the divine and so provided an importantly and unusually personal dimension of ancient religion. This fact is not, perhaps, as widely appreciated as it should be.

However, it was not only gods with whom one might make a special kind of contact at oracles, which is why I have chosen to use the broader term 'the supernatural' in my working definition. By 'the supernatural' I mean not only gods but also the **dead,** with heroes comprising a special class of the dead.[4]

---

[2]With the traditional exception of Elijah who according to II Kings 2.11 'went up by a whirlwind into heaven'. Something similar was said to have happened to Enoch, but it is more questionable as to whether he should be regarded as a prophet.

[3]Unless there is an obvious reason to understand it otherwise, 'gods' should be taken to mean 'gods and goddesses' throughout.

[4]I use 'heroes' here in the broader, ancient sense rather than the modern one. Not all heroes performed 'heroic' deeds when alive. Some were healers, some were seers, and some were rulers, but, as with heroes in the narrower sense, they were regarded as special people.

During the early centuries AD, oracles of **letters** became increasingly common. A good example can be found at **OLYMPUS**. Here, 24 lines were inscribed on a tomb, one for (and beginning with) each letter of the Greek alphabet. By some process, one of these would be selected as the answer to the enquiry. It was presumably believed that the dead ancestor within the tomb was being consulted by this means. It was widely assumed that the dead had special knowledge, but the problem was how to obtain access to it.

The tombs of heroes enjoyed a special status, in the same way that their occupants had enjoyed a special status while alive. While there are few, if any, tombs of ordinary individuals with other than dice or letters oracles attached to them, the tombs of heroes generally offered services more akin to those provided by gods. This may reflect the fact that some heroic figures are thought to have originally been gods who were subsequently 'downgraded' for some reason. Indeed, the principal difference between oracles of gods and oracles of heroes was that individual gods might have many of them, while heroes were usually restricted to one, since they only had one tomb each. So the only oracle of **Protesilaus** was at **ELAIUS**, but he was able to afford personal advice on any subject.

A dice oracle such as that at Termessos, which was erected in a public place, might be thought to have had no connection with either the gods or the dead. However, the responses it furnished were taken to be pronouncements of the gods themselves, collected and arranged for this purpose. The connection with the supernatural is indeed more tenuous in such places, but it is not lacking altogether.

Why did people consult oracles?

Although oracles might have provided a special kind of religious experience in the ancient world, people did not go to them just to have a religious experience. Overwhelmingly, perhaps exclusively, they went to them to seek some kind of assistance. Such assistance can be broken down into three basic types.

The first type of assistance consisted of a decision on religious or political matters (the two were often difficult to separate in the ancient world). Here the oracle (always that of a god in this case) was regarded as the highest authority on a particular subject, and its word was regarded as final. In Egypt, gods might be consulted on matters of state such as which candidate for high office should be selected. One of the earliest known oracles was delivered by **Amun** at Egyptian **THEBES** in support of **Hatshepsut**'s claim to the throne in the fifteenth century BC. The god's oracle at **NAPATA**, far to the south, is known to have been performing the same function nearly a thousand years later. In Greece, the oracle of **Apollo** at Delphi came to enjoy a position of pre-eminence in religious matters, even though Apollo was not regarded as the supreme god (that position was firmly occupied by **Zeus**). A common enquiry sent in from the various city-states concerned which gods they should sacrifice to on a particular matter, or which gods should have shrines erected to them. Delphi was also said to have been approached on many occasions to make a decision as to where city-states should found their colonies. This might, perhaps, be seen as a request for advice rather than a decision, but it would be a bold community that simply disregarded the answer it received.

However, more mundane advice or information was often what was sought, and these constitute the second kind of assistance oracles provided. While requests for this kind of assistance might come from communities, more often than not they reflected the concerns of individuals. There is a certain touching (or perhaps depressing?) timelessness about many of these. Whom should I marry? How should I make a living? Who has stolen my bed? Is my wife's child mine? And so on. As in all societies, the inhabitants of ancient ones sought advice and information from the best sources available (or at least the best they could afford). If human resources proved inadequate to the task, supernatural ones could be invoked. Often, of course, what was sought was not so much advice as reassurance. Questions might be phrased in such a way as to indicate the desired answer, and those involved in the delivery of oracular services were doubtless sensitive to such promptings. It seems unlikely, for example, that when the otherwise unknown Asclepiades approached the oracle of **Sobek** asking whether he should marry the equally unknown Tapetheus, he received an answer other than the one he desired.

The third kind of assistance related to matters of health, and this was in great demand. Some are inclined to distinguish healing centres from oracles and treat them as a quite separate phenomenon, but this is easier said than done. I have included healing centres in this book for two main reasons. First, although certain gods and heroes specialised in healing, they might also deliver oracles on other matters. In the same way, 'non-specialists' might also pass on the occasional health tip. Consequently, there is no hard and fast demarcation line. Secondly, the principal healing god, **Asclepius**, indisputably operated in an oracular fashion, usually delivering his responses directly to enquirers through the medium of dreams. To exclude Asclepius from a book on oracles would therefore present a very distorted view of the subject, especially since he is the most represented god here, with over a hundred entries to his name. This is perhaps not surprising, since health is probably one of the more universal human concerns. Of course, people did not regard the sanctuaries of gods such as Asclepius as the only places where they could be healed. There were other sources of help in such matters, such as the schools of medicine in the tradition of **Hippocrates**. However, the two often appeared and functioned alongside each other, as at **KOS**, for example.

How did people consult oracles?

There was no one single method by which oracles were consulted. On the other hand, some methods were more commonly used than others, and there were certain features of the process that were relatively uniform. Apart from some dice oracles, which might be consulted on a fairly casual basis (although not enough is really known about them to be at all sure of this), there would usually be some form of ritual, and this would normally involve some kind of sacrifice. To approach an oracle was to approach the powers of the supernatural, and this was not an exercise to be undertaken lightly. They were powers to be feared, and preparations for a consultation reflected this fact. Standard elements of these preparations would include sacrifice and purification. Sacrifice had a double function. First, by carrying it out (or by having it carried out on their behalf), enquirers sought to put the gods or dead in the right mood to be consulted. Secondly, the sacrifice was also a payment for the services sought (and not always the only one). Purification might be a purely ritual matter, or it could include actual bathing. Sometimes special diets might be followed and forms of abstention practised too. All this would be intended to make the enquirer not only worthy but also safe to come into closer contact with the supernatural. Those who approached in the wrong state were thought to be at risk of suffering serious harm.

Once the preliminaries had been observed, consultation might take place in a number of ways. The variety of methods in part reflected local and regional preferences, in part individual idiosyncrasies. In Egypt, for example, there was a tradition of ordinary people (as opposed to priests and pharaohs) consulting the gods when their images were being carried around outside their temples. The movements of the image, up or down or forwards or backwards, indicated the god's responses. Some (but by no means all) of Apollo's oracles employed a human medium who would utter the words of the god. At the sanctuaries of Asclepius (and many others), **incubation** was practised. Here the enquirer would sleep in a special room overnight in the hope of receiving a message from the god in a dream. It is thought that in at least some of the temples of **Sarapis**, for example that at **PERGAMON**, the voice of the god was heard through the mouth of his cult statue. The method of consultation of the oracle of **Demeter** at **PATRAI**, on the other hand, which involved a mirror and a well, appears to have been unique to it.

At some oracles (perhaps many), more than one method of consultation was employed. At **CANOPUS**, for example, it was possible to consult the god Sarapis either through the process of incubation, or by the simpler method of a **lot** oracle. Although the lot oracle was undoubtedly cruder (it seems to have been only a **binary** one), it was also apparently considerably cheaper. It is thought that even at Delphi petitioners could avail themselves of a lot oracle (involving beans or pebbles) instead of awaiting the pronouncements of the Pythia.

In a broader sense, the 'method' of consulting an oracle could also include a considerable journey. While it is true that there were many oracles, it is also true that there was far from being one on every street corner. Furthermore, the special prestige enjoyed by such as those at **DODONA** and **SIWA** meant that their services might be sought out in preference to those of more convenient ones. Journeys to both of them were arduous and not to be undertaken lightly. Even Delphi, which was relatively easy to reach, involved something of a trek for most of those who visited it, in an age when long-distance travel was neither particularly easy nor particularly common. The whole process of consulting an oracle might therefore take days, and sometimes weeks.

When did people consult oracles?

This question may be understood in two different ways, depending on whether it is the lifespan of oracles or their individual 'opening times' that is meant. And within the question concerning lifespans, it is possible to distinguish between the duration of the institution of oracles as such, and the periods during which individual oracles functioned. All of these issues will be dealt with.

To take the biggest question first, the oracle of Amun concerning Hatshepsut's claim to the throne of Egypt mentioned above is the earliest known, and is dated to the fifteenth century BC. However, it cannot be assumed that there were none before that, so the actual starting date of oracles as an institution in the ancient world must remain a matter of speculation. At the other end of the timescale, the oracles of **Isis** at **MENOUTHIS** and **PHILAE** seem to have survived until at least the end of the fifth century AD. This was despite an edict of the emperor **Theodosius the Great** in 385 that ordered all remaining oracles in the Roman Empire to be closed down. Two thousand years of oracular activity is therefore a reasonably safe claim.

As to the lifespans of individual oracles, the information available is very patchy. It is thought that some of the great oracles of Greece such as Dodona and Delphi existed in some form or other before the end of the second millennium BC, but precise dates are not remotely available. On the other hand, the cult of Asclepius seems to have emerged either in or not long before the fifth century BC, and it is known to the exact year when sanctuaries to the god were established in **ATHENS** and **ROME**. Similarly, the cult of Sarapis appears to have been instituted at around the beginning of the third century BC, and so more is known about when temples to him were first built than is known about those of Isis, with whom he was often associated, whose cult was considerably older.

When it comes to endings rather than beginnings, the picture is often not much clearer. Some oracles seem to have simply faded away, perhaps because of a lack of reliability, perhaps because of the growing popularity of oracles of letters and dice, and doubtless for many other reasons as well. For those that made it through to the fourth century AD, there was the challenge of Christianity to face. Once **Constantine the Great** had laid the foundations of a Christian Roman Empire, the way was open for the powers of the law and the state to be used against what came to be seen as pagan practices. He seems to have been present in person at the destruction of the sanctuary of Asclepius at **AIGAI (2)**. Sometimes mobs took the law into their own hands, as happened when **ALEXANDRIA**'s great temple of Sarapis was razed to the ground in 391.

The demise of some oracles, however, was more apparent than real. At **GRAND**, for example, the demise of the healing cult of Apollo **Grannus** was replaced by that of St Libaire, who continued to heal people down to at least the eighteenth century. At **TITANE**, a church dedicated to St Tryphon, another healing saint, stands on the spot previously occupied by a sanctuary of Asclepius. And there are many more examples, especially in the context of healing. This perhaps reflects the fact that the 'folk' dimension of religion tends to be both more flexible and more persistent than its more formal ones. Certainly the presence of a church dedicated to a healing saint or **Zoodochos Pigi** has served more than once as a helpful clue in tracking down the site of an ancient oracle.

As to when, during the periods of their existence, particular oracles were available for consultation, the picture is again very mixed. Presumably one of the attractions of dice and letter oracles (apart from their cheapness) was the fact that they were constantly available. On the other hand, many Egyptian oracles could only be consulted (at least by the general public) during limited periods, which often coincided with a special festival of the god in question. At Delphi, it is thought that the oracle could originally only be consulted once a year, but that this subsequently rose to at least once a month (except in winter). Asclepius sanctuaries, so far as is known, seem to have operated throughout the year. The distinctive nature of these places meant that people might spend months at a time at them, as happened with **Aelius Aristides** at Pergamon. Oracles based around springs presumably only operated when the waters flowed. It is said that the spring at **DIDYMA** had dried up completely until miraculously restored to life by the visit of **Alexander the Great**. Less dramatically, presumably seasonal springs permitted only seasonal consultations.

Why did some places have oracles and not others?

The sacred geography of the ancient world, as embodied in the distribution of oracles across it, yields no clear single pattern. Their locations depended on too many different factors, many of them long forgotten, for any kind of generalisation on the subject to be remotely persuasive. Nevertheless, the establishment of an oracle in a particular place is unlikely ever to have been a random matter, and some determining factors are easier to identify (or at least intelligently guess) than others.

Natural features were certainly a consideration in many cases, and some of these can be mentioned. Caves were a popular choice for oracles connected with the dead or the gods of the underworld. Despite the fact that there was sometimes obvious evidence to the contrary, they were often thought to constitute entrances to subterranean realms. The oracles at **BAIAE** and **LEBADEIA** may have been examples of this phenomenon, and at Delphi, one view is that the oracle was originally at the Korykian Cave, a few kilometres away from the main site. For reasons that are less obvious, lakes were often viewed in the same way. The explanation may be this. If water was seen to run into a lake (from streams or rainfall), but not to run out, then there was an apparent mystery as to why the level of the lake did not rise as a result. In the absence of an understanding of evaporation, the conclusion might be drawn that below water level there had to be an outlet through which it drained into the underworld. Lake **AVERNUS** was thought to be such a place.

If openings in the ground constituted one possible location, so conspicuous pieces of high ground constituted another, although perhaps not as often as might be expected. Zeus, for example, was originally a sky god whose cult centres might reasonably be looked for in high places. However, his oracle at Dodona lies in a sheltered valley, because the sanctuary had originally belonged to **Ge**, the earth goddess. At Siwa, on the other hand, the temple of Amun can still be seen perched on top of a large outcrop of rock rising above the oasis floor. The oracles of **Pan** at **LYKAION** and of **Dionysus** at **PANGÆUM** were established at or near the tops of mountains, but these are relatively unusual. The sanctuaries of Asclepius at both **ALIPHEIRA** and **KASSOPI** enjoyed elevated locations, but this was most likely because they were set up in cities already founded in such places (presumably for strategic reasons).

The presence of one or more springs seems to have been a guiding factor in the selection of many sites. There were at least two reasons for this. First, since they issued forth from below the ground, they could be seen as providing a channel of communication with the underworld. Secondly, they were often useful, if not essential, for purificatory or therapeutic purposes. Certainly the sanctuaries of Asclepius in Athens and probably the oracle of Apollo at **EUTRESIS**, for example, owed their precise locations to the presence of springs. Then as now, hot and/or mineral springs were especially highly regarded from the therapeutic point of view and formed the focal point of many a healing sanctuary, as at **LEBENA**. Rivers were in many ways seen as poor relations of springs, but could still be instrumental in the selection of a site. Unusually, the temple of Sarapis at Pergamon was built over one, while many sanctuaries in France are located near one, sometimes with the god of the sanctuary being the god of the river too, as at **FONTES SEQUANAE**.

In many cases, however, the selection of a site doubtless derived from other concerns. Unless they ousted other already existing ones, the sanctuaries of relatively late cults such as that of Sarapis had to establish themselves in whatever space was left. In Egypt, most buildings and most people were forced into a narrow strip of land either side of the Nile offering little by way of variety of landscape. In some cases, sanctuaries existed before they became oracular, in which case specifically oracular considerations could have played no part in the selection of their location. One of the most extreme examples of this was at **EPHESUS**, where an oracle of Apollo was introduced into the city's **prytaneion**. In principle, therefore, there would appear to have been nowhere where an oracle might not be set up if there existed sufficient will to do so.

In the case of oracles attached to the cults of heroes rather than gods, the situation is simpler. At least in theory, the oracle was centred on the tomb of the hero and nowhere else, and tombs did not move.[5] However, heroes' supposed tombs were sometimes to be found in very unexpected places. Quite how **Menestheus** ended up being buried in **GADEIRA**, for example, is a mystery. On the other hand, the claimed location of Protesilaus' tomb at Elaius was wholly in keeping with the tradition that he died in the war against **Troy**.

---

[5]Very occasionally the remains of a hero might be transferred from one place to another. The supposed bones of Theseus were brought back to Athens from their original resting place at some time around 475 BC.

Finally, it may be pointed out that the presence or absence of oracles to some extent reflected regional religious and cultural preferences and practices. Oracles were far more common among the Greeks and Egyptians than among the Romans. Apart from those belonging to imported cults, the Romans had few oracular sites of any kind.

Why did some gods and heroes have oracles and not others?

It is noteworthy that some gods had many oracles, some a few, and some none at all. Apollo and Asclepius, Isis and Sarapis stand out as clearly having the most. At the other end of the spectrum comes Hephaestus, the Greek god of fire usually identified with the Roman Vulcan. Neither had a single oracle of any kind, despite enjoying considerable prestige in other respects. In between come such as Zeus, **Pluto** and **Poseidon** with a handful each.

It is perhaps understandable that the cult of Asclepius, once established, spread quickly and widely. Healing was a commodity in great demand, and the supply grew to meet it. The efforts of Isis and Sarapis in the field of health doubtless did their popularity no harm either. The case of Apollo is more complicated, but may be explained at least in part by the fact that, among other things, he was regarded as a god of wisdom, and so as the most appropriate source of advice. That in itself, however, is not sufficient to explain why and how his oracles actually emerged, although at Delphi, and in some other places too, his cult probably took over an existing oracular sanctuary. Sometimes these transferences of oracular allegiance are suggested by mythology, sometimes they are confirmed by archaeology.

In Egypt, some major national and regional gods seem to have been oracular almost as a matter of political necessity. Through their wealth and influence, temples such as that of Amun at Egyptian Thebes were often centres of considerable power. Since, technically at least, the temples belonged to the gods rather than the priests, the gods were in effect obliged to be political players. This meant that some acknowledged means had to exist whereby they could make their views known. Another specifically Egyptian phenomenon occurred in the Faiyum, the oasis area that begins about 40 km SW of Cairo. It was home to a number of local crocodile god cults, of which many were oracular, as at **KARANIS** and **TEBTUNIS**. Most Egyptian oases had at least one oracle, but nowhere are they found in such proliferation as in the Faiyum. Quite why this should be so remains a mystery.

Beyond these few points, it is not easy to say much about the oracles of gods. When it comes to heroes, however, the picture is rather clearer. Many of those who patronised oracular cults had reputations as healers or seers when alive. So it is no great surprise to find that such as **Machaon** and **Polemocrates** carried on their occupation of healing after they had died (at **GERENIA** and **EUA** respectively), or that the great seer **Teiresias** continued to prophesy posthumously at **ORCHOMENOS**. However, it is considerably less obvious why individuals like **Achilles** and Protesilaus should have been connected with oracles at **LEUCE** and Elaius after their deaths when their lives afforded little or no evidence of any such potential.

Could oracles be trusted?

This question may be looked at in two different ways. First, did people trust oracles? Secondly, should they have trusted them? The answer to the first must be overwhelmingly in the affirmative. It is hard to see how an institution could persist for at least two thousand years without people having some faith in it. However, the fact that oracles in general enjoyed such a lengthy career does not mean that all oracles were trusted equally all the time. As in many areas of life, success breeds success. Oracles that were felt to deliver the goods doubtless attracted more custom, and lasted longer, than those that were perceived as unreliable. The length of an oracle's lifespan and the amount of wealth it accumulated may therefore be taken as rough and ready yardsticks of the extent to which it was trusted.

In some cases there is more explicit and more direct evidence of trust. While some kind of payment was usually required before a consultation, what happened afterwards was more at the discretion of the individual petitioner. At many sanctuaries of Asclepius, such as **EPIDAUROS**, it became customary for those who had received cures to write brief testimonials to that effect, which were then recorded in inscriptions at the site. Many of these have been found, and there can be no doubt that those who composed them were convinced that the god had been responsible for their recoveries. At some other healing sanctuaries, such as **ESSAROIS** and **VEII**, quantities of **votive** objects have been found, donated in gratitude by those who attributed their improvement in health to the presiding gods.[6] While it is possible that some of these gifts might have been made before a cure was effected, even then the sheer volume of them would indicate a massive degree of confidence in the powers being called upon.[7]

It therefore seems beyond dispute that many oracles enjoyed a great deal

---

[6]Of course, the numbers of those who did not receive the desired cures and who left no evidence of their visits are unknown.

[7]The same phenomenon can be observed in many Roman Catholic and Orthodox churches today, where tiny metal representations of parts of the body are attached by the faithful to paintings of those asked for, or thanked for, a cure.

of popular trust, sometimes for very considerable periods of time. Whether this trust was deserved is another matter. If the testimony of **Lucian** is to be trusted, the oracle of Glykon-Asclepius at **ABONUTEICHOS** was a total fraud. There is also some evidence at such places as Karanis and Siwa that human agency may have played a rather greater role in the consultation process than was publicly acknowledged. The fact that so little is known about the working methods of many oracles may reflect, at least in part, the desire of those who ran them to keep their secrets to themselves. There are also accounts of fraud at Delphi, where the expedient of bribery was employed on occasions in order to secure a desired pronouncement. Of course, the mere fact that some of the operating procedures of oracles appear highly dubious to modern eyes does not in itself mean that those who carried them out were guilty of bad faith or intentionally tried to deceive. Nevertheless, it is difficult to avoid the conclusion that, even if many oracles were honestly run, the potential for fraud was enormous. But the extent to which that potential was fulfilled must remain a matter of conjecture.

With regard to such institutions as dice or letter oracles, the situation is somewhat different. At these, what you saw was what you got. The obvious problem with them was that what you saw was often not very much. A letter oracle had only 24 possible responses to any question that could be asked. Dice oracles usually offered more, but still only a relatively limited variety. A degree of interpretative imagination might well be required to fit the answer to the question, although the questions themselves would presumably be put in such a way as to make it possible for the oracle to answer them. Comparisons might be made to the Chinese *I Ching*, with its 64 basic responses, or a daily astrological column in a newspaper with a total of only 12 scenarios designed to cover everyone.[8] On the face of it, there is little to choose between them in terms of trustworthiness.

It may, perhaps, be helpful to distinguish between the more subjective and the more objective dimensions of trustworthiness. At the subjective level, if people received what they needed, wanted and expected from oracles, then it seems harsh to judge them as wrong to trust them, whatever dubious practices may have been taking place behind the scenes. At the objective level, if the evidence were available it would be possible to judge how often the information vouchsafed by oracles was correct, and how many who sought cures obtained them. Unfortunately, this is not an option. However, it does not seem unreasonable to surmise that the inhabitants of the ancient world had some idea, at least at the local level, of which oracles were more reliable

[8]The *I Ching* does, however, employ a system of 'fine tuning' whereby the number of possible responses is increased considerably, although still limited.

than others. If, as I suggested earlier, success bred success, then presumably persistent failure would lead to an oracle's decline and demise. Perhaps that is all that can usefully be said on the subject.

What is left of the oracles today?

Apart from those that became transformed into Christian shrines, as happened at **OXYRHYNCHUS**, most oracles just ceased to exist. That does not mean that all oracular sites were abandoned, however. At both Dodona and Epidauros, for example, Christian churches were built within the confines of the ancient sanctuaries, although they did not take over their oracular functions. Some were plundered for their stone, some were built over, some were just abandoned, and so on. In one way or another, most oracles were forgotten. The situation began to change in the seventeenth century, when a new interest in classical culture began to develop in western Europe. At first this took the form of a desire to visit, record, and sometimes remove bits of what could still be seen of it. Around the beginning of the nineteenth century, a decisive turn was taken towards looking for what could no longer be seen, and the era of archaeological excavation began, which has continued ever since. Two hundred years ago, most of the sites that can be visited today were covered over by hundreds of years of subsequent history and debris. While the sites of some oracles have been lost, many have now been rediscovered.

Each oracle suffered its own fate, and this is reflected in what can now be seen. Some sites, such as Ephesus and **OLYMPIA** have been extensively excavated, and have been subsequently well maintained. It is possible to walk around them and get at least some sense of how they must have been when they were functioning sanctuaries, even if few buildings stand to any great height. At Epidauros this situation is being addressed by actually reconstructing some of the principal edifices. In other places, such as **PTOON** and **CYANEAE**, excavations have been carried out and much has been revealed, but the sites have since become overgrown again so that they are more difficult to explore and reconstruct in the imagination. Some sites, for example **KRANNON** and **THESPIAI**, comprise little more than nondescript piles of rubble of various sizes by the side of a road or in the middle of a field. Finally, there are others such as **ICHNAE** that have not been found at all, and whose existence is known only through literary references.

Sometimes it is possible to identify a site in general terms, but not to pinpoint the location of the oracle itself. At Kassopi, for instance, it is relatively easy to find the ruins of the city, set in their elevated position. However, the **Asclepeion** there has not been identified, and presumably lies in an unexcavated area. Consequently, it remains a matter of conjecture as to exactly where it was. At **SURA**, on the other hand, the site of the oracle can clearly be seen lying far below the ancient acropolis, but actually reaching it is something of a challenge. It has to be a matter of personal judgement as to whether the descent is worth it, although I happen to think it is.[9]

The only thing that can safely be said about what is left of oracles today is that each site has its own individual characteristics. There is everything from the vast sprawl of the temple of Amun at Karnak to a few stones in a field at **KAOUS**. Each, perhaps, has its own charm for those who are susceptible to it, and the most dramatic ones are not necessarily the most atmospheric.

Finally, I should point out that the length of an entry in the gazetteer should not be taken as an automatic guide to how much is left to be seen at any particular site. Because the more famous sites such as Delphi have had plenty written about them elsewhere, I have kept the entries on them shorter than they could have been in order to make room for others about which it is harder to find information.

Which oracles are included in this book?

Any author who claims to offer an exhaustive treatment of a subject is asking for trouble. Despite years of dedicated searching, I continue to stumble across new ones. There are doubtless many oracles still unknown to me, and they are obviously not included here. Furthermore, as I pointed out near the beginning of this introduction, it is not entirely easy to pin down exactly what an oracle is. I have operated within my own working definition, but those who subscribe to different ones may feel I have included either too many or too few. From my own particular point of view, the major difficulties I have experienced have been with healing centres. While many seem to me to have been clearly oracular, some are more questionable. Many such centres were based around springs thought to have therapeutic qualities, and it is not always easy to know whether the healing that took place at them was attributed to the waters themselves or to the supernatural intervention of some deity associated with them. Only in the latter case would the place constitute an oracle in my understanding of the word. I have therefore sought to exclude healing centres that do not fulfil this criterion, but there is not always enough information available to be confident that it has been applied consistently.

[9]One of the aims of this book is to give the reader an idea of how much there is to see at each particular site, and how easy it is to find it, in order to provide the information needed for making such personal judgements. Unfortunately, I have not yet been able to visit all of the sites, so I have sometimes had to rely on the information and judgements of others.

The cults of Asclepius, Isis and Sarapis pose special problems. It seems evident from **Pausanias** that there were shrines and temples dedicated to Asclepius other than those attached to fully-fledged sanctuaries. The total number of his temples in existence at one time or another is reckoned in the hundreds. It cannot be automatically assumed that all of these were oracular, although doubtless many were. Often there is simply not enough evidence about a particular site to be able to judge one way or the other. I have therefore tried to focus on the most important ones and the ones about which most is known, but also tried to give some sense of the widespread nature of his cult. The selection to be found here is therefore reasonably representative, but does not claim to be comprehensive. There is a definite bias towards sites in Greece since, thanks to Pausanias, more tends to be known about these.

In the cases of Isis and Sarapis similar difficulties arise. There is often no direct evidence that a particular temple dedicated to one or the other of them was a centre of oracular activity, healing or otherwise. On the other hand, it seems clear that there was a strong tendency for them to be so. Indeed, I would suggest that the popularity of their cults was in no small measure due to that fact. They offered a dimension that most other cults conspicuously failed to do (with that of Asclepius being an obvious exception). Again I have sought to provide a representative sample. A significant class of exceptions (and this applies with respect to Asclepius as well) is comprised of those cases where there seemed to be nothing to say about a sanctuary other than that it had existed, and where there was little else of interest to see at the site either. I would not claim to have been scrupulously consistent in my judgements and selections, and I hope that continuing excavations will lead to some of them having to be reversed. (I have included some lost sites as challenges for intrepid oracle hunters.) On the other hand, even when there is something to say, it is sometimes difficult to know what it means. Not all references to oracles in works of literature need be equally based on fact. It is entirely possible that some oracles that remain undiscovered never actually existed, but the failure to find them so far proves nothing either way. I should also add that the selection of sites in general reflects the fact that my own principal interests and experience lie in Egypt, Greece and Turkey, which means that other countries may be relatively under-represented.

I have used the term 'ancient world' more than once in this introduction without providing any definition of it, but geographical factors have also played a part in deciding what to include here. Oracles have played (and in some cases continue to play) an important role in many places and cultures other than those covered by this book. As a rule of thumb, I have taken 'ancient world' to mean that area contained at one time or another within the

Roman Empire, which achieved its greatest extent during the reign of **Trajan**, but whose borders regularly fluctuated. Only those oracles listed in the gazetteer under Iran seem never to have been part of the Roman world, either actually or notionally. However, one, at **ECBATANA**, relates to Asclepius, while the other is mentioned by **Strabo**, and marks his sole modest foray beyond the limits of the empire. To have omitted them would have seemed as arbitrary as to include them.

As to the scope of the book in terms of time, there was obviously no particular date on which the 'ancient world' came to an end (neither is it clear when it began). For present purposes, however, the year 400 is as good as any. With a few exceptions, such as Philae and **HELIOPOLIS**, all of the oracles I discuss had closed down by then.

How to use this book

This book is intended for the armchair traveller as well as for the more energetic one. At its heart is the gazetteer, which is arranged alphabetically by country, and then similarly within each country. Sites are listed under their ancient names where known, and under modern ones when they are not. The Index of Sites contains all the sites in a single list in alphabetical order. The names of all individuals mentioned more than once (and some mentioned only once) can be found in the Glossary, which also gives an explanation of technical terms used. Those who have a background knowledge of the ancient world may find all or much of it redundant, but it is designed for those who do not. The Concordance of Oracles and Sites can be consulted to find out which gods and heroes had their oracles where. Oracles of the dead, letters, and so on are also listed there. Finally the Bibliography contains books, articles and other resources I have drawn on, which can be used as a guide to further reading and research.

For those actually wishing to visit the sites, or even just wanting to get a clearer sense of where they are, decent maps are essential. For major cities such as Rome and Athens, street maps are available, but most of the sites are in more remote locations. In such cases, a map with a minimum scale of 1:750,000 is desirable, and something nearer 1:250,000 is much to be preferred. Much of Europe is covered by Michelin maps at scales of between 1:200,000 and 1:400,000, and these are sufficient where available. For those European countries not covered in detail by Michelin, the Roger Lascelles 'Red Cover Series' usually provides an acceptable alternative. For Greece, the 1:250,000 series recently issued by Road Editions is indispensable. For Western Turkey, the 1:750,000 AA Baedeker map is generally adequate, although it is not without the odd inaccuracy, and not all sites are marked on it. The supplementary information given in the book, however, should be sufficient to identify their locations. The AA South West Turkey Leisure Map, at a scale of 1:435,000, contains a bit more detail on the smaller area it covers. Readers and travellers alike should be aware that both Greece and Turkey have shown a tendency to change the names of places from time to time, and in Greece alternative spellings of the same place name may exist.

For sites outside Europe (and Asian Turkey), decent detailed maps can be harder to find. For Egypt, the best are the 1:1,000,000 one published by Roger Lascelles, and the 1:800,000 Insight Travel map from Geographic Publishers. Both omit some of the smaller sites. In Egypt, you may sometimes need to get close, then ask. It being Egypt, someone will probably take you there. For Algeria and Tunisia, the Michelin 1:1,000,000 contains all that is necessary. Roger Lascelles also covers them, as well as Israel. The sites in other countries are sufficiently major that they can be found on 1:4,000,000 scale maps. Michelin cover African countries, while the VWK map of the Middle East covers everything else. Other and better options may exist of which I am unaware. Where maps fail, the directions given in the book should prove adequate.

For a number of reasons, and not without some regrets, it has not proved feasible to include site plans in the book. However, this should not prove too problematic. Major sites are generally well signed, while minor sites are usually easy to negotiate. A particularly helpful policy operative in many places in Greece is the provision of a small site plan with the entry ticket. Where directions are required, those given in the book are intended to be adequate, although a compass is sometimes necessary to derive maximum benefit from them. A smattering of the local language is always helpful to have, but being able to ask for directions is unfortunately not the same as being able to understand them when they are given. Fortunately, the conventions of pointing appear to be universal. I have also omitted information on the opening times of particular sites. These are liable to change, and even posted times are not always reliable. The majority of minor sites are unfenced and so always accessible. The more significant the major site, the more likely it is to be open every day. For those that are not, Mondays are the most common day for being closed.

Another resource for the traveller is the ever-growing mass of dedicated guidebooks to the countries in question. The ones I have used are listed in the bibliography. As a general principle, however, the Blue Guides are the best for learning about what there is to see, while Lonely Planet and Rough Guide publications contain less detail, but are stronger on practicalities such as public transport and places to stay. The expanding Footprint series is also useful. For those visiting Turkey, the books of George Bean are excellent for the areas they cover. As Bean died in 1977, some sections of them are now a bit out of date, because excavations have continued at a number of sites since then. In central and southern Greece, Peter Levi's annotated translation of Pausanias is a very agreeable travelling companion, although, again, not entirely up to date. However, as all sensible authors of guidebooks point out, things are always changing, and that is just a fact of life (and travel publishing) that has to be accepted. Speaking as (I hope) a sensible author, I would be delighted to hear from anyone who finds any information in this book either outdated or unreliable, or who knows of oracles I have missed.[10]

The search for oracles is an enjoyable and rewarding one. Those who pursue it may find themselves treading in some very venerable footsteps.

[10]I can be contacted via the publisher, or via email at t.curnow@ucsm.ac.uk.

Gazetteer

ALBANIA

APOLLONIA: a sanctuary of **Asclepius** and oracle of the **Nymphs** in S Albania (40 40N, 19 28E). The site of Apollonia is to be found near Pojan, about 80 km S of Tiranë and 30 km N of Vlorë. The city was founded in 588 BC and possessed a famous school of rhetoric. Its most celebrated and successful pupil was doubtless the emperor **Augustus**. The city walls are reasonably well preserved to this day, and the remains of a number of buildings can be found within them, including an impressive stoa. The sanctuary of Asclepius has yet to be identified. There is a small museum, located in a **Byzantine** monastery built over what is thought to have been the site of a temple to **Apollo**. (Unfortunately, most of the exhibits have been removed to Tiranë.) The location of the oracle of the Nymphs has not been found, but one would expect to find it in the vicinity of a spring. It is said that the consultation process there involved the use of a special kind of incense in some way.

BUTHROTUM: a sanctuary of **Asclepius** in S Albania (39 47N, 20 00E). Buthrotum is now known as Butrint, and lies in the extreme S of the country, by a lagoon of the same name. The beach resort of Sarandë is about 20 km to the N. According to legend, the ancient city was founded by **Helenus** of Troy. Like his twin sister **Cassandra**, he had the gift of prophecy, supposedly acquired when snakes licked their ears when they were children. However, it seems more likely that it was founded by colonists from Kerkyra (modern Corfu) which lies only a short distance away to the W. In any event, despite Helenus' life as a seer, there is no known tradition of posthumous prophecy. A cult of Asclepius did exist here, however, and the ruins of a small temple dedicated to him have been found on the site of the ancient acropolis. It was originally constructed in the third century BC, but was rebuilt in the first or second century AD, with an unusual arched roof. It stands in the S part of the city, just to the W of the well-preserved theatre. Asclepius was one of the major gods of the city and fragments of a large statue, presumably of him, were found near the temple.

ALGERIA

CHERCHELL: a sanctuary of **Isis** in N Algeria (36 36N, 2 11E). Much of ancient Cherchell lies under the modern city of the same name on Algeria's N coast. However, the site of the forum, a theatre, baths and a temple, among other things, have been clearly identified, although unfortunately the dedication of the temple, at the W end of the site, has not. The most distinctive feature of the cult of Isis here was that the temple had its own resident crocodile.

LAMBAESIS: a sanctuary of **Asclepius** in NE Algeria (35 25N, 06 17E). The site of Lambaesis is now sometimes known as Tazoult, sometimes as Lambèse, and sometimes as Tazoult-Lambèse! It lies about 11 km SE of Batna, in the Aurès mountains. Lambaesis began life as a legionary camp in the first century AD and subsequently developed into a sizeable town. The ruins are extensive and reasonably well-preserved. The sanctuary of Asclepius lay to the S of the amphitheatre. The remains of the semicircular temple can still be seen and a bathing complex is clearly identifiable nearby. The sanctuary dates from 162 AD, and so is relatively late. Statues of both Asclepius and **Hygeia** have been found, and can be seen in the local museum. An inscription was also found bearing the exhortation, 'Bonus intra, melior exi' ('Enter good, leave better'), which seems to have as much to do with moral as with physical health.

Other inscriptions found at the site indicate that many other deities including **Isis** and **Sarapis** were worshipped here, as was **Jupiter** Dolichenus, although none of their sanctuaries have been found. Jupiter Dolichenus was a Roman adaptation of a Syrian cult based at Doliche (now Dülük, near Gaziantep in Turkey). Although he evidently enjoyed a period of popularity, few traces of his cult remain anywhere. It seems to have offered some kind of **lot** oracle, with a blindfolded priest picking out lettered tiles. The sight of the temple in Dülük has been identified but not excavated.

AUSTRIA

CARANTANUS, Mount: a sanctuary of **Isis** in S Austria (46 45N, 14 18E). The goddess was known here as Isis Noreia, her cult having been merged with that of a local deity, the patroness of this region known as Noricum in antiquity. It was renowned for the savagery of its inhabitants, who were only tamed in the time of **Tiberius**. The sanctuary stood on top of the mountain, which lies about 9 km N of Klagenfurt. It is now known as Ulrichsberg after the saint whose ruined church occupies the site. A fragment of an inscription built into the church wall above the door records a **votive** offering to the goddess.

Excavations revealed the remains of a complex of first-century AD buildings including a temple. Within the temple was a large basin, suggesting that water played some kind of role in cult practices, which would be consistent with a healing function. Other buildings are thought to have provided accommodation for priests and pilgrims. From the evidence of later ruins on the site, it appears that the sanctuary passed from pagan to Christian hands in the late fifth century. However, it is thought that the Four Hills Pilgrimage which takes place annually on the second Friday after Easter may continue a pre-Christian practice. Ulrichsberg is the second of four mountains to be climbed in 24 hours. If, as some believe, this ritual began in connection with some form of sun worship, then its origins are probably very ancient indeed.

BULGARIA

PAUTALIA: a sanctuary of **Asclepius** in W Bulgaria (42 16N, 22 42E). Pautalia is today known as Kyustendil, and lies near the border with Macedonia. The town grew up around a group of mineral springs, and was a popular spa in Roman times. The emperor **Trajan** came here on account of a skin complaint that was troubling him, and left cured. It is probably not a coincidence that most of what remains is thought to date from after that time. Trajan's visit and endorsement may well have transformed the fortunes of the area's establishments, and led to a substantial building or rebuilding programme. Among the buildings erected during the second and third centuries AD are those collectively known as the **Asclepeion**, the remains of which can be found on Hisarlâk Hill, in the SE of the town. However, it is now thought that this was not the Asclepeion itself, but a large bathing complex. If this is so, then the Asclepeion has yet to be found. On the other hand, it seems likely that the baths may have played some role in the therapeutic process since large numbers of **votive** objects have been found in the vicinity. It is thought that in addition to an Asclepeion in Pautalia itself, there were other smaller centres dedicated to the god scattered about the surrounding district.

PHILIPPOPOLIS or **TRIMONTIUM**: a sanctuary of **Asclepius** in S Bulgaria (42 08N, 24 45E). Philippopolis was founded by **Philip II** of Macedonia in 342 BC on the site of an earlier Thracian settlement. Later it was called Trimontium by the Romans, who made it their capital of Thrace. Today it is known as Plovdiv. The ancient city was sacked more than once, and little remains to be seen of it. In the NE part of the modern city there are the ruins of a theatre built during Roman times. The sanctuary of Asclepius stood to the E of this. Some local finds are in the city's archaeological museum.

CYPRUS

PAPHOS: an oracle of **Aphrodite** in SW Cyprus (34 45N, 32 26E). The site of Aphrodite's temple is in what is now known as Old Paphos, near the village of Kouklia, about 14 km SE of modern Paphos. The goddess was said to have emerged from the sea near here, and her temple at Paphos was perhaps the most famous dedicated to her in the ancient world. According to **Pliny the Elder** [II.210], the rain never fell on it. The site of the temple has been located and excavated, but there is not a great deal to see. It can be found in the SW part of the excavated area. Although the goddess' cult was celebrated on this site from at least 1500 BC, the visible remains of her temple are mainly from the early centuries AD. Inscriptions found in the area confirm the existence of the oracle, but not its precise whereabouts or mode of consultation. In the absence of evidence to the contrary, it is reasonable to assume that it was based at or near the temple itself. Items found here are exhibited not only in the site's own museum, but also in those of modern Paphos and Nicosia. Because of their reputation for licentiousness, involving practices such as temple prostitution, centres of the goddess's cult were frequent and early targets for the opponents of paganism.

SOLOI: a sanctuary of **Isis** in NW Cyprus (35 08N, 32 49E). Soloi, or Soli, lies near the beach resort of Yedidalga (formerly Potamos tou Kambou). This was a rich area in ancient times owing to its copper mines, and many temples were built here. Excavations in the 1920s uncovered a number of them, but they were subsequently covered in again. The city's ancient theatre has also been uncovered, and heavily restored. Above it are the remains of a temple to **Aphrodite** and Isis. A second-century BC statuette of Aphrodite was discovered here, but can now be found in the Cyprus Museum in Nicosia.

EGYPT

ABU SIMBEL: an oracle of **Ramesses II** in S Egypt (22 21N, 31 38E). The two temples at Abu Simbel were carved into the rock and completed in around 1265 BC. They are perhaps best known for having been dismantled and reassembled at a higher level to prevent them being flooded by the waters of Lake Nasser in the 1960s. They lie in the extreme S of Egypt, close to the border with Sudan. While notionally dedicated to a number of gods, they are principally and practically dedicated to Ramesses himself. Little is known about the oracle in this remote place, but there is evidence of its consultation during the twelfth century BC, when the god's statue's views were sought concerning the appointment of certain officials.

ABYDOS: oracles of **Bes**, **Sarapis** and **Ahmose I** in S Egypt (26 11N, 31 55E). The remains of Abydos are about 60 km SE of Suhag, on the W bank of the Nile. The god Bes was portrayed as a dwarf, and was especially connected with household matters. His oracle was located in the structure known to the Greeks as the Memnonion, but more commonly referred to today as the temple of **Seti I**. It is one of the best preserved buildings on the site. Although originally built as a temple to serve the posthumous cult of the pharaoh, it apparently became used more generally for the cults of **Osiris**, then Sarapis, then Bes. There may have been a degree of overlap between their periods of occupation. Whether it was oracular in the time of Osiris is not known, but some people clearly came to seek healing from Sarapis, probably through **incubation**. Exactly when Bes arrived here is not known either. The best information available about his oracle relates to its later years. According to **Ammianus Marcellinus** [XIX.12] it could be consulted either in person or through the delivery of a written enquiry by an intermediary. At least some of the oracle's responses came through the medium of dreams, but it seems unlikely that this was the only method of communication. For some reason, there was an unusual preponderance of athletes among those who came to seek the god's advice. Bes also had special associations with procreation and childbirth, and the Greeks identified him with **Priapus**.

Some of the written enquiries submitted to Bes were forwarded to the emperor **Constantius II** in 359, occasioning a treason trial, so inflammatory did he find their contents to be. An old philosopher called Demetrius was tortured on the rack during the subsequent investigation. He insisted throughout that he (and others) only sought the aid of Bes through their sacrifices to him, and were not seeking to know the future. He was eventually released and sent home. Whether or not his story was true, it was certainly plausible. Abydos clearly functioned as a major pilgrimage centre for centuries, and the seeking of oracles was only one of the possible reasons for visiting it. The oracle itself survived until the late fifth century, when it was closed down by local Christians.

The exact location of the oracle within the building complex is uncertain since inscriptions relating to it are to be found in more than one place. If oracular activity took place before the arrival of Sarapis and Bes, then an obvious focal point for it would lie at the rear (SW) of the temple where there are seven chapels. Counting from the southernmost, the fifth of these was dedicated to Osiris, and it gave access to a further set of rooms dedicated to him.

Pharaoh Ahmose I also had a posthumous oracle at Abydos, although its precise location is unknown. Ahmose himself was buried in Egyptian **THEBES**. There is evidence of the oracle being consulted in the time of **Ramesses II**, some 300 years after Ahmose's death. How long it functioned before or after that is unclear.

The ruins at Abydos are substantial and relatively well preserved. Unfortunately, they lie in an area of Egypt where visits are not encouraged at the moment, although they are not impossible.

ALEXANDRIA (now El Iskandariyah): a sanctuary of **Sarapis** in N Egypt (31 12N, 29 53E). The foundations of the temple have been located, as have some underground galleries connected with it. They were the final resting places of the temple's sacred **Apis** bulls. Excavations reveal that it was built by **Ptolemy III**, and it was probably destroyed in the anti-pagan riots of 391. Not enough remains to get a sense of how the temple looked, let alone of how the oracular function of the establishment worked. The ruins are to be found at the well-known Pompey's Pillar archaeological site in the W of the city, about 2 km SE of Midan Orabi.

BACCHIAS: an oracle of **Sobek** in N Egypt (29 32N, 31 00E). The scant ruins of Bacchias lie in the S part of Kom el Asl, about 30 km NE of Faiyum City. The temple there was dedicated to Sokonnokonni, a local version of Sobek. What can be seen today is the remains of the third-century BC temple that was built over the site of an earlier one. Evidence of oracular activity comes from papyri that were found here. The temple itself seems to have been abandoned during the fourth century AD after a period of decline. The ruins are not extensive, but the layout of the temple can clearly be made out.

BERENICE or **BERENIKE** a sanctuary of **Sarapis** in SE Egypt (23 50N, 35 28E). Berenice lay on the Red Sea coast, due E of Aswan. It was founded as a port for the trans-shipment of goods by **Ptolemy II** in 275 BC and named after his mother. Caravans departing for **KOPTOS** faced a journey of a week before reaching their destination. Sarapis was the principal deity of the ancient city, and his temple was its grandest. It was rebuilt during the first century AD, and it is the remains of that building that can be seen today, just outside modern Baranis. A bust of the god was unearthed in excavations there, along with a figurine of **Harpocrates** and many other fragments of sculpture. The area around Berenice was also famous in antiquity for its emerald mines, and the ruins of these can be found at nearby Wadi Sakait.

BUTO (now Tell el Fara'in): an oracle of **Leto** in N Egypt (31 13N, 30 44E). The site of Buto lies in the northern delta region of the Nile, about 25 km inland from the shores of Lake Burullus. The nearby modern village of Ibtu takes its name from it. Buto had been the capital of Lower Egypt before the country was unified. Even when political power moved elsewhere, it retained its religious importance as the centre of worship for the cobra goddess **Wadjet** who remained the official protectress of northern Egypt. The Greeks called her (and the city) Buto, but also came to identify her with Leto, the mother of **Apollo** and **Artemis**. It is under this name that **Herodotus** tells of her oracle. According to him [II.83], it had the greatest repute of any oracle in the country. Its most remarkable feature [II.156] was a massive block of stone in the shape of a cube, many metres long on each side. Indeed, everything about the temple seems to have been on a grand scale. Unfortunately, Herodotus gives no indication of how the oracle worked. The site of the temple has been identified, but little remains to be seen of it, let alone giant monoliths, and Buto itself now lies well off the beaten track.

CANOPUS: an oracle of **Pluto** (or **Osiris**, and later **Sarapis**) in N Egypt (31 19N, 30 04E). What remains to be seen of Canopus is near the town of Abukir on Egypt's Mediterranean coast. Much of what used to exist of Canopus is now underwater, but recent (and continuing) explorations by Franck Goddio and others are bringing ever more of it to light. The town was once linked by road and canal to neighbouring **ALEXANDRIA**. In its heyday the city earned a reputation for riotous and loose living, which it seems to have generally deserved. It was for this reason, among others, that its temple was destroyed by Christians in 389.

The philosopher **Heraclides of Pontus** mentions an oracle of Pluto there. Pluto, as god of the underworld, was identified by the Greeks with Osiris (who performed a similar function in Egypt) to whom the temple at Canopus was dedicated. How long it had been there is not known. Later, in 238 BC, the temple was rededicated by **Ptolemy III** to Sarapis, and the cult statue of Osiris was removed to another temple in nearby Herakleion. At Canopus, the cult of Sarapis became very much a healing one, and **incubation** was practised. (**Tacitus** suggests that this led to many identifying him with **Asclepius**.) However, there was a simpler (and cheaper) **binary lot** oracle as well that could provide a positive or negative answer to any suitable question. How much of this activity constituted a break with, or continuation of, previous practice is not known. An oracle of **Isis** was located in nearby **MENOUTHIS**.

COPTOS: see **KOPTOS**

DIONYSIAS: an oracle of **Sobek** in N Egypt (29 25N, 30 25E). The site of Dionysias is today known as Kasr Karun, and lies about 45 km NW of Faiyum City, beyond the W extremity of Lake Karun. It was originally situated at the water's edge, but the lake has retreated some 4 km since then leaving Kasr Karun dry if not particularly high. The main feature of the site is a temple from the **Ptolemaic** period dedicated to Sobek. Although its outward appearance and design are relatively plain, inside there is a complex arrangement of rooms and passageways, and its roof is still intact. There are concealed chambers in some of the walls, and this has led to the suspicion that oracular activities may have taken place here. Given that the crocodile god cults at nearby **SOKNOPAIOU NESOS** and **KARANIS** are known to have been oracular, a similar arrangement at Dionysias is entirely possible.

Most of the remains at the site are from the Roman period, and the city seems to have gone into terminal decline in the fourth century AD. Among the more interesting finds in the area were several moulds, dated to 315 AD, which may have been used for counterfeiting purposes.

ELEPHANTINE: an oracle of **Khnum** in S Egypt (24 05N, 32 53E). Elephantine is the island facing Aswan (ancient **SYENE**). The ruins of the sanctuary of Khnum are at the S end of the island, and it clearly dominated the ancient town of which it formed a part. Little remains above foundation level. Although there was a temple on this site from the third millennium BC onwards, what can be seen now dates only from the fourth century BC when it was rebuilt for the last time. Documentary evidence indicates that oracles were issued from this island, and it is also known that the cult of Khnum was oracular in at least some of its temples. Consequently it seems likely that this temple was a centre of oracular activity.

HEFAT: an oracle of **Hemen** in S Egypt (25 28N, 32 31E). The remains of Hefat lie at El Mualla, 23 km SW of Luxor along the banks of the Nile. Now there is little to be seen there apart from some rock tombs dating to around 2100 BC. However, it was once the main centre of the cult of Hemen, an early and almost forgotten Egyptian god. Sometimes portrayed as a falcon, his cult eventually merged with that of **Horus**. He was sometimes depicted killing a hippopotamus (representing the forces of evil) with a harpoon. Evidence of the oracular nature of his cult comes from a papyrus dated to around 770 BC. However, it is possible that the oracle in question was delivered in Egyptian **THEBES** rather than in Hefat itself.

HERACLEOPOLIS MAGNA: an oracle of **Harsaphes** in central Egypt (29 05N, 30 56E). Heracleopolis was known as Henen-nesut to the ancient Egyptians, and today is the village of Ihnasya el Medina. It lies to the S of the Faiyum and about 15 km W of Beni Suef. The site was occupied from the earliest days of Egyptian history, but the temple that can be seen there dates from the time of **Ramesses II**. Harsaphes was a ram-headed god whom the Greeks identified with **Heracles**. Oracular activity is known to have taken place here at least as early as the fourth century BC.

KARANIS: an oracle of **Sobek** in N Egypt (29 31N, 30 54E). The ruins of Karanis lie in the Faiyum area just to the N of Kom Aushim (or Oshim), 30 km N of Faiyum City, on the main road from Cairo. Karanis boasted two temples, both of which are relatively late. Neither is dedicated to Sobek as such, but among their several dedicatees were Soknopaios, Pnepheros and Petesouchos, and, like Sobek, they were all crocodile gods. It is largely a matter of interpretation whether they are regarded as independent local divinities, or simply different versions of Sobek. The cult of the crocodile, in its various forms, was a distinctive and widespread phenomenon of the Faiyum in antiquity.

The N temple was dedicated to Soknopaios, although probably not to him alone. The remains of a statue of **Isis** were found in the inner part of the temple, while an altar dedicated to the composite god **Sarapis-Zeus-Amun-Helios** was uncovered in the outer part. Its axis lies roughly on a line running from N to S, with the entrance at the S end. The S one, dedicated to Pnepheros and Petesouchos, lies even more roughly (it is at least 10 degrees out) on a line running from W to E, with the entrance at the E. It was probably built during the first or even second century AD. Inscriptions on the temple date to the reigns of **Nero**, **Claudius** and **Vespasian**. The temples seem to have fallen into disuse during the third century, and the town itself was apparently abandoned before the end of the fourth century.

The designs of the two temples are broadly similar. They both stand on raised platforms and, in typical Egyptian fashion, the most important parts of the temples are those furthest from the entrance. The walls of both still stand to a sufficient height to get a clear idea of the temples' plans. However, their innermost sanctuaries are now open to the sky whereas in antiquity they would have been very gloomy places indeed. Each sanctuary has an altar, and each altar has a cavity beneath it big enough to conceal a person. It is possible that these cavities played a role in the oracular functions of the temples, as places from which at least to hear, if not to speak. However, if Egyptian traditions were maintained, it is unlikely that any but the most privileged enquirers would have been allowed this far into the temple.

Consultation through the submission of written questions was probably the method most frequently used, and examples of these have survived. So it is known that in 6 AD someone called Asclepiades wanted the advice of Soknopaios on whether he should marry Tapetheus. The god's response is not known, and neither is the method by which he communicated it.

In addition to the remains of the temples, the ruins of a considerable complex of attendant buildings lie around them, and there is a small museum nearby. Many finds from the site are also to be found at the Kelsey Museum of Archaeology in Ann Arbor, Michigan (the University of Michigan excavated Karanis in the 1920s). Those wishing to visit **SOKNOPAIOU NESOS** 50 km away need to make arrangements at the museum in Kom Aushim.

KELLIS: an oracle of **Seth** in S Egypt (25 31N, 29 05E). The ruins of Kellis lie at Ismant el Kharab in the Dakhla Oasis, about 300 km due W of Luxor. The precise location of Seth's oracle is unclear, although it was presumably connected with one of the two temples that can be found in the SW of the extensive site. As his name appears on an inscription in the temple of **Tutu**, who also had oracular connections (at **SHENHUR** at least), it may have been based there. Some remains of the temple's walls and altars can be seen. It is apparent that Seth's cult enjoyed considerable popularity throughout the whole oasis, and it is possible that the god was consulted in more than one place. Ruins dating from almost the whole history of ancient Egypt are scattered around Dakhla. It is known that the cult of Seth was oracular in this area as far back as at least the eighth century BC.

KOPTOS: oracles of **Isis** and **Min** in S Egypt (26 00N, 32 49E). The site of Koptos (or Kebto, to give it its earlier name) is at Qift, 23 km S of Qena on the E bank of the Nile. It was a major centre of the cult of Min. The remains of no fewer than three temples have been uncovered here, and the earliest remains date back to the second millennium BC. Three early statues of the god found during excavations are now in the Ashmolean Museum in Oxford. One of the temples is dedicated to Min jointly with Isis. Construction on it began in the reign of **Ptolemy II**, and work on it continued on and off for the next 300 years. The town itself probably owed its origin to the quarries and mines in its immediate vicinity. It is known that Isis had an oracle here as far back as the thirteenth century BC. The main evidence of Min's oracular activity dates from the first century BC, when a special shrine seems to have been constructed specifically for this purpose in the southernmost of the three temples.

KYSIS: an oracle of **Sarapis** and/or **Isis** in S Egypt (24 35N, 30 43E). The ruins of Kysis are to be found at Dush, which lies at the S end of the Kharga oasis in Egypt's Western Desert. Most of what can be seen above ground consists of the remains of the temple to Sarapis and Isis, built during the second half of the first century AD. The town itself was probably founded at the same time, and survived until the fifth century when, for whatever reason (possibly insufficient water), it was abandoned. Excavations have revealed that an interesting development took place at the temple sometime during the later part of the fourth century. A brick extension was built onto the S end of the temple and, at the same time, a hole was made in its original S wall. This hole provided a direct channel of communication between the old temple's inner sanctuary and the new rooms added on to it. Through this channel people could consult the oracle of the god (or gods) within. Whether the temple was oracular before this time is not known, but it seems likely. The new arrangement is most easily understood as making access to an existing oracle easier. It is also not known whether it was Isis or Sarapis who presided over the oracular function of the temple, or whether they shared these duties between them.

MAHARRAQA: see **PSELCHIS**

MEMPHIS: sanctuaries of **Ptah, Imhotep** (or **Asclepius**) and **Apis** in N Egypt (29 51N, 31 15E). Memphis lay about 25 km S of Cairo. Many of the ruins that can be seen are in the vicinity of the modern village of Mit Rahinah. However, this is only part of the area the ancient city once covered during its long history. Saqqara, 2 km away to the W, was one of the burial grounds of the city. There can be found the step pyramid of **Djoser**, one of the first great stone buildings. Its architect was Imhotep, who later came to be identified with Asclepius. A healing cult seems to have developed around the site of his tomb. Although the origins of the two cults seem to have been completely independent of each other, Imhotep, like Asclepius, carried out his healing through the medium of dreams. Unfortunately, no traces of the sanctuary of Imhotep/Asclepius have been found.

The principal god of Memphis was Ptah, and he also had a reputation for healing. He, too, apparently used the medium of dreams for this work. While it is not known exactly how this worked, it is at least possible to see the general area where it took place. Although parts of it now lie underwater, the enclosure of the temple of Ptah comprises and contains a large part of what can be seen at Mit Rahinah. It was once one of the greatest temples of Egypt, but little of its glory remains. On the W side are parts of a monumental entrance. In the SW corner of the enclosure are the ruins of an embalming house connected with the cult of Apis, the bull god. The actual temple of Apis which it served was somewhere nearer to Saqqara, although it has not been found. Those who consulted the oracle of Apis first prayed to the god inside his sanctuary, but then received their responses from children outside it. Exactly how this happened is not clear. **Pausanias**, however, has a different account of the procedure followed. According to him [VII.22.2], it more closely resembled that employed at **PHARAI (1)**.

MENOUTHIS: an oracle of **Isis** in N Egypt (31 19N, 30 04E). Menouthis lay close to **ALEXANDRIA** and **CANOPUS** and, like the latter, now lies underwater. While **Sarapis** presided in Canopus, Isis held sway in Menouthis, its smaller and newer neighbour. However, what was on offer was very much the same in both places. **Incubation** came at the top end of the price range, while a cheap **lot** oracle was at the other. Menouthis enjoyed a certain reputation for licentiousness, which probably attracted rather more people than it repelled.

There is no mention of the temple before the second century AD, which makes it a very late foundation. However, while the temple of Sarapis in Canopus was destroyed in 389, the cult of Isis in Menouthis survived significantly longer. It was not until 495 that it seems to have been stamped out there altogether. In its place there arose a 'new' healing tradition (also employing incubation) based around a local church, in effect giving the cult a new lease of life. This tradition continued at least until the time of the Arab conquest in 640, but its fate thereafter is unknown.

OMBOS: an oracle of **Horus** in S Egypt (24 27N, 32 56E). The city known as Ombos to the Greeks was called Nebet by the ancient Egyptians, and now goes by the name of Kom Ombo. It lies on the E bank of the Nile, about 50 km N of Aswan. Its temple was dedicated to both **Sobek** and Horus (who was known here as 'the good doctor'), but the oracular activity seems to have been principally, and perhaps solely, the domain of Horus. The sanctuary was a healing one, and **incubation** may have been practised. Certainly those who came seeking the help of the god seem to have spent the night there. What is unclear is whether they slept or not. It is also unclear how much oracular activity other than that directly concerned with healing went on. The temple is in a reasonable state of preservation, and its unusual layout reflects its dual dedication. The cult of Horus occupied the W half of the building. A curious arrangement of passages may have provided hiding places for priests, although there may also be a more innocent explanation.

OXYRHYNCHUS: oracles of **Sarapis** and **Taweret** in N Egypt (28 32N, 30 40E). Located near modern El Bahnasa, about 200 km S of Cairo, it appears that ancient Oxyrhynchus may have had oracles of both Sarapis and the goddess Taweret. As evidence for both is primarily from the **Ptolemaic** period, it seems likely that they operated there at the same time. The oracle of Taweret seems to have delivered its messages in more than one way, both through **incubation**, and through the more traditional Egyptian method involving her image being carried on the shoulders of priests. It may be that the practice of incubation indicates some crossover between the two cults. Unfortunately, all that can be seen now are the fragmentary remains of a Roman theatre. The site is notable principally on account of the large number of papyri discovered there and which are now to be found dispersed among various museums around the world. One of them reveals that people were still bringing written requests for divine guidance here as late as the seventh century, although by this time, of course, it was the Christian god who was being consulted. The city's unusual name (meaning 'of the sharp-nosed fish') commemorates a local species of pike.

PHILAE: an oracle of **Isis** in S Egypt (24 01N, 32 53E). Philae lies to the S of Aswan, ancient **SYENE**. The buildings of the temple complex were relocated during the construction of the high dam, but an island setting has been preserved, so the approach to the temple is still by boat. It was one of the main centres of the goddess's cult, and the earliest parts of it have been dated to the seventh century BC. Oracular activity at the temple is not directly attested, but seems likely, given what is known to have happened at many other centres. However, there is direct evidence of at least an oracular connection. When **Theodosius the Great** attempted to close down all pagan temples at the end of the fourth century, Philae resisted. In the end, a treaty was agreed in 453 recognising local religious freedoms. At a certain time of the year the **Blemmyes** were entitled to remove the statue of the goddess from the island and take it elsewhere, although exactly where is not known. (One possibility is **TALMIS**, a short distance to the S, which seems to have been their main religious centre.) There it was used as an oracle, perhaps as part of a religious festival. This probably continued until the sixth century when the Blemmyes were displaced by their traditional enemies, the Nobatae.

PSELCHIS: an oracle of **Thoth** in S Egypt (23 11N, 32 45E). Since he was the Egyptian god of both wisdom and healing, the existence of an oracular dimension to the cult of Thoth is only to be expected. Unfortunately, the actual evidence for one is neither particularly strong nor particularly clear. However, there does seem to have been an oracle at his temple of Pselchis. Pselchis is generally identified with El Dakka, and lay about 100 km S of Aswan. It now lies under Lake Nasser. The temple at El Dakka was one of those rescued from the lake's rising waters, and it was reconstructed on its W bank 40 km further S near El Sabu el Gadid ('New Sebua'). The border between Egypt and its southern neighbour shifted periodically, and work on the temple at Pselchis began in about 220 BC when it lay outside Egyptian territory. It was founded by **Arkamani**, a king of Meroë, and dedicated to Thoth 'of Pnubs'. Some have identified El Dakka itself with Pnubs, but this seems unlikely. There is no agreement as to the exact location of Pnubs, but it is generally thought to have lain far away to the S, perhaps at or near Kerma in modern Sudan. It may be that the temple there also had an oracle. The temple at Pselchis was not finished by Arkamani, and further work on it was carried out by first the Ptolemies and then the Romans.

It is known that the oracle at Pselchis was available for consultation at the time of the god's special annual feast, but the extent of its availability at other times is unclear. It is also known that there was a special connection between Pselchis and **PHILAE**. The **Blemmyes** used to consult Thoth in order to ascertain the most auspicious time for their annual ritual of borrowing the image of **Isis** from her temple on Philae.

The temple from El Dakka now stands together with those from Maharraqa and El Sebua. The former has also been relocated here from an original location some 50 km to the N. Being dedicated to **Sarapis** and **Isis**, it may also have had some oracular or healing function. It was begun in the time of **Augustus**. Never finished, it became converted into a Christian church. The ancient name of Maharraqa was Hierasykaminos ('Sacred Sycamore'). Most contemporary visitors to the temples approach them from the water. New Sebua is about nine hours by boat from the Aswan end of Lake Nasser and eight from Abu Simbel.

SAIS: an oracle of **Neith** in N Egypt (30 58N, 30 46E). The scant remains of Sais, which the ancient Egyptians called Zau, can be found at Sa el Hagar, about 30 km NW of Tanta in the Nile Delta. At first briefly (727-715 BC) and then later for a longer period (664-525 BC) it was the country's capital. The goddess's temple was built on the grand scale, and claimed to be the place where **Osiris** was buried. There is nothing of it to be seen, although stones from the site have been reused in local buildings. The cult of **Isis** also seems to have had a firm foothold in the city. As Neith was associated with, among other things, wisdom, it is not surprising to find that she had an oracle, but very little is actually known about it.

SHENHUR or **SHANHUR**: an oracle of **Tutu** in S Egypt (25 50N, 32 45E). Shenhur is now a small village on the E bank of the Nile about 20 km N of Luxor. The remains of its ancient temple lie at the village's edge. Its construction took place in various stages, mainly during the first century AD. It was dedicated to **Isis**, but the cult of Tutu seems to have been conjoined with hers here, and oracles were delivered in his name rather than hers. The older parts of the temple, including the central sanctuary, are the most intact, and presumably provided the focal point of the oracular function.

SIWA: an oracle of **Amun** (or **Zeus**) in N Egypt (29 12N, 25 31E). The name 'Siwa' seems to date only from the middle ages. Ancient writers generally referred to the place simply as the oasis of Amun, in honour of the oracle. It lies about 500 km W of Cairo, and is usually reached from Mersa Matrouh (about 300 km away by road) on the Mediterranean coast. The ancient Greeks identified Amun with Zeus, and Siwa was one of his great oracles. Its origins are obscure. A legend recounted by **Herodotus** [II.53ff] claims that it was founded from Egyptian **THEBES** at the same time as **DODONA**. However, it was **MEMPHIS** that exercised religious control over it. Both places were a considerable, and arduous, journey away, and whatever its religious connections, Siwa was for practical purposes substantially independent. The earliest buildings that can be seen today have been dated to the sixth century BC, and were probably constructed to local designs by Greeks from **CYRENE**. According to Herodotus [I.46ff] the oracle of Amun at Siwa was one of those consulted by **Croesus**, although it failed his test.

The most famous visitor to Siwa (and, arguably, to anywhere else he went) was **Alexander the Great**, who came here in 331 BC. His preparedness to make the long trek across inhospitable desert when his ambitions lay in the opposite direction is considerable testimony to the importance he attached to the oracle. He had a private audience with the god, a privilege granted to very few, but never revealed what he was told. He did, however, indicate that he was pleased with the response he received, which would doubtless have given the god's blessing to his conquest of Egypt. (It seems likely that it would have been drafted in Memphis and sent on ahead of him from there.) Perhaps it was because of this that he later expressed his wish to be buried here. Most people are convinced that his final resting place was elsewhere, but that has not stopped others searching for his tomb in the vicinity.

The standard (and typically Egyptian) method of operation of the oracle seems to have involved the god's image being borne aloft in its shrine by a number of priests. The movement of this procession in some way indicated the god's response. This suggests that the responses were either limited to a 'yes' or a 'no', or else perhaps extended to choosing from however many options were laid before it

The ruins of the temple can be found in Aghurmi, a couple of km E of Siwa town. There are in fact two temples of Amun there. The oracular one was built on a large outcrop of rock. It is quite well preserved, and its layout can easily be seen. Its innermost room (at the N end) was presumably where the god's image was kept, and where oracles were also delivered to those of the most elevated status. A disparity between the heights of its external and internal walls suggests that this room may have had a false ceiling, designed to accommodate priests eager to overhear questions being put to the god.

The other temple stands a little distance away on lower ground, and is today known as Umm Abayda. It is also dedicated to Amun, and its scant remains date to the middle of the fourth century BC. Excavations in the area have also uncovered evidence of a processional way linking the two temples, and it is presumably along this that the image of the god would have been carried in its public outings during which most consultations would have taken place.

SOKNOPAIOU NESOS: an oracle of **Sobek** and **Isis** in N Egypt (29 32N, 30 40E). The ruins of Soknopaiou Nesos (now known as Dimeh or Dimai) can be found in the Faiyum area of Egypt, about 50 km from those of **KARANIS**. Permission to visit the site must be obtained from the museum in Kom Aushim. The remains of a temple can be found within its high surrounding wall. To the N of it can be seen the foundations of another. There is nothing on the site to indicate how the oracle worked. However, two pieces of papyrus dating to the middle of the second century BC have been found (now in the Ashmolean Museum, Oxford) that were clearly used in a consultation there. They reveal that someone called Teshnufe wanted advice on whether to plough a particular piece of land or not. One piece of papyrus contained the question and a positive response, the other the same question and a negative response. By some means or other one of them would have been selected and returned to Teshnufe. It is not known which he received.

SYENE: a sanctuary of **Isis** in S Egypt (24 05N, 32 54E). Even though a major centre of her cult lay nearby at **PHILAE**, Syene (modern Aswan) had its own temple to the goddess. Built during the second half of the third century BC, it lies to the E of the railway station, near the road leading to the northern quarries. The building has had a varied history, having been converted into a Christian church during the sixth century and more recently served as a store for the Department of Antiquities.

TALMIS: an oracle of **Mandulis** in S Egypt (23 33N, 32 52E). Talmis became known as Kalabsha, and with the construction of the Aswan High Dam its temple was taken apart and rebuilt at New Kalabsha. This lies about 13 km S of Aswan, and is only a little to the S of the dam itself. The temple's original location is another 40 km to the S, under the waters of Lake Nasser. Although usually known by his Greek name Mandulis, the god was in fact of Nubian origin and known to the Egyptians (who sometimes identified him with **Horus**) as Merwel. The temple that can be seen today was built in the first century BC, on the site of another founded a thousand years earlier. It was dedicated to **Isis** as well as Mandulis, but he alone seems to have exercised the oracular function. The god was consulted through the process of **incubation**, but this is only attested between the first and third centuries AD.

Outside of that time, little is known concerning what took place there. However, it is thought that Talmis was for some time the major religious centre of the **Blemmyes**, and its recorded oracular history falls within the period of their occupation. Eventually, during the sixth century AD, part of the temple was converted into a Christian church.

TEBTUNIS: an oracle of **Sobek** in N Egypt (29 07N, 30 45E). Tebtunis was a city founded by **Ptolemy I** in the third century BC on the site of a far earlier Egyptian settlement known as Beten. Today the place is known as Umm el Breigat, and lies in the extreme S of the Faiyum area SW of Cairo. Sobek was known here as Soknebtunis, one of the many local names or identities he assumed in this region. The temple itself has almost entirely disappeared, but the sanctuary wall surrounding it can still be seen, as can the ceremonial way approaching it. However, the evidence for an oracular cult here comes from the enormous number of papyrus documents and fragments discovered in the area. On the basis of this evidence it is apparent that the cult was oracular as far back as the late fourth century BC at least. The later history of the cult is obscure, but it is known that the temple continued to function until the fourth century AD. Oracles were obtained through submitting alternative answers to a question on separate pieces of papyrus. The answer that was selected (by whatever method) and returned was the one sanctioned by the god. Most of the papyri that have been found date to the third century BC, and by far the most frequently asked questions relate to matters of theft, with the god being asked to identify the guilty party.

TENTYRA or **TENTYRIS** (modern Denderah): a healing sanctuary of **Hathor** in S Egypt (26 08N, 32 40E). Often visited on a day trip by boat from Luxor (about 60 km away to the S), the temple of Hathor, the cow goddess, at Tentyra is one of the best preserved in the whole of Egypt. Most of what can be seen was built in the first centuries BC and AD. Next to it, at its S end, is a temple to **Isis** built by **Augustus**. However, from the point of view of oracles, the most interesting building is what remains of a mud-brick structure (of which little survives) lying near the NE corner of Hathor's temple. This has been identified as an ancient sanatorium. To this place the sick would come to seek help through the medium of dreams, which were perhaps induced by the use of psychoactive chemicals (or magic, depending upon your perspective). Water also apparently played a significant role in the process. Although the precise relationship that obtained between the sanatorium and the temple is unknown, Hathor did have some associations with healing. It seems likely that similar healing centres might have been built near to other temples, but have not survived.

THEADELPHIA: an oracle of **Sobek** in N Egypt (29 21N, 30 34E). The site of Theadelphia lies at Batn Ihrit, about 30 km W of Faiyum City. Sobek was worshipped at the temple here under the name of Pnephoros, one of his various identities. Relatively little remains to be seen today, but the temple at Theadelphia has been an important source of our knowledge of Egyptian oracles. A wall painting found at the temple, showing the god's image being borne aloft on men's shoulders, seems to provide clear confirmation of one of the ways in which an oracular god could be consulted. It is known that questions might be put to a god when its image was being carried around outside its temple, and that the movements of the image (or, more precisely, of those carrying it) could then be regarded as an oracular response. This process seems to be the subject matter of the painting.

THEBES: oracles of (in alphabetical order) **Ahmose Nefertari**, **Amenhotep I**, **Amun**, **Hatshepsut**, **Khonsu**, **Montu** and **Mut** in S Egypt (25 42N, 32 38E). A positive plethora of oracles seem to have been at work in this ancient city, once called Waset by the Egyptians and Great City of **Zeus** (with whom Amun was identified) by the Greeks. Geographically, ancient Thebes was divided between the east bank, modern Luxor and Karnak, and the west bank, the Valley of the Kings, Deir el Bahri, and Deir el Medina. The two will be dealt with separately here.

(i) East Bank. Thebes was the centre of the cult of Amun, and his temple at Karnak one of the greatest dedicated to any god anywhere. The oracle of Amun seems to have been principally consulted on matters of state, and its first known pronouncement dates from the fifteenth century BC when it obligingly endorsed Queen Hatshepsut's claim to the throne. Thereafter it continued to give advice, when asked, for well over a thousand years.

The complex of buildings at Karnak was constructed over an enormous period of time. The oldest parts of the precinct of Amun date back to at least the reign of Hatshepsut herself. Work on the temples continued right through until Roman times, and the ruins are both extensive and impressive. Although the temple of Amun forms the most important part of the complex, other deities are represented there too. In the SW corner of Amun's precinct is a temple dedicated to his son Khonsu, a moon god. He seems to have specialised in healing. During the reign of **Ramesses II** the god's statue was apparently sent on a long journey away from Thebes on a mission to cure the pharaoh's sister-in-law. A thousand years later, **Ptolemy IV** also sought, and received, the god's medical assistance.

The temple of Khonsu is one of the better preserved parts of the complex, and was probably founded in the fourteenth century BC, although what can be seen now is of later origin. It stands to a considerable height, and it is possible to climb up onto its roof. The stairs are just to the E of the temple's sanctuary, and a statue of the god was discovered under its floor. It is now in the Egyptian Museum in Cairo.

Montu and Mut also had their temples at Karnak, to the N and S of Amun's respectively. They evidently also delivered oracles from time to time.

(ii) West Bank. In general terms, the ancient Egyptians regarded the E as the place of life and the W as the place of death; hence the great burial ground of the Valley of the Kings lies on the W bank of the Nile. Being carved into the rock, tombs have survived better than free-standing buildings. However, there were once many temples in this area serving the posthumous needs of those buried there. The temple of Hatshepsut in the locality known as Deir el Bahri is a surviving (and much restored) example. At some time this seems to have been a centre of oracular activity, perhaps because it was built on the site of an earlier temple dedicated to Ahmose Nefertari and Amenhotep I.

For reasons that are not entirely clear, these two (mother and son) enjoyed considerable popularity on the west bank, especially in the area now known as Deir el Medina. It was in this village that those who worked on the tombs and temples lived. One possible explanation for the cult of Amenhotep I, at least, being prominent here is that he may have been responsible for the village's original foundation. The area around the village evidently contained many shrines to him, large and small. Almost all traces of these have disappeared, but there remains one temple in Deir el Medina in which the cult of Amenhotep I (among others) was celebrated. Built in the third century BC, it survived partly because it became converted into a Coptic monastery, and it is well preserved to this day.

   Also preserved is what appears to be a picture of the oracle of Amenhotep actually being consulted. It is to be found in the tomb of Amenmose, a twelfth-century BC priest of the deified pharaoh's cult. It is one of what are known as the tombs of the nobles (number 19) that lie near the Valley of the Kings. In the wall painting, the statue of Amenhotep I is clearly shown being carried on the shoulders of priests, which would be typical for an Egyptian oracular consultation.

FRANCE

ALBAECE REIORUM APOLLINARIUM: a healing sanctuary of **Apollo** and **Asclepius** in SE France (43 50N, 06 07E). The site is now known as Riez and lies in the Alpes de Provence, about 80 km N of Toulon. It was originally the capital of the Reii tribe, then refounded by **Augustus** as a Roman town. Modern buildings obscure most of the remains of the ancient ones, but not all of them. In the W of the town there are some columns from what was probably the temple of Apollo, while nearby is a large spring where an inscription to Asclepius was found. Since they were regarded as father and son, and very closely associated in places like **EPIDAUROS**, it may be that the two cults operated together in some way here. The local museum contains finds from the excavations.

ALESIA: a healing sanctuary of **Apollo** Moritasgus and **Damona** in E France (47 30N, 04 38E). The site of Alesia is to be found just to the E of Alise-Ste-Reine, 65 km NW of Dijon. Its most famous appearance in ancient history is in **Julius Caesar**'s description of his conquest of Gaul, for it was here, in 52 BC, that he forced the great Gaulish leader **Vercingetorix** to surrender after laying siege to the city. Not surprisingly, perhaps, most of the ruins that can be seen there now date from after this time. The remains of a temple, houses, shops and a theatre have all been found in the area. The healing sanctuary was at the E end of the site, based around a spring. It seems likely that **incubation** was practised here, but the discovery of ancient surgical instruments in the vicinity suggests that a wider range of treatments was on offer. Apollo Moritasgus (an **epithet** meaning 'masses of sea water') was only one of the deities worshipped here, and he shared the healing functions of the site with **Damona**.

ALLONNES: a healing sanctuary of **Mars Mullo** in N France (47 57N, 00 09E). Allonnes is about 5 km SW of the centre of Le Mans, and the ruins to be found there come from the period between the second century BC and the fourth century AD. They lie just outside the town, on a small wooded hill overlooking the river Sarthes. Mars Mullo was a composite of a Roman and a Gaulish god, and his cult was particularly popular in what are now Normandy and Brittany. How many of his sanctuaries practised healing is not known, but at Allonnes many **votive** objects have been found indicating that people came to him because of eye problems. Excavations have revealed the layout of the sanctuary, which was centred on a large square courtyard. The temple stood at its W end, and its central part was circular in plan. Around the N and S sides of the courtyard were a number of rooms whose purpose remains unknown. All of the buildings date to the second century AD, although they seem to have replaced earlier ones on the same site. Parts of a baths complex were uncovered in the nineteenth century, but there is now nothing to be seen of them. Movable items found at the site are on display in the town hall.

AQUAE: a healing sanctuary of **Borvo** in SE France (45 40N, 05 54E). Aquae is now better known as Aix-les-Bains, but little remains to be seen of its ancient history. The foundations of a temple have been found, as has a baths complex. Objects found in the excavations are now in the local museum. Inscriptions reveal the presence of the cult of Borvo, but other healing deities may have been worshipped here too. Small bronze statuettes found near a spring in the vicinity suggest that he may have been identified locally with **Heracles**.

CHAMALIÈRES: a healing sanctuary of Maponos in central France (45 45N, 03 01E). Chamalières lies just to the W of Clermont-Ferrand. The ancient name of the site is unknown, and, apart from an enclosure wall, there were apparently no permanent structures there. The connection with Maponos is not entirely certain, but excavations carried out in the late 1960s unearthed a lead tablet inscribed with his name. Maponos was a youthful Gaulish deity, sometimes identified with **Apollo**. Chamalières is the site of therapeutic springs, and many wooden items depicting afflicted parts of the body have been found in their vicinity, indicating healing activity. The items have been dated to a relatively limited period, roughly 50 BC to 50 AD. Quite why this should be so is something of a mystery, as a far longer healing history seems guaranteed. Even today the town boasts more than one thermal establishment (in the areas to the W and NW of the railway station). The precise locality of the sanctuary is known as La Source des Roches, but there is nothing to be seen there apart from water. Finds from the site are in the Musée Bargoin in Clermont-Ferrand.

ESSAROIS: a healing sanctuary of **Apollo** in E France (48 03N, 04 33E). The site is at Essoyes, about 20 km NW of Châtillon-sur-Seine. The god was worshipped under two different forms here, as a god of springs (the source of the Cave river is nearby) and as Apollo Vindonnus ('clear light'). To reflect this dual identity, there were two separate temples close to (but not actually touching) each other. Most of what has been found dates to the first centuries BC and AD, and includes a number of thin bronze plates depicting eyes and arms. Carved items of wood and stone have also been found in the shapes of arms, legs and other limbs. Most of these are now in the museum in Châtillon-sur-Seine. Apollo Vindonnus seems to have had a special appeal to those suffering from eye problems. It is assumed that the nearby springs played some part in the healing process.

FONTES SEQUANAE: a healing sanctuary of Sequana in E France (48 30N, 04 45E). The sanctuary, of which only a few traces of the foundations remain, lies about 2 km SE of Saint-Germain-Sources-Seine, 35 km NW of Dijon. Sequana was a river goddess of the Sequanae tribe. (In the sixth century AD she reappears, after a change of both sex and religion, as St Sequanus.) She shared her name with, and personified, their principal river (now known as the Seine), and was particularly associated with the river's source, where her healing cult was located. The archaeological evidence unearthed at the site indicates that it was well patronised from the first to the fourth centuries AD, after the Roman conquest of Gaul. The pre-Roman history of the sanctuary is far less clear. It was situated on a terraced cliff, with the temple on the highest level. Healing took place through the medium of **incubation**, and a little lower down the cliff lay sleeping accommodation for visitors. Right at the bottom there seems to have been some kind of shop. Over two hundred objects have been found at the site, made from wood, stone or bronze, representing parts of the body. Given in thanks by those who received cures, they may have been purchased in the shop.

GLANUM: a healing sanctuary of Glanis in S France (43 46N, 04 51E). The ruins of Glanum lie 2 km S of St Rémy de Provence, about 30 km NE of Arles.

In a curious footnote to the history of art, the site was captured in oils by Vincent van Gogh in his 'Olive Trees with the Alpilles in the Background'. Since excavations there began only after his death, the painting preserves an image of Glanum in its undisturbed state. The sanctuary of Glanis lies at the far S end of the site. The remains of a complex of buildings can be seen there, though nothing stands to any great height. What survives was built between 125 BC, when the town was destroyed, and 270 AD, when it was destroyed again. Glanis was a local god, and his healing cult was based around a spring in the sanctuary.

GRAND: a healing sanctuary of **Apollo Grannus** in E France (48 24N, 05 33E). Grand lies about 60 km SW of Nancy and 16 km W of Neufchâteau. The site's ancient name is unknown. Grannus was a Celtic healing god who was usually found in association with therapeutic springs. In Roman times he was often connected with, or even replaced by, Apollo, and that seems to have happened at Grand. Certainly Apollo was not the first deity to be worshipped here. As with many healing cults, that of Grannus practised **incubation**.

Within the sanctuary was an amphitheatre seating around 17,000 people, which may give some indication of the considerable popularity it enjoyed during at least part of its history. Among its more illustrious visitors was the emperor **Caracalla** who visited in 213, laden with gifts. The long-term benefits that may have accrued to his health as a result are difficult to gauge as he was murdered a few years later. It is also widely thought (although not universally agreed) that the emperor **Constantine the Great** came here in 309 and received a vision of Apollo himself. The details are scanty and disputed, but the incubatory history of the site gives the claim that such a thing happened here a reasonable degree of plausibility.

In any event, it seems likely that many people came here for more than just healing. A well at the site yielded many fragments of ivory that were pieced together to form four astrological tablets. Interestingly, some of the writing on them is in Coptic, indicating a connection of some kind with Egypt. Presumably they were used in the process of casting horoscopes. They formed two pairs, one now in the museum at Epinal, the other in the museum at St-Germain-en-Laye. Some other finds can be seen in a museum at the site.

Excavations have also uncovered the foundations of what was presumably Apollo's temple. It lies just to the SW of the modern village's square. To its W are the remains of a basilica with mosaics, while to its S lay a bathing complex. It is thought that incubation took place in the area between the temple and the baths. Little is known about how the sanctuary functioned, but water seems to have played a significant role in its cultic practices. Dramatic evidence for this can be seen in the system of underground aqueducts that has been discovered.

The site survived the advent of Christianity. According to tradition, a certain Libaire was martyred here in 362, and a healing cult continued to operate under her name until the eighteenth century. It was based around a spring which curiously seems to have dried up in 1789, the year of the French Revolution. (Goodbye Libaire, hello liberté?) A church at the E extreme of the village is still dedicated to her.

GEORGIA

LEUCOTHEA or **LEUKOTHEA**: an oracle of **Phrixus** in W Georgia. **Strabo** [XI.2.17] tells of an oracle in the Moschian part of Colchis, an area that lies near Georgia's border with Turkey. Leucothea has not been located with any certainty, but some have identified it with Vani (42 05N, 42 30E), which lies about 180 km W of Tbilisi and 20 km SW of Kutaisi. Excavations at the site indicate that it was a major city before being destroyed soon after 100 BC. Such a date is at least consistent with Strabo's observation that the temple there was robbed by **Pharnaces** who ruled Pontus (Strabo's homeland) at about that time. He also mentions the fact that rams were never sacrificed at this temple. Although the precise reasons for this are left unclear, there was a legendary connection between Phrixus and this animal. Phrixus had been about to be sacrificed when he was rescued by his mother, and given a ram with a golden fleece (a present to her from **Hermes**). The ram carried him off to safety in Colchis. Although he sacrificed that particular animal in gratitude for his escape, he may have developed an appropriate sympathy for the species thereafter. (The golden fleece itself was saved, and subsequently sought by the **Argonauts**.) **Leucothea** was the name of a goddess ('the white goddess'), and Strabo says that the oracle of Phrixus was located in her temple (which Phrixus had founded). She was often identified with **Ino**, and had her own oracle at **THALAMAE**.

GERMANY

AQUAE MATTIACAE: a healing sanctuary of **Diana** Mattiaca in W Germany (50 06N, 08 10E). A spa since Roman times, the place is now known as Wiesbaden. One of the few signs of its antiquity the modern city possesses is a stretch of wall known as the *Heidenmauer* ('heathen wall'), which was probably built in the reign of **Diocletian**. However, it is known that a large bathing complex was constructed here during the first century AD. Before

Roman times, this area was the stronghold of the Mattiaci tribe, and Diana Mattiaca takes her name from them. She was worshipped here as a goddess of healing, but no temple to her has been located.

AUGUSTA TREVERORUM: a healing sanctuary of **Lenus Mars** in W Germany (49 48N, 06 36E). Lenus Mars was a composite god. Lenus was the principal healing god of the people known as the Treveri, and his cult had existed long before his identification with Mars. His principal centre was at the place the Romans called Augusta Treverorum, and later Treveris, but which is now known as Trier. However, while the Roman city was on the E bank of the Mosel, the sanctuary of Lenus Mars lay on the other side of it, in a small wooded valley. The site can be found about 1 km W of the bridge that crosses the river from the end of Karl Marx Strasse. Here a sizeable temple was constructed in the second century, with an altar on a similar scale, along with a number of other attendant buildings, including a theatre. Excavations have indicated that these were constructed over an older and much more modest sanctuary. The principal remains to be seen at the site are the foundations of the temple and altar. A healing spring lay a little above them, and the waters flowing from it were channelled into a small bathing complex. Beliefs in the curative properties of the spring continued long after the buildings around it had fallen into ruin. Excavations at the site unearthed many **votive** objects, and the city's Rheinisches Landesmuseum contains many local archaeological finds from the Roman period. The city itself still boasts some impressive monuments to its long history.

HOCHSCHEID: a healing sanctuary of **Apollo** in W Germany (49 52N, 07 13E). The remains of the sanctuary are to be found in woods to the SW of Hochscheid village, which lies S of the Mosel about 45 km ENE of Trier. Its ancient name is not known. Inscriptions on two altars found there indicate that the sanctuary was dedicated to Apollo, in conjunction with **Sirona**, a Celtic healing goddess with whom he was sometimes found in association in this part of the world. On one of the altars, Sirona is shown with a snake coiled around her left arm. (This animal was also associated with **Asclepius**.) The site consists of the ruins of a temple constructed around a spring. The temple was probably built during the second century AD and destroyed during the third. The sanctuary was evidently well endowed. Given its relatively remote location, this might indicate the support of a wealthy local patron. Although usually called Hochscheid, after the nearest village, the sanctuary itself is known locally as *Heiliggeist* ('holy spirit').

POMMERN: a healing sanctuary of **Lenus Mars** in W Germany (50 13N, 07 20E). Pommern lies about 70 km NE of Trier, on the W bank of the Mosel. The sanctuary stands on top of a hill known as the Martberg, commemorating its ancient association with Mars. Excavations have revealed the remains of an impressive complex of buildings, one of which may have served as an **abaton**. There were probably several other sanctuaries of Lenus Mars scattered about the countryside around Trier, but apart from those of Pommern and **AUGUSTA TREVERORUM**, none have survived to any significant extent.

GREECE

ABAI or **ABÆ**: an oracle of **Apollo** in Boiotia, central Greece (38 33N, 22 57E). This isolated hilltop site is NW of **ORCHOMENOS**, about 2.5 km W of Exarchos. The city was evidently of some importance in its heyday and, according to legend, had been founded by **Abas**. However, apart from some impressive sections of wall and a gate, little has survived that is recognisable. The oracle itself was situated in a sanctuary by the road leading to neighbouring Hyampolis, whose ruins crown a nearby hill. Excavations were carried out in an area some 600 m NW of Abai at the end of the nineteenth century and the remains of a **stoa** and two temples were found. It seems probable that they belonged to the sanctuary of Apollo, but there is not much left to see of them now.

The oracle clearly enjoyed a considerable reputation. According to **Herodotus** [I.46-50], it was one of only five on the Greek mainland consulted by **Croesus**. He also tells how it was visited by **Mys** on the orders of **Mardonius**, a Persian general [VIII.134]. He describes the oracle as having been wealthy, and as still active in his own time [VIII.33]. According to **Pausanias** [IV.32.5], it was consulted by the Thebans before the battle of Leuktra, which took place in 371 BC. In none of these cases has the oracle's answer been recorded, although Croesus evidently found its response to his enquiry unsatisfactory. According to **Stephanus Byzantius**, it was older than the oracle at Delphi, but it apparently ceased to function before Pausanias visited it, and nothing is known about how its responses were delivered. Despite its eminent past, Abai receives few visitors.

ABDERA or **ABDIRA**: an oracle of **Apollo** in Thrace, NE Greece (36 46 N, 24 48E). Abdera was on the coast, about 26 km S of Xanthi, and about 5 km S of modern Avdira. The city was said to have been founded by **Heracles**, but the archaeological evidence points to a date somewhere in the seventh century BC. It produced some celebrated philosophers (**Leucippus, Democritus,**

Protagoras), but was generally renowned for the dullness of its inhabitants, which was attributed to its unwholesome climate. Excavations have uncovered the city walls and the remains of some buildings within them. Some restoration work has taken place. Next to nothing is known about the oracle here, including its location. Archaeological finds from the area are mainly on display in the museum at Komotini, about 50 km to the E.

ABIA or **ABIÆ**: a sanctuary of **Asclepius** in Messenia, S Greece (36 54N, 22 10E). The site is now known as Avia and lies on the coast about 8 km SE of Kalamata. The town had once been known as Ira (or Ire), and appears as such in **Homer**'s *Iliad*. **Pausanias** says [IV.30.1] there was an **Asclepeion** here, but it has so far eluded proper identification. The city was better known for its splendid sanctuary of **Heracles**, but there is not much left of anything.

ACHLADOKAMPOS: a sanctuary of **Asclepius** in Argolis, S Greece (37 28N, 22 35E). **Pausanias** [VIII.54.5] observed a shrine of Asclepius on the road from **ARGOS** to Tegea. He gives the place no name, but it is thought to have lain near the village of Achladokampos. While the modern road from Argos to Tripoli, near which the village stands, is easy to find, the line of the ancient road is not so clear and the site has not been found. However, a possible location lies about 2 km E of Achladokampos, at a place called Kefalari. Here there is a church of the **Zoodochos Pigi** which may occupy the site of an ancient therapeutic establishment. The church stands isolated with a spring flowing by the side of it and trees providing plentiful shade. It is evidently a popular local picnic spot.

AEGINA or **ÆGINA** or **AIGINA** (now Egina): a sanctuary of **Asclepius** on an island in the Saronic Gulf in S Greece (37 44N, 23 26E). In his play *Wasps* (lines 120-1), **Aristophanes** has a character say:

> We sailed to Aegina to have him sleep
> A night in the temple of Asclepius.

This confirms not only the presence of an **Asclepeion** on the island, but also that **incubation** was practised there (as was normal in such places). **Pausanias** [II.30.1] enigmatically says only where the Asclepeion *isn't*, making it clear that it was *not* near the shrines of **Apollo**, **Artemis** or **Dionysus**.

Although remains of temples have been found on the island, and although there has been some dispute over their dedications, none has so far been attributed to Asclepius.

AEGIRA or **ÆGIRA** or **AIGEIRA**: a sanctuary of **Ge** in Achaia, S Greece (38 7N, 22 23E). The evidence for an oracle of Ge here is rather confused. **Pliny the Elder** [XXVIII.147] clearly believed there was one, and that it operated according to a somewhat bizarre practice whereby the prophetess first drank bull's blood and then descended into a cave. Since bull's blood was generally supposed to be lethal, there are strong undertones of death here, which are reinforced by the act of descent into the cave. However, **Pausanias**, who took a keen interest in oracles, describes things differently [VII.25.8]. He suggests that the drinking of bull's blood was part of the procedure whereby the prophetess was *selected* rather than functioned. The drinking of the blood was a test of the candidate's truthfulness. The main topic on which the truth was sought concerned the candidate's sexual history. She was not allowed to have had more than one lover and, if selected, was to have none thereafter. On the question of how she prophesied, Pausanias is entirely silent. He also indicates that the sanctuary, whose location he calls Gaios, was not in Aegira itself but outside it. No obvious candidate for the cave in question (if cave it was) has been found.

According to Pausanias [VII.26.3] there were also statues of **Asclepius** to be found in a temple at Aegira, but it is unclear as to whether the temple itself was dedicated to him. The remains of ancient Aegira can be found near modern Egira.

AIANI: an oracle of **Pluto** in Macedonia, N Greece (40 09N, 21 54E). The site of Aiani lies 18 km S of Kozani. The modern village of the same name is noted mainly for its **Byzantine** churches. On top of a nearby hill can be seen a few remains of some far older structures. Not enough is known about the ancient sanctuary of Pluto to determine its location. It is possible that one of the churches now occupies it. Certainly an elevated site is less likely for the god of the underworld. As was usual at his oracular sanctuaries, **incubation** was the established procedure for consultation.

AIGION: a sanctuary of **Asclepius** in Achaia, S Greece (38 14N, 21 59E). According to **Pausanias** [VII.23.5], this sanctuary had statues of both Asclepius and his daughter **Hygeia**. These statues (along with the sanctuary itself, perhaps) obviously enjoyed a special reputation as they were reproduced on the local coinage. No remains of either the sanctuary or the statues have been found, however, and most of the ancient city lies firmly buried under the buildings of modern Egio, on the coast 30 km due E of **PATRAS**. In his observations about the place, Pausanias recollects a conversation he had there with a Phoenician, during which they agreed that

Asclepius could be thought of impersonally as the health-giving fresh air rather than as a god.

AKAKESION: an oracle of **Pan** in Arkadia, S Greece (37 23N, 22 03E). The site lies about 13 km W of **MEGALOPOLIS**, and 1 km E of the ruins and village of Likosoura. **Pausanias** [VIII.37.11] visited it, but says that the oracle had ceased to function by his time. However, he does mention that Pan had not operated alone in his oracular capacity here, but had employed a local nymph, Erato, as his mouthpiece. This is consistent with the fact that Pan often appeared in the company of **Nymphs**. The area has yet to be excavated and there is little to see apart from the remains of an ancient cistern by the side of the road. The sanctuary of Pan lay somewhere between the cistern and the walls of ancient Likosoura higher up.

AKARNANIA: an oracle of **Amphilochus** in central Greece. Akarnania is a region, but within it there was a town called Argos Amphilochicum (38 55N, 21 13E), which was the capital of the area known as Amphilochia. This town was said to have been founded by Amphilochus. However, there are two characters called Amphilochus who are both possible candidates for this role. One was the son of **Amphiaraus** (the possessor of an oracle of his own at **OROPOS**), the other was his grandson. Whether the oracle was located in or near this town is not known, but seems likely. It was a dream oracle, which was commonly the case for heroes (as opposed to divinities). There was another oracle of Amphilochus at **MALLUS**. For a hero to have more than one oracle was certainly *not* common, since such institutions were generally based around their (supposed) burial sites. As the son of Amphiaraus is clearly associated with Mallus, it may be safest to assume that the shrine in Akarnania belonged to his grandson. The modern town of Amfilokhia should not be confused with its predecessor. The ancient settlement lay about 10 km to the N, about 1 km off the main road, near the village of Loutro. The remains are scant, although some substantial foundations have been exposed in places.

ALIPHEIRA: a sanctuary of **Asclepius** in Arkadia, S Greece (37 31N, 21 52E). The ruins of Alipheira lie about 3 km S of modern Alifira, NW of Andritsena. It is mentioned by **Pausanias** [VIII.26.6], although he says little about it. The extensive site was excavated in the 1930s and much can be seen. Following the clues of Pausanias, a temple dedicated to Asclepius was discovered at its N end. It is very modest in scale (less than 10 m long, less than 6 m wide), and the remains of an altar stand in front of it. The altar has been dated to the fourth century BC, while the temple itself is thought to have been built around 300 BC. To the SE of the altar were found the remains of another building, which may have played a role in the healing function of the establishment. It may have been that **incubation** took place there. At the other end of the site is a large temple of Athena, and the remains of a variety of buildings lie in between. The principal buildings are helpfully labelled. The place is remarkably peaceful and offers some spectacular views.

AMPHIKLEIA or **AMPHICAEA**: a sanctuary of **Dionysus** in central Greece (38 38N, 22 43E). According to **Pausanias** [X.33.5], it had once been known as Ophiteia, owing to the benevolent intervention of a snake in ancient times (the Greek word for snake is *ophis*). The modern town was known as Dadi until it renamed itself in honour of the adjacent ruins. Dionysus supplied both prophecies and healing here. The healing function worked through **incubation**, while the oracular function was performed by a priest who became periodically possessed by the god. The city was also noted in antiquity for the special mysteries of the god that were celebrated there. The site lies on the N side of Mount Parnassus, while **DELPHI**, which also had connections with Dionysus, lies to the S. However, unlike Delphi, little of significant interest has been uncovered in Amphikleia and there is nothing to indicate where Dionysus worked his wonders.

ANAPHE: a sanctuary of **Asclepius** in the Cyclades (36 22N, 25 45E). Anaphe (now Anafi) is small, and lies in the SE part of the groups of islands, about 30 km E of its more famous neighbour **THIRA** (Santorini), from which it is usually reached. Its principal modern settlement lies in the S of the island, while such ruins as there are can mainly be found in its eastern extremity. At Kastelli there are the ruins of the ancient city of Anaphe, which include the very few remains of a temple dedicated to **Apollo** and Asclepius. As there was another temple on the island dedicated to Apollo, it may be that the temple with the dual dedication was in practice primarily concerned with the cult of Asclepius. However, the evidence is too scant to know what went on there.

The island is mentioned by **Apollonius of Rhodes** [IV.1716]. He claims that the **Argonauts** visited it on their return voyage. According to him, Apollo was worshipped there with the **epithet** Aigletes ('radiant'). It is thought that the monastery of Kalamiotissa stands on the site of his temple.

ANTISSA: the site of an oracle of **Orpheus** on the island of **LESBOS** (39 15 N, 25 52E). According to legend, Orpheus was hacked to death by followers of **Dionysus**, who threw his head into the nearby river. In due course it reached the sea, and landed on Lesbos. There it was placed in an underground cave at Antissa where it made its prophecies. It continued to do so until **Apollo** came and ordered the head to be silent as it was luring too many people away from his own oracles! The modern village of Antissa is in the NW of the island. The remains of its ancient predecessor lie 7 km to the NE, on the coast. Orpheus' head, if it was ever there, is long gone. However, there is evidence to suggest that the use of skulls was a recognised (although not necessarily common) way of making contact with the underworld.

AORNOS: an oracle of the **dead** in Thesprotia, NW Greece. **Pausanias** [IX.30.3] relates the story that **Orpheus** visited it, and it is at least a possible candidate for the setting of his legendary descent into the underworld. Unfortunately its location is not known. Somewhere near modern Gliki (about 20 km E of Parga) has been suggested as one possibility, although somewhere nearer the sea is perhaps more likely. That would place it more in the vicinity of **EPHYRA**. As Ephyra was meant to have its own oracle of the dead, it may be that what appear to be two oracles were in fact one.

ARGOS: the site of an oracle of **Apollo** (and of a sanctuary to **Asclepius**) in Argolis, S Greece (37 38N, 22 42E). The modern city lies at the foot of two hills, both of which were the sites of early settlements. The oracle of Apollo was situated on the W slopes of the E hill, known as Aspis ('shield'). The god was known here by two different **epithet**s, Pythaeus and Deiradiotes. Pythaeus is a reference to **DELPHI**, and was frequently used of the god whether or not there was a specific link to that place. Deiradiotes is peculiar to Argos: a ridge joins the two hills above the city, and Deiradiotes means 'of the ridge'. Part of the ridge was landscaped into terraces, with connecting stairways, to accommodate Apollo's temple and oracle, as well as another temple dedicated to **Athena**. The oracle was not based in the temple of Apollo itself, but in a separate brick building nearby. Both were situated on the middle terrace, with the temple probably at the S end of it, where the remains of a **Byzantine** church can be seen. The site seems to have been one of some antiquity, but clear evidence of oracular activity cannot be found before the third century BC.

The oracle was still functioning in **Pausanias'** time, and he provides an account of how it operated [II.24.1]. The prophetess, who was required to remain chaste, prophesied once a month. The special attendant ritual required that a ewe-lamb be slaughtered at night, and that she drink the blood of it. This brought on a state of possession by the god. The fact that the procedure at Argos was so different from that at Delphi suggests that the two oracles had quite independent origins. In fact, the practice at Argos seems much more like that of the oracle of **Ge** at **AEGIRA**. Pausanias also testifies [II.23.4] to an Asclepius sanctuary in Argos, but its whereabouts are unknown. He claims it was founded by Sphyrus, a son of **Machaon**.

ASINE: a sanctuary of **Asclepius** in Argolis, S Greece (37 30N, 22 52E). The ruins of Asine lie on the coast, near the road linking modern Asini with the resort of Tolo. Although not large, the site is an ancient and interesting one. Its most notable feature is its second century BC walls, substantial sections of which survive. Within them have been found the foundations of buildings going back at least a thousand years, and artefacts another thousand years older again. Unfortunately no trace has been found of its **Asclepeion** at all, and **Pausanias** makes no mention of it. Asine has achieved a fame disproportionate to its size thanks to a celebrated poem ('The King of Asine') written about it by **Seferis**, who befriended the Swedish leader of the excavations there. Even if they are not imposing, a stroll to the ruins is an agreeable exercise should the pleasures of Tolo's beaches begin to pall. Because of the Swedish involvement in excavations at the site, finds from Asine are distributed among museums in Nauplio, Uppsala and Stockholm.

ASOPOS: a sanctuary of **Asclepius** in Lakonia, S Greece (36 42N, 22 50E). Modern Asopos lies in the extreme SE Peloponnese. Ancient Asopos was probably about 5 km to the S of it, on the coast at or near Plitra. The sanctuary, according to **Pausanias** [III.22.9], was located about 3 km outside the city and some way above it. In that vicinity the only ruins to be found are those of a monastery, but unfortunately there is no direct evidence to link it with the ancient **Asclepeion**. Pausanias makes a special point of mentioning that Asclepius was known as 'the People's Friend' in this area.

ASTYPALAIA: a sanctuary of **Asclepius** in the Dodecanese (36 38N, 26 25E). The island of Astypalaia lies about midway between **KOS** and **ANAPHE**. Its main town is also known as Astypalaia, although sometimes referred to as Chora. The town is built over its ancient counterpart, leaving nothing of the latter to be seen. However, it was here that the sanctuary of Asclepius was established. The cult of the god may have arrived here with a group of colonists from **EPIDAUROS**. The sanctuary has been lost, but some Astypalaian coins bearing the god's image have been found, indicating that the cult came to play a significant role in the island's culture.

ATHENS: sanctuaries of **Asclepius** and Amynos in Attica, central Greece (37 57N, 23 44E). Athens came to have two sanctuaries of Asclepius. The god's cult was introduced here in 420 BC, during a time of plague. The site on which his temple was built is said to have been previously occupied by a water god. It lies to the S of the acropolis, on a terrace that runs W from the theatre of **Dionysus**. Dedicated in 418 BC, it became known as the Old **Asclepeion** to distinguish it from the New Asclepeion, which lay between it and the theatre, and which was built in the third century BC. However, the two seem to have become amalgamated at some point and **Pausanias** [I.21.7] speaks of a single sanctuary. It is difficult to distinguish them now, and only one temple, one **abaton** and one **katagogion** can be clearly identified. However, two separate springs can at least be seen. At the E end of the terrace, that of the New Asclepeion lies within a small round cave, and has become a Christian chapel. At the W end there is an open spring contained within ancient walls. There was a tradition that anything thrown into one of these springs (it is not clear which, but the W one appears more likely) would emerge in the sea near **PIRAEUS**. It also seems that Asclepius did not always bother with the ritual of **incubation** at Athens. The *Suda*, a tenth-century encyclopaedia, tells of an individual named Plutarch (not the famous author) who consulted the god in around 400 AD. When he awoke from his sleep and complained out loud about the instructions he had received (which involved eating lots of pork), 'straightway Asclepius spoke from the statue in a very harmonious voice, prescribing another remedy for the illness' (Edelstein 1975, I, p.241).

Excavations have revealed another healing sanctuary at the SW foot of the Areopagus hill. It was dedicated to the comparatively obscure healing god Amynos. The dramatist **Sophocles** was said to have been a priest of it. Since he was also said to have been instrumental in bringing the cult of Asclepius to Athens, it may be that Amynos was perceived to be losing his healing powers by the late fifth century BC. The sanctuary is severely ruined and difficult to make out.

ATHOS, Mount: an oracle of **Apollo** in NE Greece. The ancient history of Mount Athos is largely obscure. While the names of some of the towns that stood on the peninsula are known, their locations are conjectural. However, on the shore near the monastery of Iviron (40 15N, 24 17E) stands a small chapel of St Basil. It is built over a spring, and this is thought to have been the site of an oracular temple of Apollo. According to Athonite tradition, the Virgin Mary herself visited the place and was responsible for the oracle's demise.

BOIAI: a sanctuary of **Asclepius** in Lakonia, S Greece (36 30N, 23 04E). The site of ancient Boiai lies about 2 km to the N of Neapolis in the far SE Peloponnese. There is virtually nothing to see, but according to **Pausanias** [III.22.13] there were shrines not only to Asclepius, but also to **Sarapis** and **Isis**. Asclepius seems to have been associated with **Maleatas** here. Pausanias relates that at nearby Etis he saw the ruins of a large sanctuary dedicated to Asclepius and **Hygeia**. Although he describes Etis as only about 1 km from Boiai (in an unspecified direction), it has not been found.

BRASIAI or **PRASIAI**: a sanctuary of **Asclepius** in Lakonia, S Greece (37 21N, 22 48E). It is probably to be identified with the modern Plaka, on the E coast of the Peloponnese, about 4 km from Leonidio. **Pausanias** [III.24.5] mentions the existence of a sanctuary there. There are some ruins to be seen, but nothing specifically identifiable as an **Asclepeion**. Inscriptions also link the place with **Maleatas**.

BURA or **BOURA**: an oracle of **Heracles** in Achaia, S Greece (38 09N, 22 11E). The name of the ancient city lives on in that of the Vouraikos river, which enters the Gulf of Corinth near Diakofto. For part of the way it flows through its own spectacular gorge, which also provides the route for the Kalavrita railway. The city lay some way inland on a hill top. Even in **Pausanias'** time it had been the victim of earthquakes, and they have done more damage since, so that ruins are difficult to find or identify. However, the oracle itself was located in a cave or grotto somewhere between the city and the sea, near the river. Some think the cave in question was one destroyed by earthquakes in the nineteenth century, and so permanently lost. Others identify it with another near the village of Zachloritika, about 1 km SW of Diakofto. However, this is a very modest affair and does not seem to be a particularly persuasive candidate, although it is certainly in the right general area.

The oracle was still functioning when Pausanias made his visit [VII.25.6], and he gives an account of its operation. Inside the grotto was a statue of Heracles, before which the enquirer first prayed. Then four dice were selected from the large number available, and they were thrown. For each possible outcome, there was a response that could be read from a board. (No priests or functionaries of any kind seem to be involved here.) It is not clear whether it made a difference which dice were chosen, and so it is impossible to know how many different outcomes and responses were on offer.

CHIOS: an oracle of **Apollo** in the E Aegean (38 25N, 26 03E). Exactly where on the island the oracle lay is uncertain. However, two temples dedicated to the god have been found there, and they are the most likely candidates so far. One is at Emporio and the other at Kato Fana, both in the S part of the island. The latter is the site of ancient Phanai, from which the god derived his local **epithet** Phanaios.

CORINTH: a sanctuary of **Asclepius** in Corinthia, S Greece (37 54N, 22 53E). Although it lay (just) inside the walls of the ancient city, the remains of the **Asclepeion** are well off the modern beaten track. They lie unmarked nearly 1 km N of the main site, in an area that is substantially overgrown. Fortunately, they are relatively well preserved. The sanctuary occupied two levels. On the higher level stood the temple. Archaeological evidence indicates that there had been an earlier temple of **Apollo** on this site. It is surmised that the cult of Asclepius may have been introduced here at some point during the fifth century BC. Given Asclepius' close association with (his father) Apollo, it was far from unknown for places dedicated to the latter to be occupied by the former, jointly and/or subsequently. The outlines of the principal structures that were built on this level can be picked out.

However, it is the lower level that is in many ways more interesting. It could be reached either by steps or ramp from the upper level (depending on one's degree of mobility, presumably), or through its own separate entrance. What can be seen is the remains of a courtyard, once colonnaded along each side. Dining rooms lay off it to the E, while to the S there were basins supplied from reservoirs, whose tunnels can still be explored (with caution). The impression is of a modest size spa complex, which is what it was. The waters were supplied by both a spring and such local precipitation as could be collected and stored by the reservoirs. The buildings on both the upper and lower levels seem to date from a late fourth-century BC rebuilding programme.

Near the forum, and the main archaeological site of ancient Corinth, is a museum containing the results of excavations in the area. Of particular interest is a selection of terracotta **votive** items. The volume of such materials found at Corinth amounts to something in the region of 10 cubic metres. Most of the pieces are life size, and most parts of the body are represented. Arms, legs, female breasts and male genitals are among the items discovered and displayed.

Above the site looms the massive rock of Acrocorinth with its impressive fortifications. According to **Pausanias** [II.4.7], **Isis** and **Serapis** each had two sanctuaries along the way up to it, but nothing remains of any of them.

DELOS or DILOS: oracles of **Apollo, Anios** and Glaucus, sanctuaries of **Asclepius** and **Sarapis** (37 23N, 25 17E). Delos lies near the centre of the

Cyclades, about 3 km SW of Mykonos, from which it is usually reached. According to legend, this tiny island was the birthplace of Apollo (and of his sister, **Artemis**). Although this claim was disputed by both **PATARA** and **TEGYRA**, Delos enjoyed a religious significance out of all proportion to its size on the basis of it. Partly because of this, the island had a turbulent history, sometimes independent, sometimes dominated by others. On two occasions (once in the sixth century BC, and for a second time in 426 BC) the island was 'purified' at the insistence of the Athenians. On both occasions this involved the removal of tombs: the first time from around the sanctuary of Apollo, the second time from the remainder of the island. After the second purification, it was announced that no further births or deaths should take place on Delos. (This was a common restriction imposed on sanctuaries: the implication of the policy seems to be that the whole island was to be regarded as a sanctuary at this time.)

The sanctuary of Apollo lies on the W of the island, near both the ancient and modern harbours. This area was originally a Mycenaean settlement, but became the focal point of the cult of the god from at least the early seventh century BC onwards. The sanctuary is unusual in having three temples dedicated to the same god. The first of these, which is also the smallest, was built in the sixth century BC, and is known as the Porinos Naos. Next to it stands the Temple of the Athenians, which was constructed between 426 and 417 BC. Finally there is the southernmost, and largest, of the temples, sometimes called the Great Temple or the Delian Temple. Work on it was begun in around 475 BC, but was then halted and not recommenced until after 314 BC. It was never completed. There is thought to have been an earlier temple on this site, located to the E of the House of the Naxians, which is the oldest building of the surviving sanctuary complex. There are remains of several other buildings, but their original functions are not always apparent. Some of the items uncovered in the excavations on the site are in the museum on the island, others are in the National Museum in Athens.

The history of the oracle itself is very obscure. It is mentioned in a hymn to Apollo, which is probably to be dated to the middle of the seventh century BC. It may have ceased to operate by the fifth century BC, but been revived in the early centuries AD. **Virgil** describes a visit to it by **Aeneas** [*Aeneid* III.70-100]. The emperor **Julian** is said to have consulted it. It seems reasonable to suppose that the oracle was based within the sanctuary, but the unusual proliferation of temples on the site makes it difficult to be more specific.

The oracle of Anios is even more obscure, and even its existence has been doubted. Anios was a legendary prophet who told **Menelaus** that it would take the Greeks ten years to capture **Troy** (and, of course, he was right).

However, he is described not only as a prophet, but also as a priest, a son of Apollo, and a king of Delos. This might mean that he served at the god's oracle (as Virgil indeed says he did), rather than that he ever had one of his own. On the other hand, the idea that a seer might have a posthumous oracle was certainly not unknown. **Teiresias**, **Mallus** and **Kalchas** were all said to have done this (at **ORCHOMENOS**, **MALLUS** and **Mount GARGANUS** respectively). Archaeology has produced no evidence of the oracle of Anios.

No traces of the oracle of Glaucus have been found either. However, as he seems to have been associated with **Nymphs** here, somewhere in the vicinity of a spring is a possible location. Exactly which Glaucus had an oracle here is uncertain. There was more than one character of that name in Greek mythology, and more than one of them had connections with prophecy. Perhaps the most likely candidate is the Glaucus who was once a fisherman but became a sea god. According to one legend he was the father of the **Sibyl** of **CUMAE**, and another says he made his underwater home off the coast of Delos. That might suggest that his oracle was not by a spring but rather by the sea itself.

The remains of a sanctuary of Asclepius can be found towards the S end of the island. It was built in the fourth and third centuries BC and the remains of a temple and other buildings can be seen.

At a surprisingly early date, the island began to play host to a number of foreign gods, and of these the most significant were Sarapis and **Isis**. There is evidence of the worship of Isis from at least as early as the third century BC. In due course a number of temples were built, most of them in the inland area between the sanctuary of Apollo and the summit of Mount Kynthos. Three separate sanctuaries of Sarapis have been identified. The most important and biggest (known as Serapeion C) was constructed in the second century BC, and a temple dedicated to Isis stands nearby. Given that this god and goddess were closely connected with the activities of prophecy and healing, it seems likely that at least one of their establishments on the island was involved with one or both of them.

DELPHI: oracles of **Apollo**, **Poseidon** and **Ge** in Phokis, central Greece (38 29N, 22 29E). Delphi is the best known oracle of all, although what is actually known about it is a matter of considerable dispute. What is not in dispute is the position of pre-eminence it achieved and sustained over many centuries. Although usually connected with Apollo, the oracle also had associations with Poseidon and Ge. According to **Pausanias** [X.5.3], Ge was the original occupant of the site, with Daphnis, a nymph, as her prophetess. He also relates the legend that at one time it was shared by Ge and Poseidon, with Ge doing her own prophesying and an individual named Pyrkon operating as the mouthpiece of Poseidon. Ge gave her share in the enterprise to **Themis**, who gave it to Apollo, who also acquired Poseidon's stake in it by giving him Poros in exchange. The goddess Ge was the central and dominating figure of early Greek religion, and there are many well-substantiated cases of sanctuaries originally belonging to her being subsequently taken over by others. Poseidon was, among other things, the god of earthquakes, and it may have been for this reason that he developed a connection with Delphi, a place that gets more than its fair share of seismic activity.

However, other legends suggest that Apollo's arrival was rather more violent. The prophetess at Delphi was always known as the **Pythia**, and it was said that Apollo had slain a great snake or dragon (called the Python, and connected in some way with Ge) that guarded the site. Whenever **Homer** mentions the place, he calls it not Delphi but Pytho (and Pythian or Pythaeus was an **epithet** often used of the god). The fact that he does mention it, and explicitly identifies it as an oracle of Apollo, means that the god was almost certainly established there by 700 BC, and perhaps substantially earlier.

The origins of the specifically oracular dimension of Delphi are explained in a similar way by both **Diodorus Siculus** [XVI.26.1-5] and Pausanias [X.5.3]. It is said that a goatherd noticed his animals behaving strangely when they went near a certain place. When he investigated, he found himself acquiring the gift of prophecy. The traditional explanation of this phenomenon described gases emanating from a natural chasm. This story was widely believed until excavations in the late nineteenth and early twentieth centuries revealed no evidence for it at all. However, research at the site led and undertaken by Jelle de Boer and John R. Hale at the end of the twentieth century has revived the credibility of the ancient account through its geological findings.

The first stone temple dedicated to Apollo on this site was probably built during the seventh century BC. One tradition has it that Trophonius was involved in its construction. (He later came to have his own oracle at **LEBADEIA**). What can be seen on the site today is the remains of a later temple completed in around 330 BC. Originally the oracle seems to have been available for consultation only once a year. This later became at least once a month, except in winter when it did not function at all. (At this time of the year, Apollo seems to have been open for business at **PATARA**.) Central to operations was the Pythia, who took her place in the temple on the appropriate days. Usually there was only one, but there appear to have been times (presumably when the oracle was at its busiest) when there were reserve or supplementary ones too. They were older women (aged over 50), chosen from the local community. They were required to be of good character, and after appointment they were expected to live a chaste existence in accommodation specially provided for them. Originally Pythias were chosen from among younger women, but they seem to have found chastity more of a challenge.

Exactly how the oracle functioned is unclear, and a matter of some dispute. Opinions are strongly divided on such subjects as the nature of the Pythia's possession by the god, the question as to whether responses were usually or unusually given in verse, and the degree to which the oracle's pronouncements tended towards the enigmatic. On this last point, Joseph Fontenrose in particular has sought to argue that, among those responses of the oracle that can reasonably be taken as genuine (because recorded at or around the time when they were made), there is nothing in the way of ambiguity and little in the way of prediction. However, since his conclusion is based on an analysis of fewer than a hundred (out of what must have been thousands of) responses, it cannot be taken as definitive.

One response dismissed by Fontenrose as legendary rather than genuine is that recorded by **Herodotus** [I.46ff]. It concerns **Croesus**, who died at least 50 years before Herodotus was born. In an attempt to test out the oracles of his time, he sent the same question to seven of them, and Delphi came up with the correct answer, expressed in hexameter verse. (The oracle of **Amphiaraus** at **OROPOS** seems to have been the only other successful one, but its response was not recorded.) Whether fact or fiction, the story encapsulates the high esteem in which Delphi was generally held. There is also a story, later but perhaps no less legendary, that the last response of the oracle came in response to an enquiry sent to it by the emperor **Julian**. That the oracle finally ceased to function at around his time is, however, entirely plausible.

The site of Delphi has been thoroughly excavated, and is one of the most dramatic and popular archaeological attractions in modern Greece. It is located on a hillside, with the entrance to the sanctuary being at its lower end. A sacred way winds up to the focal point of proceedings, the temple of Apollo itself. The entrance to the temple faces E, and on consultation days the Pythia would have taken up her position in its innermost chamber. Tradition has it that one of the issues on which the oracle was often consulted, especially in its early days, concerned the prospects of founding colonies in particular places. Delphi also came to be seen as the prime authority on religious matters. Some came with questions relating to political problems. Many came with enquiries that were entirely mundane. Today many just come to look. (Even in ancient times the place seems to have been something of a tourist attraction.) Apart from what can be seen *in situ*, the adjacent museum has an important display of local finds.

In the hills above Delphi (a steep climb followed by a pleasant walk) is the Korykian Cave. Some think this may have been the oracle's original location. Independent evidence based on excavations there suggests it was the site of a **dice** oracle dedicated to **Pan** and the **Nymphs**. It is also thought that some kind of **lot** oracle may have been on offer at Delphi itself as an alternative to consulting the Pythia.

DIMITRIAS: see **PAGASAI**

DION: sanctuaries of **Asclepius** and **Isis** in Macedonia, N Greece (38 50N, 22 59E). Ancient Dion lies to the N of Mount Olympos, and about 15 km S of Katerini, near the modern village of the same name. It was the most sacred city of the ancient Macedonians. It has been partly excavated, and its general outline is easily discerned, with its main streets oriented N-S and E-W, and various buildings disposed along them. **Pausanias** [IX.30.3] relates the legend that the bones of **Orpheus** were buried there. Not surprisingly, archaeologists have not found them, but they have unearthed buildings ranging in date from the fourth century BC to the fifth century AD. **Alexander the Great** passed this way, and held a festival here before embarking on his Persian campaign. Religious activities were generally concentrated in the S part of the city, and it was here that a sanctuary dedicated to Asclepius was found. In the residential part of the city was a huge baths complex, and among its ruins was discovered a set of statues representing Asclepius' sons and daughters.

The sanctuary of Isis is also in the S part of the site. Many statues have been found there, some still carrying traces of their original paint. They can be seen in the nearby museum.

DODONA or **DODONI**: an oracle of **Zeus** in Epirus, N Greece (39 42N, 21 01E). Dodona is situated in a quiet valley about 22 km SW of modern Ioannina. **Herodotus** [II.52] thought that it was the oldest oracle in Greece, and [I.46-50] that it was one of five on the Greek mainland tested by **Croesus** (it failed). It was known to Homer who described it as 'wintry' in the *Iliad* [II.750], and in the *Odyssey* [XIV.325 and XIX.295] told of the 'great oak-tree that is sacred to the god'. The oak tree was central to the oracle at Dodona, although there are no explicit indications of the precise role it fulfilled. **Apollonius of Rhodes** [I.9.16] says that the prow of the **Argo** was made of wood taken from the tree, and that it was able to speak. Those who found the idea of talking wood too implausible were inclined to think that the rustling of the leaves of the tree somehow provided the responses of the oracle. There are also stories of bronze cauldrons emitting ominous sounds. The remains of such cauldrons can be seen in the National Archaeological Museum in Athens, along with many other bronze items found at the site.

According to one explanation of the oracle's foundation told by Herodotus [II.55ff], the importance of the tree was as a perch for a bird that flew there from Egyptian **THEBES**. (Another bird flew to **SIWA**.) However, he was more inclined to believe the story that it was a priestess from Thebes, and not a bird, who first established the oracle, with the tree playing a purely incidental role in the matter. This was how the priests in Thebes understood the matter. The story of the bird, on the other hand, was told to Herodotus by the three priestesses at Dodona itself. **Strabo** [VII fragment 1a] tells a very different story. According to him the oracle originated elsewhere, in **SKOTUSSA** (far to the E, about 30 km S of **LARISA**). When unnamed people decided to burn down the tree there, the oracle was moved to Dodona at the prompting of **Apollo**. In the *Iliad* [XVI.220ff], Homer also talks of a mysterious people called the Selloi (or Helli) who were the prophets there at some point. They did not wash their feet, and slept on the ground. This suggests that they attached importance to maintaining direct contact with the earth.

If ancient sources paint a confused picture, archaeology has uncovered clear evidence that the cult of Zeus was established at Dodona by about 1200 BC. The goddess **Ge** may have been worshipped there a thousand years before that, and the later cult absorbed elements of the former. Zeus was known at Dodona as Zeus Naios, which means 'of the earth'. Furthermore, he was associated there with the goddess Dione, who seems to have been a reinvention of Ge. Enquiries were addressed to Zeus and Dione jointly. When the site became oracular is not known. The first stone temple was built there in around 400 BC, some time after the visit of Herodotus. What can be seen today is mainly the remains of building programmes carried out in the third century BC. Strabo says the oracle was virtually extinct in his time, but it was still functioning, and perhaps enjoying something of a revival, when the emperor **Hadrian** visited it in 132. Over 200 years later the emperor **Julian** is said to have consulted it, but this may have been near the end of its long existence. There is evidence to suggest that the oak tree was finally uprooted at the end of the fourth century.

If it is unclear as to how the oracle responded, it is at least known how questions were put to it. In 1952 excavations at the site turned up a number of small lead tablets. Measuring about 75 mm by 25 mm, most of them have been dated to the period between 500 and 300 BC. A selection of them can be seen in the Archaeological Museum in Ioannina. Questions were written on the lead, which was then folded. Most of the questions found on them relate to familiar everyday matters such as marriage, careers, stolen property, the weather and paternity. However, although this was clearly *a* way in which questions were put to the oracle, it may not have been the *only* way. It was certainly not unknown for more than one method of consultation to be employed at an oracular centre.

The most impressive remains at Dodona are not those of the oracle but of the theatre, which is still sometimes used for performances. It is one of the largest and best preserved in Greece. By comparison, the temple of Zeus to the E of it is a very modest affair. Indeed, it is almost an exaggeration to call it a temple at all. It was originally very tiny, although it was later rebuilt on a slightly grander scale. More significant, and much larger, is the enclosure into which it protrudes and in which the tree stood. (The tree that can be seen there today is of recent origin. The original was destroyed centuries ago.) The slightly clumsy layout of the precinct suggests a sacrifice of symmetry for the sake of the oak, which grew near the E wall.

Despite its antiquity, and despite being an oracle of the supreme god Zeus, Dodona never achieved the kind of significance or wealth of places like **DELPHI** and **DIDYMA**. This must have been in large part due to its location on the geographical fringes of the ancient Greek world, far from the places that were the movers and shakers of their time, and far from the sea which provided the principal means of long-distance travel. No wonder strange stories developed to explain the existence of an oracle in such an unlikely spot. Even today the site can have an air of remoteness about it, partly due to the curiously poor public transport links with Ioannina.

EPHYRA or **EPHYRE**: an oracle of the **dead** in Thesprotia, NW Greece (39 15N, 20 32E). The site is sometimes just referred to as 'the Nekromanteion', but this is misleading. In the first place, Nekromanteion (or more properly 'Nekyomanteion') simply means 'oracle of the dead', so it is a description rather than a place name, and more than one oracle of the dead was thought to exist. (There may even have been another close by at **AORNOS**.) Ephyra is the name of an ancient city whose scant ruins lie near the modern village of Mesopotamos, some 20 km to the SE of the resort of Parga. Nearby is the Acherontos river, the Acheron of antiquity, supposedly one of the rivers of Hades. Consequently, the site is sometimes referred to as the Nekromanteion of Ephyra, or the Acheron Nekromanteion. However, whatever name is attached to it, it is now disputed whether the site, 600 m S of Ephyra, was that of a Nekromanteion at all.

The ruins to be seen there were discovered in the 1950s under the church of St John, which stands on a hill of the same name, and is now suspended on girders over the excavations. They are the remains of a complex structure dating back to the third or fourth century BC, apparently destroyed by fire in the second century AD. Buried among them were a variety of foodstuffs, animal bones, agricultural tools, bits of machinery and some terracotta figurines of **Persephone**. Under one of the complex's rooms, located at the end of a labyrinthine passageway, is a substantial vaulted chamber.

The combination of labyrinth, subterranean chamber, Persephone, and nearness to Ephyra led to the belief that this was the Nekromanteion, and other finds were interpreted in that light. The bits of machinery were thought to come from some kind of contraption designed to stage elaborate illusions in the subterranean chamber. It is now generally agreed, however, that in fact they were parts of ancient catapults. In line with this reinterpretation, it is further argued that the ruins are not of the Nekromanteion at all, but of some kind of fortified farmstead, hence the stores of food and the tools.

In the absence of any inscriptions found at the site, the ruins have to speak for themselves. Indeed, it could be argued that the precise absence of any inscriptions might suggest a private rather than a public structure. On the other hand, the work that was evidently required for the levelling of the site, the excavation of the subterranean chamber and the construction of the buildings suggests that it was a place of some importance. And the need for such an elaborately fortified structure so near to the protective walls of Ephyra might be questioned. Were the church of St John an ancient structure, then it might be reasonable to suppose that it had been erected over an ancient pagan site. Unfortunately, the present building (which is not without its own modest interest) dates only from the eighteenth century, and any earlier history is unknown.

The very least that can be concluded is that the identification of the site is problematic. Fortunately, that does not detract from its interest, and the ruins are fascinating to explore, whatever they are. And if excessive imagination is to be avoided by the archaeologist, at least the casual visitor is free to indulge in it. Items of a movable nature unearthed there are mainly to be found in the archaeological museum in Ioannina.

EPIDAUROS: a sanctuary of **Asclepius** in Argolis, S Greece (37 38N, 23 09E). Epidauros is the pre-eminent sanctuary of Asclepius on the Greek mainland. Its only rivals are **KOS** and **PERGAMON** which are island and Asian centres respectively. It is close to the modern town of Ligourio: the ancient and modern settlements of Epidauros are further E on or near the coast. The city of Epidauros owned and managed the sanctuary. (Hereafter 'Epidauros' should be taken to refer to the sanctuary rather than the city.) Epidauros contested with **TRIKKA** for the right to be recognised as the birthplace of

Asclepius. The dispute was resolved by the oracle at **DELPHI**, which was wholly appropriate since **Apollo** was Asclepius' father. As the cult expanded many centres were established as direct offshoots of Epidauros, with its blessing.

As was often the case, the cult of Asclepius was grafted on to an existing cult of Apollo at Epidauros. On a hill near the sanctuary of Asclepius (about 600 m NE of its theatre) are the remains of an older one dedicated to Apollo **Maleatas**, dating back to perhaps the eighth century BC. When Asclepius arrived at Epidauros is not known: it was no later than the fifth century BC, but could have been significantly earlier. Evidence suggests that before having his own temple at Epidauros, Asclepius had an altar at the temple of Apollo. The gods are often addressed jointly in inscriptions that have been found on the site. When and why a new sanctuary was established so near to, yet separate from, the old one of Apollo, no one knows. It may simply be that the new, more level, site afforded greater possibilities for expansion for a cult that was growing in importance and popularity.

The buildings whose remains can be seen at Epidauros today are mainly from the fourth and third centuries BC. One of the first to be built was the temple of Asclepius itself. Next to it is the **abaton**. At some stage this was extended to the W. Because the ground falls away in that direction, the newer part had two storeys. Another building, known as the thymele, stands to the S of the abaton and W of the temple. Unusually in ancient Greek architecture, the thymele was circular, and its foundations are labyrinthine in design. Despite considerable conjecture, its precise purpose remains undiscovered. Both the abaton and thymele are being restored and rebuilt.

Two large buildings lie in a SE direction away from this complex. There has been some disagreement over the use of the first (gymnasium and dining hall are the two main candidates), but the second is generally agreed to have been a **katagogion**. Further to the SE again is the most famous building of all at Epidauros, its theatre, one of the most impressive in Greece. The size of all of these buildings indicates that considerable numbers of people were catered for. Naturally not all of them were cured, but some certainly were. At Epidauros it became customary for grateful beneficiaries of the god's curative prowess to leave behind them testimonials to that effect. These would indicate what problems they came with and how they were cured. They were then copied onto stone tablets which were displayed around the sanctuary, and some of them have been found. Blindness and baldness are among the problems to which the god is said to have found the answer. The museum at the site displays these and other finds.

At some point in its history, the sanctuary welcomed the cult of **Isis** within its boundaries. The remains of a complex of brick buildings dedicated to her can be found in the overgrown NW part of the site.

The sanctuary seems to have gone through some hard times in the first century BC, and been plundered on more than one occasion. However, the early centuries AD saw something of a revival of fortunes, and in the second century a considerable amount of repair and restoration work was carried out. The third century saw further damage done, and in the fourth century came the final decline. The last known priest at Epidauros, named Mnaseas, dedicated an altar there to Asclepius of Aigai in 355. The temple of Asclepius at **AIGAI (2)** had been ordered destroyed by **Constantine the Great**, and perhaps Mnaseas intended to make a gesture of defiance in response. **Themistius**, writing perhaps a little before this time, noted that there were very few sanctuaries of Asclepius left to visit. How many, or how few, years after 355 Epidauros continued to function is not known. However, the site itself was not abandoned, and the ruins of a substantial **Byzantine** church can be found at its N extreme, near the original ceremonial entrance to the sanctuary.

An extensive rebuilding programme is being pursued at Epidauros, along with considerable archaeological survey work. This means that substantial areas of the site are off-limits to visitors, and are likely to be for some time. To those of us who like our ruins ruined, the reconstructions seem unnecessary and unwanted.

EPIDAUROS LIMERA: an oracle of **Ino** and sanctuary of **Asclepius** in Lakonia, S Greece (36 45N, 23 03E). Confusingly, Epidauros Limera ('harbour') is nowhere near Epidauros, but instead lies about 6 km N of Monemvasia in the SE Peloponnese. It is also known as Palaio ('old') Monemvasia. There are quite substantial remains to be seen, especially the walls of the ancient city's acropolis. The sanctuary of Asclepius was located somewhere inside them, but has not been identified. The oracle, however, was located outside the walls at a place known, according to **Pausanias** [III.23.8], as Ino's Water. This may be the small deep pool to be found about 500 m NE of the acropolis. The oracle could only be consulted once a year, at the time of the goddess's festival, and the procedure was a curious one. Those seeking advice had to throw loaves of bread baked from barley into the water. If they sank, it meant that Ino had accepted them, and the omens were good. If they floated, she had rejected them, and the omens were bad. It is interesting to speculate on the extent to which outcomes were dependent on the skills (or whims) of the local bakers.

EPIRUS: an oracle of **Apollo** in NW Greece. **Aelian** mentions an oracle of Apollo located somewhere in Epirus where the behaviour of sacred snakes was examined for **omen**s. He says no more about it, and neither does anyone else. It was apparently situated in a sacred grove, but there are no indications as to its precise whereabouts. While the snake had some specific associations with **Asclepius** and some more generic ones with omens and prophecy as in the cases of **Melampus** and **Helenus**, it does not normally appear in the cult of Apollo, except in the special case of **DELPHI**. Everything about this oracle, if it existed, is a mystery.

ERETRIA: a sanctuary of **Isis** in central Greece (38 23N, 23 50E). The ruins of ancient Eretria lie next to the modern town and resort of the same name about 23 km SE of Halkida. The city was one of considerable antiquity, being mentioned by **Homer** in the *Iliad* [II.537]. Its history was an eventful one, being destroyed by both the Persians in 490 BC and the Romans 300 years later, but managing to produce a school of philosophy in between. Surprisingly, perhaps, quite a lot remains to be seen, although some of the ruins are in the midst of modern buildings. The foundations of the temple of Isis are to be found in the S of the town, W of the **agora** and near the shore. The earliest parts are dated to around 300 BC, making it relatively early for this part of the world. Its proximity to the ancient harbour suggests it may have been established by or for those involved in maritime activities, which seems to have been frequently the case with the cult of Isis. It was rebuilt and expanded some time after 198 BC, and second-century BC mosaics were found in one of the ancillary buildings of the complex. A clay statue of the goddess was discovered inside the temple itself. The local museum contains finds from the general area, but unfortunately nothing from the sanctuary of Isis itself. An inscription has been found indicating the existence of a temple of **Asclepius** in Eretria, but nothing is known as to its whereabouts.

EUA or **EVA**: an oracle of **Polemocrates** in Argolis, S Greece (37 19N, 22 37E). According to legend, Polemocrates was the son of **Machaon** (who had his own oracle at **GERENIA**), and Machaon was the son of **Asclepius**. As might be expected, the grandson of Asclepius concerned himself with healing. **Pausanias** [II.38.6] specifically says that he cured *local* people here, which suggests that the sanctuary did not have a particularly widespread reputation. On the other hand, since healing centres were not a rarity, many (if not most) of them would presumably have catered primarily for the demand of a relatively small catchment area. Eua is described by Pausanias as a village, and it is thought to have been on the site of the Moni Loukou monastery, which lies about 3 km W of Astros in the NE Peloponnese. Stones from earlier structures are incorporated into the fabric of the monastery church, although these may have come from the nearby villa of **Herodes Atticus** rather than the sanctuary of Polemocrates. In the courtyard outside the church is an interesting old spring. Inside are some beautiful icons and frescoes. One icon has many tiny metal plates attached to it bearing depictions of limbs and organs. Clearly many still believe the place to possess healing powers.

EUTRESIS: an oracle of **Apollo** in Boiotia, central Greece (38 17N, 23 10E). The remains of Eutresis can be found on top of a hill about 15 km SW of Thiva on the road to Lefktra. Most of what can be seen relates to the foundations of the city walls, although there are also the sparse remains of a heavily excavated acropolis, now topped by a concrete pillar. There was apparently a famous oracle here, but it must have ceased to exist long before **Pausanias'** time as he makes no mention of it at all. The oracular shrine may never have had a temple, in which case there is nothing of it to find. However, a number of **votive** vases and terracotta figurines (mainly dating from the fifth to third centuries BC) have been unearthed which are probably connected with visitors to the oracle. An inscribed stone found at the site suggested that consultations probably took place in its vicinity. A spring about 500 m SE of the acropolis, just outside the line of the city walls, is regarded as the most likely candidate. Some of the finds from the excavations at Eutresis are on display in Thiva's museum.

GERENIA: an oracle of **Machaon** and a sanctuary of **Asclepius** in Messenia, S Greece. Machaon was the son of Asclepius and, like his father, a healer. The family tradition was carried on by his son **Polemocrates** who had a healing shrine of his own at **EUA**. Gerenia may have stood on the site of modern Stavropigi (36 53N, 22 12E), about 20 km SE of Kalamata in the S Peloponnese. **Pausanias** says [III.26.9], without further explanation, that the place where the sanctuary stood was called 'The Rose', and contained a bronze statue of the healer. According to **Strabo** [VIII.4.4], the temple of Asclepius here was a copy of the one in **TRIKKA**. Puzzlingly, Pausanias does not mention the **Asclepeion** and Strabo does not mention Machaon. One possible explanation is that father and son shared the same premises, either concurrently or consecutively. The village's principal landmark is the fifteenth-century Zarnata Castle. Within its boundaries is a **Byzantine** church dedicated to **Zoodochos Pigi**, which may mark the site of the ancient healing sanctuary of Machaon, Asclepius or both.

GONNOS: a sanctuary of **Asclepius** in Thessaly, N Greece (39 49N, 22 33E). The remains of Gonnos lie 2 km NE of modern Goni, about 30 km N of **LARISA**. It stands near the SW mouth of the Tempi gorge. It is possible to see sections of city wall built in the time of **Philip II**. The foundations of a number of buildings have been uncovered, one of which may have been the temple of Asclepius, although no firm identification has been established.

GORTYNA or **GORTYN** or **GORTYS**: an oracle of **Apollo** and a sanctuary of **Asclepius** in Crete (35 07N, 24 58E). Gortyna lies about 45 km S of Iraklio and 16 km E of Phaistos. During the Roman period, it was the biggest and most important city on the island. It was built on either side of what was then called the Lethaios river, but most of what remains is to be found on the E side, and S of the modern road that runs E-W through the site. The temple of Pythian Apollo was the main sanctuary, and lies about 100 m S of the road, in what was the centre of the ancient city. The earliest parts of the temple probably date to the seventh century BC, but restorations and enlargements followed, and what can be seen today is a composite structure put together over several centuries. Presumably the oracle functioned at or near the temple. In later years (no earlier than the first century AD) a temple of **Isis** and **Sarapis** was built a little to the N of it, which may also have performed an oracular function at some stage.

The sanctuary of Asclepius was situated near the river, N of the church of St Titus. (Titus was a friend of **St Paul**, and the first bishop of Gortyna.) There is little evidence of it on the ground, but a statue of Asclepius was found in its vicinity and is on display in the museum in Iraklio.

GORTYS or **KORTYS**: a sanctuary of **Asclepius** in Arkadia, S Greece (37 31N, 22 01E). Gortys lies near the very centre of the Peloponnese, about 6 km NE of the village of Elliniko. At one time it was a place of some magnitude, but it shrank to village size when **MEGALOPOLIS** was founded some distance to the S of it in the fourth century BC and some of its population was transferred there. Gortys was built along the W bank of the Lousios river, known in antiquity as the Gortynios. According to **Pausanias** [VIII.28.2] it was held to have the coldest water of any river. Two separate Asclepius sanctuaries were built, one to the S of the city's acropolis, and another to the N. The latter is the easier to find, being at the end of the road from Elliniko. The ruins of a substantial temple can be seen, along with the remains of a bathing complex nearby. Both were constructed during the fourth century BC. A heating system was added a little later. The other sanctuary is earlier. It contains the foundations of a fifth-century BC temple (slightly larger than the one to the N), and attendant buildings. However, these ruins are not at all easy to find. Pausanias only mentions the N one, which had a famous statue in it. There is some evidence that it was never finished, perhaps because of the move to Megalopolis. Apart from the N **Asclepeion**, the site of Gortys is now very overgrown and difficult to explore.

GYTHION: a sanctuary of **Asclepius** in Lakonia, S Greece (36 45N, 22 31E). The remains of ancient Gythion lie above modern Githio, about 40 km S of **SPARTA**. Apart from its theatre, there is not much to see. Legend has it that **Paris** and **Helen** became lovers near here. According to **Pausanias** [III.21.8] the temple of Asclepius here had a bronze statue and no roof. An adjacent spring belonged to it, but it is not clear whether this played any role in healing.

HALIEIS or **ALIS**: a sanctuary of **Asclepius** in Argolis, S Greece (37 20N, 23 13E). The remains of Halieis lie at the S tip of the peninsula that extends SE from Nauplio, near modern Portocheli. Much of the ancient settlement now lies under the waters of the bay that separates the ancient site from the modern one. The remains of a temple of **Apollo** have been found below sea level, but this seems to have been destroyed in the fifth century BC, and not rebuilt. Sanctuaries of Asclepius were sometimes established in the vicinity of temples to Apollo. There is no specific evidence of that here, but no other candidates for the site have been identified either. The town seems to have been abandoned at the end of the fourth century BC, which probably explains why **Pausanias** makes no mention of it. The sanctuary at Halieis was an offshoot of **EPIDAUROS**, about 40 km to the N. The results of excavations here are mainly in the museum at Nauplio.

HERMIONE or **HERMION**: an oracle of the **dead** in Argolis, S Greece (37 22N, 23 15E). The remains of ancient Hermione are about 8 km E of Kranidi in the NE Peloponnese, and about 15 km NE of **HALIEIS**. The ruins occupy a wooded promontory at the E extreme of the modern town of Ermioni. The area had strong associations with the underworld. There was a tradition that the distance from Hermione to the underworld was so short that there was no need to pay **Charon** for his services. There was a temple to **Demeter** here, and near it were two further sanctuaries, one dedicated to **Pluto**, the other to Klymenos. **Pausanias** [II.35.5] was inclined to think that Klymenos was just another name for Pluto. There was a Klymenos who was the son of Phoroneus, a river god, and another who was an ancient king in the NW Peloponnese, but there is no obvious connection of either with this place. However, it was in his sanctuary here that there was an opening in the ground that was said to lead to Hades. If there was an oracle to the dead in the area, then it was presumably here. The temple of Demeter may have stood in the vicinity of the small church of **Agioi** Taxiarchi (the archangels Michael and Gabriel), where some ancient foundations can be seen. Exactly where the sanctuary of Klymenos stood in relation to it is unclear. The only other remotely recognisable ruins are some distance away, and have been identified as belonging to a temple of **Poseidon**.

HYETTOS or **YETTOS**: a sanctuary of **Heracles** and **Asclepius** in Boiotia, central Greece (38 32N, 23 08E). The site of Hyettos is about 10 km NW of Kastro, and a similar distance NE of **ORCHOMENOS**. According to **Pausanias** [IX.24.3] the cult statue of Heracles here was very ancient and crude, but exactly how it worked cures is not known. The **Asclepeion** was evidently an institution of some significance, and was managed by its own body of elders. Although the location of Hyettos, which may never have been much more than a village, has been established through the evidence of inscriptions, there is nothing of it left to see.

HYPERTELEATON: a sanctuary of **Asclepius** in Lakonia, S Greece (36 38N, 22 53E). Hyperteleaton lay just to the S of modern Finiki, in the SE Peloponnese. **Pausanias** mentions it [III.22.10], but gives no description. A sanctuary of **Apollo** Hyperteleates has been found there, but nothing to directly link the site with Asclepius. The god was evidently very popular in this area, as there was another **Asclepeion** near **ASOPOS**, only 10 km away.

HYPSOI: see **LAS**

HYSIAI: an oracle of **Apollo** in Boiotia, central Greece. The exact site of Hysiai is unknown, but it was probably somewhere E of modern Erithres (38 14N, 23 20E), about 14 km S of Thiva. A location about 2 km E of Erithres, near the chapel of Pantanassa, is a possible candidate. **Pausanias** visited it [IX.2.1], and mentions an unfinished temple, dedicated to Apollo, and a holy well. He relates a local legend according to which those who drank from the well were able to give oracles.

ICHNAE: an oracle of **Apollo** in Macedonia, N Greece. The location of Ichnae is lost, but it was in ancient Bottiaea, a district that lay between the mouths of the Axios and Haliakmon rivers. This would place it around 25 km W or WSW of Thessaloniki (40 35N, 22 33E). There is also testimony to a shrine of **Themis** at Ichnae. Themis is a complex character, always encountered in connection

1. Karanis. North temple.

2. Siwa. Temple of Amun.

3. Abai. View from the citadel towards the site of the oracle.

4. Achladokampos. Church of Zoodochos Pigi.

5. Alipheira. Temple of Asclepius and altar.

6. Argos. The oracle terrace.

7. Athens. The Asclepeion: the east spring, now a Christian shrine.

8. Corinth. Asclepeion: lower level.

9. Delos. Early excavations.

10. Delphi. Temple of Apollo.

11. Dodona. Temple of Zeus.

12. Ephyra. Nekromanteion: labyrinth.

13. Epidauros. Entrance to the sanctuary.

14. Eretria. Temple of Isis.

15. Eua. Moni Loukou church.

16. Gerenia. Church of Zoodochos Pigi.

17. Gortys. North Asclepeion: baths.

18. Hermione. Church of Agioi Taxiarchi and ruins.

19. Kassopi. Katagogion.

20. Kenchreai.

21. Kos. Asclepeion in c. 1900.

22. Lebadeia. The source of the Erkyna.

23. Lykaion. Archaeological site.

24. Messene. Asclepeion.

25. Nikopolis. City walls.

26. Olympia. Site of the altar of Zeus.

27. Onchestos. Temple of Poseidon.

28. Orchomenos. Temple of Asclepius.

29. Oropos. Amphiareion.

30. Pagasai.

31. Patrai.
Entrance of shrine.

32. Perachora. Temple of Hera Akraia.

33. Phlious. Church of Zoodochos Pigi.

34. Piraeus. Temple of Asclepius.

35. Mount Ptoon.

36. Sikyon. Fountain.

37. Skotussa.

38. Sparta. Theatre.

39. Thebes (Greece). Ismenion.

40. Therapne. Shrine of Menelaus and Helen.

41. Thermos. Temple of Apollo Lyseios.

42. Titane. Inscribed stone from the Asclepeion, built into the church wall.

43. Avernus. 'Temple of Apollo'.

44. Cumae. Entrance to the Sibyl's cave.

45. Baiae.

46. Pompeii. Temple of Isis: purgatorium.

47. Puteoli. 'Temple of Sarapis'.

48. Adada. Temple of Zeus Sarapis.

49. Claros. Temple of Apollo: underground chamber.

50. Cyaneae.

51. Didyma.
Temple of Apollo.

52. Ephesus. Prytaneion.

53. Hierapolis. Temple of Apollo.

54. Limyra.

55. Magnesia on
the Maeander.

56. Olympus. Oracle tomb.

57. Patara. Temple.

58. Pergamon. The sacred way.

59. Pergamon. Temple of Sarapis.

60. Priene. Sanctuary
of the Egyptian Gods.

61. Sura. Temple and spring.

62. Termessos. Ruins
of the city gate.

63. Smyrna.
Temple of Athena.

with **Ge**, and perhaps identical with her. One of the legends at **DELPHI** claimed she had inherited the oracle there from Ge, and passed it on to Apollo. Her proximity to an oracle of Apollo at Ichnae might suggest the same pattern of development, in which case Ichnae might have begun as an oracle of Ge herself.

KAOUS: a sanctuary of **Asclepius** in Arkadia, S Greece (37 43N, 21 52 E). The village of Kaous was a ruin when **Pausanias** visited it [VIII.25.1], but its local sanctuary of Asclepius seems to have been intact. The scant remains of it can be found about 2 km N of Toumbitsi, about 35 km E of Olympia on the road to Tripoli via Langadia. The sanctuary lay near the river Ladon. Fragments of stone in the fields between the road and the river seem to be all that is left of it, although it is possible that there are a few more remains in less accessible areas nearby. The Ladon flows on to the S where it passed by another Asclepius sanctuary in the vicinity of Onkios, but of this one not even a trace has been found.

KASSOPI or **KASSOPE**: a sanctuary of **Asclepius** in Thesprotia, NW Greece (39 09N, 20 40E). The ruins of Kassopi lie about 30 km N of Preveza. The city's ancient history, which began in the bronze age, came to a relatively early end. The Romans destroyed it in 167 BC, and then, towards the end of the first century BC, forced the inhabitants of the rebuilt city to move to nearby **NIKOPOLIS**, founded by **Augustus** to celebrate his victory over **Antony** and **Cleopatra**. The ruins of Kassopi occupy an impressive elevated site with views to Nikopolis and beyond. They include a theatre, a **prytaneion** and a **katagogion**, which might have had a role to play in the cult of Asclepius. Otherwise no trace of the sanctuary has been found. However, much of the extensive site remains unexcavated.

KENCHREAI: sanctuaries of **Isis** and **Asclepius** in Corinthia, S Greece (37 52N, 22 59E). Kenchreai is located about 6 km S of the point where the main road crosses the Corinth Canal, near the modern village of Kechries. Lying by the sea, it was Corinth's port on the E side of the isthmus, and its ruins lie scattered around its ancient harbour. The sanctuary of Isis, used by **Apuleius** as the setting for a scene in his *Metamorphoses*, lay in the S of the city. A group of ruins, some partly underwater, can be seen on a promontory jutting out into the sea at the S end of the site. It includes warehouses, and a large hall that has been identified as part of the sanctuary of Isis. Other parts lie beneath the waves altogether. The sanctuary of Asclepius stood somewhere near that of Isis, according to **Pausanias** [II.2.3]. This almost certainly means that if anything is left of it, it is underwater too. The museum at Isthmia, about 4 km to the N, contains some of the finds from the area. At the N end of the site, a few remnants of sea wall and the ruins of a **Byzantine** church can be seen. The hill above it contains a number of underground Christian tombs, some of which still retain traces of their original paintwork.

KITHAERON, Mount: an oracle of the **Nymphs** in central Greece (38 12N, 23 15E). Mount Kithaeron formed the W end of the boundary between Attica and Boiotia. According to **Pausanias** [IX.3.5] the oracle had been located in a grotto called 'The Signet', and according to **Plutarch** [*Aristides*, XI] it opened towards the NW. No satisfactory identification of the cave has ever been made, and the oracle had apparently ceased to function long before Pausanias' time. It was not unusual for a variety of unusual mental states, including prophecy, to be explained in terms of possession by Nymphs.

KLEITOR: a sanctuary of **Asclepius** in Arkadia, S Greece (37 53N, 22 07E). The ruins of Kleitor are near modern Klitoria, about 25 km S of Kalavrita. They are quite extensive, and substantial stretches of wall can be seen, as can part of a theatre. Materials from the temple of Asclepius have been incorporated into a church, which may also occupy the site of the materials' source. **Pausanias** [VIII.21.3] notes that the god's sanctuary here was one of the two most distinguished of the city, but otherwise says nothing about it. The ancient city was also said to have in it a fountain whose waters instilled an aversion to wine.

KNOPIA: an oracle of **Amphiaraus** in Boiotia, central Greece. The precise location of Knopia is not known. It seems to have been a little to the S of modern Thiva (38 19N, 23 19E). In his lifetime, Amphiaraus was a seer. His mortal career ended when he was struck by a thunderbolt while fleeing from an ill-advised attack on **THEBES**, and the ground swallowed him up. This is meant to have happened near the river Ismenos. His oracle evidently enjoyed a considerable reputation. According to **Herodotus** [I.46-50] it was one of seven tested by **Croesus** and one of only two to pass with flying colours (the other was **DELPHI**). Its actual response is not recorded, but Croesus became a benefactor thereafter. If true, this story means that the sanctuary existed at least as early as the sixth century BC. According to **Strabo** [IX.2.10], the oracle was subsequently moved to **OROPOS**. This probably happened somewhere between 431 and 414 BC. Such a move was highly unusual as oracles were normally firmly tied to particular places. Although it was very close to Thebes, people born there were not permitted to consult it. Consultation was by **incubation**. **Pausanias** [IX.8.2] saw a small ruined enclosure to the S of Thebes which local people believed to mark the spot where Amphiaraus had vanished, and he says that animals gave the place a wide berth. This might have been the location of the oracle, although Herodotus [VIII.134] seems to suggest that it was a grander affair than anything Pausanias encountered there, even allowing for a prolonged period of deterioration.

KORONE: a sanctuary of **Asclepius** in Messenia, S Greece (36 55N, 21 58E). Korone stood on the hill that rises above modern Petalidi, about 20 km W of Kalamata in the S Peloponnese, and was the safest port in the region. There are few recognisable ruins, the principal exception being a brick-built structure that appears to be the remains of a bathing complex. It is possible that the baths were in some way connected with the sanctuary of Asclepius, as was the case at **GORTYS**. Otherwise there is no obvious evidence of its likely location.

KORONIA or **KORONEIA**: an oracle of the **dead** in Boiotia, central Greece (38 24N, 22 59E). The remains of ancient Koronia can be found to the SE of **LEBADEIA**, about 6 km N of modern Koronia. They lie in the middle of fields, and are generally unremarkable. A section of wall is visible from a distance, but promises more than it delivers. Some foundations of a temple have been uncovered, but where the oracle was is unknown. **Pausanias** makes no mention of it, suggesting that it had ceased to function before his time.

KOROPE: an oracle of **Apollo** in Thessaly, central Greece (39 16N, 23 09E). The site of ancient Korope was next to modern Koropi, which lies about 25 km SE of Volos, below Mount Pelion. The oracle was an ancient one, and continued to function right through into Roman times. At some point, the sanctuary came under the control of **DIMITRIAS** (about 30 km away), which was founded in 290 BC. An inscription dated to around 100 BC reveals that by that time (if not before) the process of consultation was a lengthy one. There was first a procession from the city to the temple, followed by the obligatory sacrifice. Enquirers wrote their questions on small tablets and spent the night in the sanctuary. The answers (which were limited to a simple positive or negative response) somehow eventually appeared on the tablets. On the second day, the procession returned to the city. The site of the sanctuary was discovered in the early twentieth century, below the hill known as Petralona. Excavations revealed parts of walls and many terracotta items. However, the site was filled in again afterwards, so there is nothing to see *in situ*. Portable items have found their way to the archaeological museum in Volos, although only a few are on display.

KOS: a sanctuary of **Asclepius** in the Dodecanese (36 54N, 27 19E). Kos was by far the most important centre of the Asclepius cult on the Greek islands. Curiously (or perhaps not?), it was also the birthplace of **Hippocrates**, regarded as the founder of scientific medicine. The sanctuary is about 4 km SW of Kos town (the capital of the island), and is known as Asklipion.

As was the case in many other places, the cult of Asclepius first attached itself to that of Apollo. The sanctuary of Asclepius developed around that of Apollo Kyparissos ('of the cypress tree' – the trees still grow around the site), with Asclepius' presence being first marked by an altar there. It was only after the middle of the fourth century BC that a dedicated Asclepius sanctuary began to develop. It evolved into a complex of three interconnected terraces. The lowest was mainly concerned with the provision of bathing facilities, and rooms in which the sick might rest. The middle terrace was the site of the altar to the god, and it is also possible to see on its W side the remains of a fourth-century BC temple dedicated to him. The upper terrace was the location of the much larger temple built in the second century BC, when an expansionist building programme took place. It may have been modelled on that at **EPIDAUROS**. Below the lower terrace there are later Roman baths.

It is not known when the sanctuary ceased to function. Much of the damage done to it was the result of earthquakes. The main temple became adapted for Christian use at some stage, but eventually the site was abandoned and forgotten. It was rediscovered right at the beginning of the twentieth century. Not only has it been thoroughly excavated, but some parts of it have also been reconstructed. This means that there is a lot to see, although some of the restoration work may owe at least something to romanticism. There is a museum containing local finds situated in Kos town.

Although the principal and typical form of healing on offer at the sanctuaries of Asclepius involved **incubation**, on Kos it seems more mundane methods were also used (although the practical balance between the two is unclear). Physicians were employed at the sanctuary to treat those who arrived with their various ailments. They presumably drew on the expertise of Hippocrates and his successors. The sanctuary of Asclepius on Kos would therefore have constituted one of the most important medical centres of the ancient world.

KRANNON: a sanctuary of **Asclepius** in Thessaly, N Greece (39 28N, 22 18E). The ruins of Krannon lie about 3 km SW of the modern village of Kranonas, which is 20 km SW of **LARISA**. The site lies unannounced on either side of an unpaved road, in the midst of cotton fields. Most of what can be seen consists of excavated tombs and nondescript piles of rubble. The foundations of the temple of Asclepius were discovered during excavations, but now defy recognition. It is known that the temple was one of the repositories of the city's official archives, suggesting that the cult enjoyed a special significance there. However, the city's glory days ended relatively early, and after the fifth century BC it lost its independence to Larisa. Confusingly, Krannon is sometimes known as Palaio-Larisa ('ancient Larisa'). The cults of **Isis** and **Sarapis** also enjoyed some popularity in Krannon, but their temples have not been found at all. An isolated church stands near the site.

KYLLENE: a sanctuary of **Asclepius** in Elis, S Greece. The exact site of ancient Kyllene is unknown. Modern Kyllini (37 56N, 21 10E) is situated close to the westernmost tip of the Peloponnese, about 13 km W of Andravida, but the remains that lie around it are medieval rather than ancient. Kyllene was a port, so any remains may be underwater. Somewhere in the area NW of Kyllini seems the most likely place for ruins of it to be found. Beyond noting its existence, **Pausanias** [VI.26.5] reveals nothing about the sanctuary itself, but notes that the local people worshipped **Hermes** in the shape of a phallus.

KYPHANTA: a sanctuary of **Asclepius** in Lakonia, S Greece. **Pausanias** [III.24.2] says that the sanctuary here was in the form of a cave, located 2 or 3 km inland. A spring and some carved rocks have been found about that distance in that direction from the village of Kiparissi in the E Peloponnese (36 55N, 22 48E). However, neither the findings nor Pausanias' directions are sufficient for a clear identification of the place as the site of Kyphanta. A cave is an unusual site for a sanctuary of Asclepius, being more often associated with the **dead**.

LARISA or **LARISSA**: a sanctuary of **Asclepius** in Thessaly, N Greece (39 35N, 22 27E). Ancient Larisa lies under the modern city of the same name. (It should not be confused with Palaio-Larisa, the name sometimes applied to **KRANNON**, some 20 km away.) As a consequence, there is little to be seen *in situ*, although there are some ruins in the NW of the town, near the cathedral and the river. These include remains of a theatre and an unidentified temple. Local finds are to be found in the archaeological museum that has been established in an old mosque on the market square. Nothing of the sanctuary of Asclepius has yet been found.

LAS: a sanctuary of **Asclepius** in Lakonia, S Greece (36 41N, 22 28E). The site of Las lies about 9 km SW of Githio, at the place now known as Pasavas. The remains of a thirteenth-century castle occupy it, incorporating fragments of far older buildings. The sanctuary of Asclepius was built on the summit of one of the surrounding mountains. The castle itself has enormous well-preserved walls, but most of what can be found inside them now dates only from the eighteenth century. According to **Pausanias** [III.24.8], there was another sanctuary of Asclepius about 7 km away at Hypsoi. Although many ruins are scattered around the area, neither **Asclepeion** has been found.

LEBADEIA (modern Levadia): an oracle of **Trophonius** in Boiotia, central Greece (38 26N, 22 53E). This was one of the most famous oracles of antiquity. According to **Herodotus** [I.46-50] it was one of those selected for consultation by **Croesus** (although it was unable to give him the correct answer to his question). The origins of the oracle are obscure, and the legends concerning Trophonius confused. One says he was the son of **Apollo**, another that he had a human father. He is generally credited with having a brother, Agamedes, with whom he is often linked. They are said to have built the first temple of Apollo at **DELPHI** (about 50 km from Lebadeia) and died there soon afterwards. Another story says Trophonius robbed a king and was swallowed up by the ground at Lebadeia during his attempt to evade capture. However, the real story may be that Trophonius was originally a local god of the underworld. The way his oracle functioned is consistent with this. The oracles of heroes, even of those later elevated to divinity like **Asclepius**, tended to use the medium of dreams. What happened at the oracle of Trophonius was very different, and **Pausanias** gives a firsthand account of it.

According to him [IX.39.4], before the consultation could take place there were days of preparation to be gone through. While religious ritual in ancient Greece almost always involved animal sacrifices, here it was given a special significance. After each sacrifice, the entrails of the slaughtered animal would be examined for omens. The more positive the signs, the greater the hope of a satisfactory outcome. When the big moment finally came, the enquirer would be dressed in special clothes (including heavy boots!) and lowered into a chamber. From this a narrow opening led into a further one, which had to be entered feet first. There things would be heard, and sometimes seen as well, before departure by the same route and method. The experience was evidently a traumatic one, and those emerging had to be looked after by officials and friends. After a suitable period of recovery, enquirers had a record of their experiences inscribed on a piece of wood which was kept at the site. None of these have survived, and unfortunately Pausanias does not reveal what he heard and saw there either. However, he does give an example [IV.32.5] of an oracle said to have been delivered by Trophonius in verse to the people of Greek **THEBES** in 371 BC. In it, he predicted that they would triumph in a coming conflict with **SPARTA**, which they duly did.

The oracle of Trophonius was evidently highly regarded for a very long time, and the setting for intense and dramatic personal experiences. The extent to which these experiences were stage-managed is unknown. This is because the location of the oracle itself remains unknown (or at least highly disputed). Pausanias' directions are inadequate to pinpoint the spot. One of the problems is establishing whether the oracular chambers lay below the ground or were constructed above it. Different interpretations of Pausanias have led to people looking in very different areas.

There are some natural landmarks to guide the search. The river Erkyna runs through Levadia, and it can be followed uphill to its source. The springs that feed it played a role in the consultation of the oracle, as enquirers drank from them. Nearby is a substantial hill furnished with medieval fortifications. At the top of it is a small church supposedly built over the remains of a temple dedicated to **Zeus**. Claims have been made for the vicinity of the temple as the obvious site for the oracle, while others argue that it was some way below it. Pausanias says only that it was on the hill and above a sacred wood. Unfortunately it is literally impossible to see the wood for the trees, as they now reach right to the top of the hill. Any sign of any kind of opening in the ground has been seized upon as a possible candidate for the oracle site, but so far no convincing cases have been made. If the oracular chambers were built above ground, it is most likely that all traces of them have long since disappeared. But the search goes on and the area between the springs and the hill top is interesting (if exhausting) to explore. When the oracle ceased to function is not known, but it seems likely that it lasted until at least the third century AD.

LEBENA (modern Lendas): a sanctuary of **Asclepius** in Crete (34 55N, 24 55E). Lebena lies on the coast about 30 km S of **GORTYNA**, and served as its harbour. The hot springs to be found in the area make it an obvious location for a healing centre. A chemical analysis of the water there has revealed traces of arsenic (*not* arsenic trioxide, which is the poisonous variety). This is meant to be beneficial to the blood. The remains of many buildings can be seen on the site.

The temple of Asclepius itself dates from the fourth century BC, which is probably when the sanctuary was first established. Much of what can be seen of the sanctuary today, however, comes from a substantial rebuilding programme carried out during the second century AD. The remains of two **stoas** and a treasury can be seen, and some sections of mosaic paving have been found intact. Although their precise functions are not always easy to discern now, these buildings were obviously intended to serve both the temple and the visitors to the sanctuary. The more easterly of the stoas (known a little confusingly as the North Stoa) yielded many inscriptions recording successful cures attributed to the god. It is thought that it may have functioned as an **abaton** for at least part of its useful life. The springs lie near the E end of the stoa. According to **Pausanias** [II.26.7] the cult of Asclepius was brought here from **BALAGRAI**.

LESBOS: an oracle of **Apollo**. The god had a temple on the island where he was known by the **epithet** Napaios ('of the woods'). The remains of a sanctuary have been found at Klopedi (39 20N, 26 15E), a village about 5 km W of **Agia** Paraskevi and reached by a track from there. Many think this may have been Apollo's, although nothing has been found to make the identification definite. The ruins of two temples have been uncovered and dated to the sixth and fifth centuries BC. Wherever it was on the island, legend has it that **Pelops** visited Apollo's oracle here. Items excavated from the Klopedi site (and from elsewhere on Lesbos) are in the museum in Mytilene, the island's capital situated at its E extreme.

Mytilene had a temple of **Asclepius**, which was the most important in the city, and there may also have been a healing shrine of **Artemis** here. Neither has been found, but there is a church of **Agios** Therapon. He is (as his name suggests) a healing saint whose cult goes back to the third century. The present church on this site was begun only in the nineteenth century, although it contains icons dating back to the fourteenth and fifteenth centuries. The presence of a church of St Therapon in a place known to have had a temple of Asclepius may not be a coincidence. In the town of Agia Paraskevi, the church of the same name may have been built on the site of another ancient shrine of Asclepius. The god's cult also had a centre in Eresos, in the W of the island, while **ANTISSA**, in the NW, was associated with an oracle of **Orpheus**.

LEUKTRA: a sanctuary of **Asclepius** in Lakonia, S Greece. According to **Pausanias** [III.26.4], Asclepius was the principal god worshipped here. He speculates that the place may have been named after Leucippus who, according to one story, was the grandfather of Asclepius. The site of Leuktra is now known as Leuktron, and lies near Stoupa (36 47N, 22 19E), about 35 km SE of Kalamata in the Peloponnese. Most of what can be seen today consists of the remains of a medieval castle built on top of the hill that formed the ancient city's acropolis. Nearby was found an inscription that apparently came from the sanctuary of **Machaon** at **GERENIA**.

LISSOS or **LISOS**: a sanctuary of **Asclepius** in Crete (35 14N, 23 40E). The site of Lissos is about 10 km E of Paleochora, on the S coast of the island. Relatively little is known concerning the history of the place, although the extent of the ruins indicates that it was a substantial city. Much of it remains unexcavated, but the area around the sanctuary of Asclepius is fortunately the principal exception to this. Although the sanctuary itself was large, the actual temple was quite small. The sanctuary was located near a healing spring, and contained ancillary buildings, including baths, in addition to the temple. This probably dates to the third century BC originally, although the mosaics found inside it are significantly later. A number of statues, especially of Asclepius and **Hygeia**, have been found in the area. Most of these can now be seen in the museums of Iraklio and Hania. The evidence suggests that the immediate cause of the sanctuary's demise was an earthquake. Despite the distance, it seems that Lissos had a special connection with **GORTYNA** in antiquity.

LOUSOI: a sanctuary of **Artemis** in Arkadia, S Greece (37 59N, 22 09E). Lousoi lies about halfway between **KLEITOR** and Kalavrita. Legend has it that the tradition of healing began when **Melampus** brought granddaughters of **Abas** here in order to cure their insanity with the aid of a nearby spring. Thereafter, the temple was regarded as a place with special powers. Its remains, and those of other attendant buildings, have been uncovered in excavations that began at the end of the nineteenth century. The sanctuary is constructed on two levels, with the temple itself on the higher one. Most of what can be seen dates from the late fourth and early third centuries BC, although the sanctuary itself seems to have been in use since at least the sixth century BC. The ruins are unspectacular, but the layout of the sanctuary can clearly be seen. There are plans to build a museum on the site to display the many finds unearthed in the area, but in the meantime they are in store in Patras.

LYKAION, Mount: an oracle of **Pan** in Arkadia, S Greece (37 22N, 21 58E). Mount Lykaion is about 20 km NW of **MEGALOPOLIS**. The sanctuary lies on the S side of the mountain, above the village of Ano Karies. The ruins are very sparse. The remains of a **katagogion** have been identified, as well as the sites of the stadium and hippodrome used in the games held here. A number of other unidentified remains are scattered around the vicinity, and much of the area is unexcavated. The oracle may have been located in a cave rather than a temple, but no trace of it has so far been found.

MANTINEIA: a sanctuary of **Asclepius** in Arkadia, S Greece (37 37N, 22 23E). The ruins of Mantineia lie about 12 km N of Tripoli. The city was destroyed by the Spartans in 385 BC but rebuilt soon after. The sections of wall still visible are from that time. Within the walls the fragmentary remains of a number of buildings have been uncovered. According to **Pausanias** [VIII.9.1] there was an unusual double temple here, half dedicated to Asclepius, half to **Leto**, but this has so far eluded discovery.

MARATHON: a sanctuary of **Aristomachus** in Attica, central Greece (38 07N, 23 58E). Next to nothing is known about Aristomachus. There are several individuals with that name in ancient Greek legend and history, but none obviously fits the bill here. His cult was evidently very local, and he seems to have been primarily a healer. The remains of ancient Marathon lie a few km to the S of modern Marathonas and consist principally of burials. The dead from the battle of Marathon in 490 BC were interred under two large mounds, which can still be seen. Between them are the remains of several considerably older tombs. However, the cult of Aristomachus seems to have been located in or around the ancient city's temple of **Dionysus**, which has not been found. It is thought that it lay somewhere between Marathonas and the coast. Aristomachus also had a sanctuary at **RHAMNOUS**, some 10 km to the NE, but **Pausanias** makes no mention of him in connection with either place. His cult seems to have gone into a terminal decline during the late centuries BC, at least partly as a result of being eclipsed by that of **Amphiaraus** at neighbouring **OROPOS**. The distance between Marathon and the centre of ancient **ATHENS** to its SW was about 40 km, as might be expected from the sporting event that takes its name from the place. The distance to the nearest point of sprawling modern Athens is considerably shorter.

MEGALOPOLIS: two sanctuaries of **Asclepius** in Arkadia, S Greece (37 24N, 22 09E). Ancient Megalopolis ('the great city') lay about 1 km N of the modest modern town of the same name in the central Peloponnese. **Pausanias** [VIII.32.4-5] tells of two separate sanctuaries of the god Asclepius here, with the second one referred to specifically as being of the *child* Asclepius. The cult statue that stood in this sanctuary appears to have been very small, only about 45 cm high. The site of this sanctuary is said to have been near a spring, but it has not been identified.

The other **Asclepeion** lay just to the NE of the city's enormous theatre, by the river. The theatre can easily be seen but little is visible of the Asclepeion itself. The more impressive ruins of ancient Megalopolis lie further N, on the other side of the river, where excavations continue.

MEGARA: an oracle of **Nyx** in Megaris, central Greece (37 59N, 23 22E). Little remains of ancient Megara as the modern city is built on top of it. **Pausanias** [I.40.5] mentions a statue of **Asclepius** here, but does not explicitly indicate the presence of a sanctuary. On the oracle of Nyx he sheds no light (perhaps appropriately since she was the goddess of night). Nothing that can be seen in the area seems likely to have had any connection with it.

MESSENE: a sanctuary of **Asclepius** in Messenia, S Greece (37 11N, 21 58E). The extensive remains of ancient Messene lie around the village of Mavromati, about 20 km N of modern Messini. (Confusingly, there is another village with the same name only 2 km from Messini.) The city was famed in antiquity for its walls, substantial and magnificent sections of which are still well preserved. The remains of the sanctuary of Asclepius lie in the area of archaeological excavations immediately below the village. The identification of the ruins has been the subject of some disagreement. What can be seen is the foundations of a temple and altar contained within a large courtyard, which had a colonnade along each side. Around the outside of this courtyard were various rooms, large and small, and at one end of it a small theatre. The courtyard was once thought to be an **agora**. However, the recognition of the temple in the middle of it as dedicated to Asclepius suggested that the whole complex was an **Asclepeion**, and this is now the generally held view. If it is correct, then it is an interesting example of one, being compact and self-contained within a city setting. According to **Pausanias** [IV.31.10], all of the best statues in Messene were to be found in the Asclepeion, including one cast in iron, an unusual medium in Greek sculpture.

MILOS or **MELOS**: a sanctuary of **Asclepius** in the Cyclades (36 42N, 24 25E). Milos lies in the SW corner of the group of islands. The celebrated Venus de Milo was found in the village of Trypiti here in 1820. The town of Milos (more commonly known as Plaka) stands substantially over the site of its ancient predecessor, but some remains of earlier settlements have been uncovered to the S and SE of it. The hill now known as Profitis Ilias was the acropolis of the city of classical times. It was in this area that the head of a statue of Asclepius (now in the British Museum) was found. Although the sanctuary of the god was also in this area, there is nothing obvious of it to be seen.

MYTILENE: see **LESBOS**

NAUPAKTOS: a sanctuary of **Asclepius** in Phokis, central Greece (38 24N, 21 50E). Naupaktos stands near the mouth of the Gulf of Corinth, on its N shore.

In the Middle Ages it was known as Lepanto, and there are some impressive remains from this period. **Pausanias** says [X.38.7] that the sanctuary of Asclepius had already fallen into decay when he visited it. However, he does relate an interesting story about its foundation. Unusually, it had been built by a private individual (named Phalysios) rather than by a community. He tells how Asclepius sent the poetess **Anyte** from **EPIDAUROS** with a sealed tablet to present to Phalysios, who was losing his sight. When he unsealed it, his sight was restored. Anyte is known to have lived in the third century BC. The site of the sanctuary is thought to have lain a little to the E of the town, where some inscriptions were found on an elevated terrace. They may still be there, but I was unable to find them.

NIKOPOLIS: a sanctuary of **Asclepius** in Thesprotia, N Greece (39 00N, 20 43E). Nikopolis ('City of Victory') was founded by **Augustus** to celebrate his triumph in the battle of Actium, which was fought nearby. This defeat of **Antony** and **Cleopatra** in 31 BC was a decisive moment in his drive for domination of Rome. The ruins of the city occupy a large area about 6 km N of Preveza. However, much of the huge site is unexcavated and under cultivation. The most impressive remains of the city are its walls, although the best preserved parts date from the sixth century rather than from the time of its foundation. Other structures are widely scattered. It is known that there was a sanctuary of Asclepius, but it has yet to be identified.

OITYLON: see **THALAMAE**

OLOUS: a sanctuary of **Asclepius** in Crete (35 12N, 25 41E). The site of Olous lies about 10 km N of Agios Nikolaos, on the N coast of the island, near the village of Elouda. From the evidence of inscriptions it is apparent that the cult of Asclepius enjoyed a measure of importance here. Unfortunately, most of the site, including the god's sanctuary, now lies underwater and only some sections of city wall remain to be seen.

OLYMPIA: oracles of **Zeus** and **Ge** in Elis, S Greece (37 37N, 21 39E). Set in the W Peloponnese, Olympia was a place of major importance in antiquity and is an enormously popular tourist destination today. It was the centre of the cult of Zeus, and the statue of him there was one of the Seven Wonders of the ancient world. However, it is evident that Zeus was not the first to be worshipped here. The oracle of Ge mentioned by **Pausanias** [V.14.10] had long ceased to function by his time, although there was still an altar of the goddess to be seen. Its location is now unknown.

The oracle of Zeus seems to have been based around his great altar which stood somewhere between his temple and that of Hera. A large tree now grows near the likely spot. The altar was constructed of the accumulated ashes of the sacrifices made at the site, and the act of sacrifice was itself the basis of the oracular process. The precise method is not clear, but it involved examining the skins or entrails of the sacrificial victims. Those who carried out this exercise were the priests based at the sanctuary. The office of priest was filled on an hereditary basis for much of its history.

As with many sanctuaries, it went into decline and was finally closed down at the end of the fourth century AD. Earthquakes and floods conspired to do a great deal of damage. However, excavations have been going on for over a century now, and there is much to be seen. Unfortunately, the oracular past of Olympia has left no visible traces. It was the home of the ancient Olympic Games, and the Olympic flame is now lit here every four years to be carried to the chosen venue of their modern successors.

OMOLION: a sanctuary of **Asclepius** in Thessaly, N Greece (39 51N, 22 39E). Ancient Omolion stood near modern Moli, at the NE end of the Tempi gorge. **GONNOS** lay 18 km to the SW at its other end. Then as now it lay near the border with Macedonia, and it was one of the places captured by **Philip II** in his expansionist programme. In 117 BC it passed into the hands of **DIMITRIAS**. What can be seen now consists of some stretches of the city walls and, within them, the foundations of a temple and a theatre. The **Asclepeion** has not been identified.

ONCHESTOS: an oracle of **Poseidon** in Boiotia, central Greece (38 21N, 23 12E). The ruins of Onchestos are tucked away in a field about 3 km SE of Aliartos, just off the old road to Thiva. The remains are neither extensive nor impressive, but the temple of Poseidon has been identified among them. Poseidon was a complex character, and was thought to be, among other things, the inventor of the chariot. At Onchestos his oracle operated by observing and somehow interpreting the behaviour of horses hitched to a chariot.

ONKIOS: see **KAOUS**

ORCHOMENOS: an oracle of **Teiresias**, and a sanctuary of **Asclepius** in Boiotia, central Greece (38 30N, 22 58E). The ruins lie in the NW of modern Orchomenos, about 12 km NE of Levadia. There are many legends associated with Teiresias, who was a celebrated seer during his lifetime. He was made blind, but there is an overabundance of explanations as to why this happened. It was also believed that he spent part of his life as a woman. Greek **THEBES** was the place most closely connected with him during his lifetime, but he is said to have died at Telphussa, which lies between Thebes and Orchomenos, and his posthumous oracle was apparently at the latter (a traditional rival of Thebes). Those credited with special powers of prophecy or healing often became transformed into the sources of oracles after death. It is said that the oracle of Teiresias fell silent during a time of disease. It is not clear as to when this is supposed to have happened, but certainly **Pausanias** makes no mention of any oracle here. Neither does he make any mention of a sanctuary of Asclepius, although a temple to the god has been found dating from the fourth century BC. This was part of a major rebuilding programme carried out by **Alexander the Great** and his father after Orchomenos had been destroyed by its Theban neighbours in 364 BC. Several parts of the ancient city can still be seen, including a theatre. The remains of the Asclepius temple lie about 500 m to the W of it, on the way up to the acropolis. Its foundations can clearly be made out.

OROBIA: an oracle of **Apollo** in Euboea, central Greece (38 47N, 23 16E). Orobia is modern Rovies, which lies in the NW of the island of Evia. The god was known here by the **epithet** Selinuntius ('of the moon'). According to **Strabo** [X.1.3], this oracle was particularly truthful, but **Pausanias** makes no mention of it, and there is nothing to see at the site.

OROPOS: an oracle of **Amphiaraus** in Attica, central Greece (38 18N, 23 49E). The ruins of the oracle of Amphiaraus, known as the Amphiareion, lie between Markopoulo and Kalamos, about 49 km N of Athens. Modern Oropos (usually known as Skala Oropou) stands about 20 km to the W. Although belonging to Oropos, the oracle was not situated in the ancient city itself, which was about 7 km away to the NW.

The oracle seems to have originally been located at **KNOPIA**, and probably moved to Oropos in the late fifth century BC. The oldest buildings whose remains can be seen there date back to the fourth century BC, and the sanctuary as a whole continued to function until the fourth century AD. In the intervening period it was visited by **Pausanias** [I.34.1-3], among many others. He tells how the method of consultation involved the sacrifice of a ram, whose skin was then slept on. (A similar method was used at **Mount GARGANUS**, at the oracle of **Kalchas**.) However, inscriptions found at the site suggest alternatives to rams were also permitted. The sacrifice itself could only be carried out after a period of preparation that involved giving up food for one day and wine for three. There was also a substantial fee to be paid. The sacrifices were performed by the sanctuary's priest when he was in attendance, but could be carried out by individuals seeking Amphiaraus' assistance when he was not (which may have been a lot of the time). Dreams seem to have been the medium of all oracles delivered there, whether they related to healing or not. There is nothing in legend to suggest that Amphiaraus had any particular affinity with healing when alive, but his oracle came to specialise in this area of activity after it moved to Oropos. According to one legend, he had become a seer by spending the night in a mysterious 'house of prophecy' at **PHLIOUS**.

The remains of the principal cult structures can be easily made out. The temple, its altar and the **abaton** lie along a line running from SW to NE through the site. The sacred spring can be found below the altar. There is a museum containing many of the inscriptions found here. However, it is only the central area of the site that has been fully excavated and substantial areas remain wholly or only partly uncovered. Nevertheless, what has been revealed shows that the sanctuary functioned as a spa as well as an oracle, and that healing by other than miraculous means was expected to take place here. One of the more curious structures found at the site, on the other side of the stream from the temple, is an enormous water clock with its bronze plug hole still in place.

PAGASAI: an oracle of **Apollo** in Thessaly, N Greece (39 22N, 22 56E). The ruins of Pagasai lie about 4 km S of Volos, on either side of the road to Nea Anchialos. It was an ancient settlement, famous in legend for being the place where the **Argo** was built. In 290 BC another city, Dimitrias, was founded to the N of it, and the two soon became one. Consequently the whole site is frequently referred to as Dimitrias. Most of what remains to be seen comes from the newer city, and of the original Pagasai little more than the odd piece of wall remains. The combined city covered a considerable area and such of it as survives is very scattered. In Volos museum there is a model of the site which is helpful in making sense of how the bits and pieces fit together. Next to nothing is known about the oracle, either how it functioned or exactly where it was. There is even some doubt as to whether it was an oracle of Apollo at all. However, what is clear is that at some point Dimitrias acquired control over the oracle of Apollo at **KOROPE**, about 30 km away to the SE. It is also thought that Dimitrias had a sanctuary of **Asclepius**, but no trace of it has been found.

PAMISOS: a healing sanctuary in Messenia, S Greece (36 59N, 22 01E). The Pamisos is the river that flows S into the Messiniakos Gulf near Kalamata.

About 20 km upstream, near the village of **Agios** Floros, was a sanctuary dedicated to curing children. The springs in this area were thought to be the source of the river. **Pausanias** [IV.31.4] mentions it, but gives no indication as to how children were cured, why only children were cured there, or which (if any) deity was associated with the place. The remains of a small temple were discovered in the area in the 1820s, and what was left of it rediscovered in the 1920s. It stood near three springs and had dedications recorded on its walls. Items found at the site were taken to the National Museum in Athens, and the excavations covered over. Consequently, there is now nothing to be seen *in situ*.

PANGÆUM, Mount: an oracle of **Dionysus** in Macedonia, NE Greece (41 30N, 24 10E). Although he is not very precise as to its whereabouts, the existence of an oracle in this area is clearly indicated by **Herodotus** [VII.111]. According to him it lay in the territory of the Satrae, a warlike and independent people who inhabited the mountains and were finally subdued only in the time of **Augustus**. They lived on and around Mount Pangæum (now Pangeo), which lies about 25 km W of Kavala and the same distance S of Drama. This area was also famous for its many mines, including gold mines. The priests of the oracle came from the Bessi, a particularly aggressive subdivision of the Satrae, and the god's responses were delivered by a prophetess. The oracle was probably situated on one of the highest parts of the mountain, but it is not possible to say exactly where. No remains have been found, but there may never have been a permanent building here. This particular area, and nearby Thrace in general, was always closely associated with the cult of Dionysus. There was apparently another oracle of the god elsewhere in Thrace, at an unknown location, where prophecy was consequent upon the consumption of wine, one of the god's special interests. The story of an oracle of Dionysus in this region being closed down by local Christians in 400 may relate to either.

PANOPEUS: a sanctuary of **Asclepius** in Phokis, central Greece (38 27N, 22 45E). The site is about 20 km W of **ORCHOMENOS**, above the village of Agios Vlasios. It now lies off the beaten track, but in ancient times the road from **ATHENS** to **DELPHI** ran through it. This proved to be a mixed blessing as it encouraged foes as well as friends to pass this way, which they did. By the early first century BC it had been destroyed three times in a little over four hundred years. The third time proved extremely unlucky and it never really recovered. **Pausanias** [X.4.1] describes it as a very run-down place. One of its claims to fame was as the home town of Epeius, said to have designed the wooden horse of **Troy**. The walls of the ancient acropolis are well preserved, but what is inside them less so. However, it is not entirely fanciful to think that a small chapel standing near two wells might have been built on or near the site of the **Asclepeion**.

PAROS: a sanctuary of **Asclepius** in the Cyclades (37 04N, 25 10E). Paros is the name of both an island and its main town (sometimes called Parikia) which lies on its W coast. The town is built over the ancient city of the same name, but is rather smaller than the earlier foundation. Unfortunately, part of what the modern city has spared has been claimed by the forces of erosion and now lies under the sea. However, the site of the **Asclepeion** has escaped both kinds of invasion and lies to the SW of the modern town, on the lower slopes of Mount Arakas (a sanctuary of Pythian **Apollo** can be found higher up). Sadly, the ruins are not very impressive, consisting mainly of a ruined terrace and two fountains dating from the fourth century BC.

PATRAI or **PATRAS**: an oracle of **Demeter** and a sanctuary of **Asclepius** in Achaia, S Greece (41 11N, 20 52E). Modern Patras stands on the N coast of the Peloponnese, atop its ancient predecessor, although a few remnants of the latter manage to show through. However, it is thought that the temple of Demeter occupied the site now known as Plateia **Agios** Andreas, which lies near the sea front, S of the fishing harbour. The square is dominated by the enormous church of Agios Andreas and attendant buildings. According to **Pausanias** [VII.21.5] the oracle here was very reliable, but it only dealt with medical matters. The method used to consult it was a curious one. A mirror was lowered by means of a cord until it just touched the surface of the water of a spring outside the temple. The mirror revealed whether the sick person would live or die. In the SW corner of the square is a small building erected over a flight of steps. At the bottom of the steps is a well fed by a deep spring, which is presumably that of the oracle. The place is now a Christian shrine and continues to receive regular visitors. Above its entrance can be seen the palindromic inscription NIΨON ANOMHMATA MH MONAN OΨIN, which exhorts those who pass under it to cleanse their souls as well as their bodies. The sanctuary of Asclepius was located near the acropolis (which can also be seen), but its precise location is unknown. The museum in Patras contains local finds.

   Strabo [VIII.7.4] speaks of another sanctuary of Asclepius, with a noteworthy temple, about 15 km SW of Patrai. It stood by or near the river Piros, perhaps in the vicinity of the modern village of Agios Stephanos, but no trace of it has been found.

PELLANA: a sanctuary of **Asclepius** in Lakonia, S Greece (37 10N, 22 21E). Pellana is situated in the S Peloponnese, near the modern village of the same name, about 27 km NW of Sparti. The location of the Asclepius sanctuary is unknown, although it caught the interest of **Pausanias** [III.21.2]. Some of the city's walls can be seen, and there are some impressive tombs in the area.

PELLENE: a sanctuary of **Asclepius** in Achaia, S Greece. The remains of Pellene are at modern Pellini (38 01N, 22 34E), about 11 km SW of Xilokastro, which stands on the Gulf of Corinth. However, according to **Pausanias** [VII.27.5] the sanctuary of Asclepius lay about 12 km from the town, but he gives no precise direction. The likely location is in the vicinity of Trikala (a collective name for what is in fact three separate villages) which lies to the SW. The name is clearly suggestive of a connection with the healing god, as a common variant of **TRIKKA**. Pausanias says that there were a number of springs at the site, with a statue of Asclepius set beside the biggest one. The highest of the three Trikala villages, Ano Trikala, is now a winter sports destination, perhaps continuing a long tradition of healthy activity.

PERACHORA: an oracle of **Hera** in Corinthia, central Greece (38 01N, 22 51E). The name Perachora now applies both to the large promontory directly N of Corinth, and a village on it. The remains of the oracle of Hera are at the tip of the promontory, about 9 km W of the village. Two sanctuaries to the goddess were located at this site. That of Hera Akraia lies near the water, with the remains of a **stoa** and small **agora** nearby. That of Hera Limenia ('of the harbour') is a little to the E of it, on higher ground. **Strabo** [VIII.6.22] says that the oracle belonged to Hera Akraia, but that it had ceased to function long before his time. Traces of the ninth-century BC temple to Hera Akraia can be seen, although rather more remains of its sixth-century BC replacement. The temple of Hera Limenia dates to the eighth century BC. How the oracle functioned is not known. Some think it was located at the rear of the temple of Hera Akraia, others have suggested a site somewhere between the two temples. It is also unclear as to how the two sanctuaries were related to each other, but a collaborative rather than competitive relationship seems likely. The sanctuary was probably abandoned during the second century BC when the Romans destroyed nearby **CORINTH**, to which it then belonged. The sharks that can sometimes be found in the adjacent waters are unlikely to have played a significant role in its depopulation.

PHALANNA: a sanctuary of **Asclepius** in Thessaly, N Greece (39 45N, 22 20E). The site of ancient Phalanna lies near the modern village of Falani, 9 km

N of **LARISA**. Apart from a few scattered stones there is nothing to see there, although at one time it was a city of some importance. However, at one time the cult of Asclepius evidently played an important part in the city's history since the names and years of tenure of the god's priests were used to date official decrees.

PHARAI (1) or **PHARAE**: an oracle of **Hermes** in Achaia, S Greece. The precise location of Pharai is uncertain, but it may be near the modern village of Fares, about 16 km S of Patras (41 11N, 20 52E). There are certainly some ruins in the area, but **Pausanias** [VII.22.2] gives directions that are difficult to follow. However, he does at least give a clear idea of how the oracle actually worked. It was centred on a stone statue of the god which stood in an enclosure. Enquirers would burn incense, fill the lamps with oil, light them, and place a coin on the altar. They would then whisper their question into the statue's ear. Having done so, they would block up their own ears with their fingers and leave the enclosure. Once outside they would unstop their ears, and the oracle consisted of whatever words they heard first. Chance words overheard were a well known, if not particularly prevalent, kind of **omen**.

PHARAI (2) or **PHERAE**: a sanctuary of **Nicomachus** and **Gorgasus** in Messenia, S Greece (37 01N, 22 09E). Pharai probably stood on the site of present-day Kalamata, and so there is nothing of it left to see. According to **Pausanias** [IV.30.3], Nicomachus and Gorgasus were sons of **Machaon**, and so grandsons of **Asclepius**. Other than this, little is known of either of them. With such a pedigree, it is to be assumed that they were thought to have been healers while alive, and people were still coming to their sanctuary for cures when Pasusanias visited it. They also appear to have been joint kings of Pharai.

PHARSALOS: a sanctuary of **Asclepius** in Thessaly, N Greece (39 14N, 22 27E). The ancient city mainly lies under modern Farsala, about 40 km S of **LARISA**, and little can be seen of it except some fragments of city wall. Achilles may have lived here, and in 48 BC **Julius Caesar** decisively defeated his rival **Pompey** nearby. Although the temple of Asclepius has not been found, a head of the god was discovered in the E of the city, along with inscriptions carrying his name. The museum at Volos contains some of the more interesting finds from the site.

PHENEOS or **PHENEA**: a sanctuary of **Asclepius** in Arkadia, S Greece (37 55N, 22 19E). The ruins of the ancient city are to be found near the village of

Archea Pheneos, about 20 km E of **KLEITOR** and 30 km directly S of **AEGIRA** (but nearly 50 km by road). The city had a long history and, according to **Pausanias** [VIII.14.5], it possessed a bronze statue of **Poseidon** claimed locally to have been dedicated by **Odysseus** himself. Curiously Pausanias makes no mention of any sanctuary of Asclepius, although its few remains constitute most of what can be seen at Pheneos today. They lie in the SE corner of the hill-top site, and comprise what is left of two separate buildings. The base of a statue dedicated to Asclepius has been found, along with the remains of a colossal statue of **Hygeia**.

PHERAI: a sanctuary of **Asclepius** in Thessaly, N Greece (39 23N, 22 44E). The site of Pherai is mainly covered by modern Velestino, 17 km W of Volos. Sections of wall and a temple of **Zeus** have been discovered. The city was famous for its springs, one of which, named Hypereia, can be found in the centre of the modern town, near the church of **Agios** Haralambos. Unfortunately, the ancient walls nearby have been identified as coming from a shrine dedicated to **Heracles**, not Asclepius. However, although not a saint particularly associated with healing, Haralambos is nevertheless regarded as a protector against epidemics. The presence of a church dedicated to him in close proximity to a spring might therefore be more than a simple coincidence, and could point to the sanctuary of Asclepius having been in this vicinity.

PHIGALIA or **PHIGALEIA**: an oracle of the **dead** in Arkadia, S Greece (37 23N, 21 51E). The ruins of Phigalia lie near modern Figalia, a village about 20 km SW of Andritsena in the central Peloponnese. **Pausanias** [III.17.9] goes into no details, but if there was such an oracle here it might have been located in a chasm lying to the S of the ruins. The city itself had something of a reputation for the dark arts, so an oracle of the dead is not implausible. The remains of some walls and towers can be seen. Although not mentioned by Pausanias, it is thought that there were sanctuaries of both **Hygeia** and **Asclepius** here, but they have not been identified.

PHILIPPI: a sanctuary of **Isis** in Macedonia, N Greece (41 05N, 24 16E). The ruins lie just outside Krinides, about 17 km NW of Kavala. Krinides (which means 'fountains') was the original name of this settlement before it was renamed (after himself) by **Philip II** of Macedon in 356 BC. In 42 BC two major battles were fought here in the struggle for control of Rome after the assassination of **Julius Caesar**. In one of them the poet **Horace** ran away in order to live and write another day. **St Paul** twice passed through the place, and, when in Rome, sent the inhabitants one of his epistles.

The site is partly on the side of a hill, and partly on the more level ground below it. On the hillside, to the NW of the theatre, are the remains of the sanctuary dedicated to Isis and other Egyptian gods. Exactly when her cult arrived here is not known, but after the battles of 42 BC she became officially recognised as the city's patroness and protectress, and Philippi became recognised as one of her main healing centres in this part of the world.

PHLIOUS: a sanctuary of **Asclepius** in Achaia, S Greece (37 51N, 22 38E). What is left of Phlious stands about 2 km NW of modern Nemea (which is about 30 km SW of Corinth) in the NE Peloponnese. A whitewashed church standing on a ridge surrounded by fields of vines is the site's only real landmark. This is the church of **Zoodochos Pigi**, which has clearly made use of materials of a more classical vintage in its construction. Both the church's dedication and its location suggest that it may occupy the site of the **Asclepeion**. According to **Pausanias** [II.13.3] the temple of Asclepius was located near, and above, the theatre. What is left of the theatre can clearly be seen, below the church, to the SW. Nearby are the remains of other buildings that may have played a role in the therapeutic process. Pausanias says little more about the place, and there is little else to see there.

PIRAEUS (modern Pireas): a sanctuary of **Asclepius** in Attica, central Greece (37 56N, 32 39E). As in ancient times, Pireas is the port of **ATHENS**, and distinctly overshadowed by its larger and more glamorous neighbour. Most of the city's ancient past has been buried without trace. Fortunately, an exception is the sanctuary of Asclepius, remains of which have been found. They lie on a hill, behind the open air Kastela theatre and opposite the Profitis Ilias church, in the SE of the city. The foundations of the temple and altar are clear, and there are a number of chambers and steps cut into the surrounding rock whose purpose is unclear. Carved reliefs were found there, some of which can be seen in the National Archaeological Museum in Athens. It is also known that there was a temple of **Isis** in the city, her cult having been introduced there by Egyptians in the fourth century BC. No trace of it remains, however.

PTOON, Mount: an oracle of **Apollo** in Boiotia, central Greece (38 29N, 23 15E). The sanctuary stands opposite the small church of **Agia** Paraskevi at the W end of Mount Ptoon, which itself lies about 3 km W of the village of Akrefnio. Akrefnio occupies the site of ancient Akraiphnia, to which the sanctuary was connected by a sacred way. Ptoos was an ancient hero, or local god, whose own sanctuary lay nearby, and with whose cult that of Apollo became locally fused to some degree. It was also said that **Teneros** had once been a prophet here. (His brother, **Ismenos**, was associated with an oracle of Apollo in Greek **THEBES**). The oracle here was an ancient one, and the first temple on the site was probably built in the seventh century BC. However, the oracle seems to have ceased to function during the first century AD (if not before) and had a long period of decline before that. Although **Pausanias** mentions it [IX.23.3], he did not rate the place worth a visit.

The sanctuary is built on three terraces. On the lowest can be seen a fountain and the remains of a number of cisterns. Here the ritual bathing necessary before approaching the oracle would have taken place. The middle one was occupied by two **stoas** and a **katagogion**, the foundations of which can be made out. On the top one is the little that is left of the temple and its altar. The temple was built in 318 BC to replace a sixth-century BC one that had been destroyed by **Alexander the Great**. It is thought that the oracles were not delivered in the temple itself, but nearby. How this would have happened is not known, but **Herodotus** [VIII.135] tells of a visit to the sanctuary by **Mys**, who claimed that the oracle spoke to him in his own language, Carian, rather than Greek. This at least suggests that the god made use of a prophet or prophetess here. The remains of a small grotto can be found near the SW corner of the temple. Although natural in origin, there are clear signs of it having been partly shaped by human hand. This is as likely a location for the oracle as any.

Many impressive statues were found at the site, most of which are now in the museums of Thiva and Athens. They were discovered in the area in front of the temple, which is presumably where they originally stood. Most are standing male figures, known as *kouroi*. The oldest statue found here is dated to 620 BC. The Thiva museum also has a useful plan of the site, which is itself very overgrown.

RHAMNOUS: sanctuaries of **Asclepius** and **Aristomachus** in Attica, central Greece (38 12N, 24 01E). Rhamnous lies near the coast, about 10 km NE of **MARATHON**, and about 50 km from the centre of **ATHENS**. It is a site much appreciated for its remoteness and beauty. Its most distinctive feature is its temple of **Nemesis**. **Herodes Atticus**, a native of Marathon, was one of its patrons. The temple lies about 400 m from the town proper and its fortifications. Much of this area is as yet unexcavated. Inscriptions have been found indicating that there was an **Asclepeion** in Rhamnous, but it has not been found. Opposite the city gate, on a small hill, is a terrace where a sanctuary of Aristomachus once stood. His was a local healing cult based at

Marathon. What activities took place at the sanctuary is not known, but it ceased to function in the third or second century BC when the cult faded away.

RHODES: a sanctuary of **Asclepius** in the Dodecanese (36 10N, 28 00E). Rhodes lies just off the SW coast of Turkey. The sanctuary of Asclepius was in the S part of the island. After heading SW from Lindos along the coastal road for about 15 km, there is a turning to the right that leads to Asklipio, about 5 km away. The site is little known and little visited, and the only obvious remains to be seen now are medieval. For reasons that are not entirely clear, but perhaps connected with advances in Greek medicine, it seems that the sanctuary on Rhodes may have closed down as early as the second century AD.

SAMOS: a sanctuary of **Asclepius** in the E Aegean (37 42N, 26 59E). Samos lies just off the coast of Turkey, opposite the resort of Kusadasi. It is best known for being the birthplace of **Pythagoras**, and proud possessor of a great temple of **Hera**. Many ancient structures have been found, but an **Asclepeion** is not one of them. By the village of Kamara, at the extreme E end of the island, there is a monastery of **Zoodochos Pigi**. This dedication is sometimes associated with ancient healing sites. However, the present foundation dates only from 1756, and the earlier history of the site is unknown.

SIKYON: a sanctuary of **Asclepius** in Achaia, S Greece (37 59N, 22 44E). The remains of Sikyon lie about 7 km inland from Kiato on the Gulf of Corinth, and about 25 km W of Corinth itself, near the village of Vasiliko. **Pausanias** [II.10.2-3] not only tells of the existence of the sanctuary, but also gives some information concerning its establishment. He says that the god was brought to Sikyon from **EPIDAUROS** on the back of a mule cart in the form of a snake. The snake was a creature frequently associated with Asclepius, and the animals were often kept at his sanctuaries. However, although he was evidently to some extent identified with them, he was always portrayed in human form. The god's sanctuary has not been found although the temple of his father, **Apollo**, has. The most impressive ruins at the site, however, are of a large gymnasium spread over two levels. The **Asclepeion** probably lay not far away from it. There is a museum nearby, but it is closed at present.

SKOTUSSA or **SKOTOUSSA**: an oracle of **Zeus** in Thessaly, N Greece (39 21N, 22 31E). The few remains of the ancient city lie about 30 km S of **LARISA**, on either side of the road between Ano Skotousa and **Agia** Triada. They consist of little more than piles of stones. The oracle itself was said to have been situated somewhere outside the city, but exactly where is unknown. As at **DODONA**, the oracle of Zeus at Skotussa was centred on a tree, although exactly what the function of the tree was is unclear. It may have been the similarities between the two that led some, as explained by **Strabo** [VII.n.1a], to believe that the oracle was at some point transplanted from Skotussa to Dodona. Certainly the connection between oracles and trees was very unusual in the Greek world. Some think that there may have been more than one place called Dodona, and that one of them lay in the vicinity of Skotussa. Perhaps all this conjecture and confusion arose because so little of the actual history of the oracle was known. It seems certain that it was in existence before the fifth century BC, but it was clearly only a very distant memory by Strabo's time.

SPARTA (modern Sparti): sanctuaries of **Asclepius** in Lakonia, S Greece (37 03N, 22 26E). **Pausanias** [III.14.2, 7; III.15.10] indicates the existence of three separate sanctuaries dedicated to Asclepius in Sparta, which seems rather excessive given the traditionally hardy nature of its inhabitants. Unfortunately, not a single one has been found, but it is known that one lay near the city's theatre. This *has* been discovered, and can be seen on the SW side of the ancient acropolis (N of the modern city). Another lay near some royal tombs. The third was in the vicinity of the racecourse, which may have been situated to the W of the city. This one was dedicated to the god under the name of Agnites, in honour of the wood from which his cult statue was carved. Part of another statue of the god can be seen in the local museum.

Pausanias also says he saw a new sanctuary of **Sarapis** in the city, but he makes no mention of any oracular activity in connection with it. **Cicero** [I.43] says that Sparta's rulers used to consult an oracle of **Pasiphae** in a field near the city. He might have been confusing this with her oracle at **THALAMAE**, although that was quite some distance away. It may be a mistake, or it may be evidence of an oracle that is otherwise unknown.

TAINARON: an oracle of the **dead** in Lakonia, S Greece (36 21N, 22 29E). Tainaron stands on the southernmost tip of mainland Greece, at the end of the Mani peninsula. The principal divinity here was **Poseidon**. Some remains of his sanctuary can be found near the ruined church of the **Agioi** Asomatoi ('bodiless powers'), which was partly constructed from its stones. The foundations of other structures can be seen nearby. This was also thought to be the place where **Heracles** brought Cerberus up from the underworld, of which he was the dreaded three-headed guard dog. **Pausanias** [III.25.5] found a cave there, but reported, rather disappointedly, that it didn't seem to lead anywhere. A cave can still be found on the beach below the church, and it still doesn't go anywhere, but if there was an oracle of the dead in this area this is most likely where it was.

TEGYRA: an oracle of **Apollo** in Boiotia, central Greece. Tegyra lay near and to the E of **ORCHOMENOS**. It was one of the places that claimed to be the actual birthplace of the god, others being **DELOS** and **PATARA**. The temple of Apollo was said to be located beside two streams, but no trace of it has been found. It evidently enjoyed a considerable reputation at least as far back as the sixth century BC, but had ceased to function by the first century AD. For some time, the site of Tegyra was thought to lie at Pirgos, about 7 km NE of Orchomenos, and the ruins of a medieval tower can be seen there. However, many now think that Polyira, which lies about half way between Pirgos and Orchomenos, is a more likely candidate. Pottery has been found there from dates corresponding to the period of the oracle's operation.

THALAMAE or **THALAMAI**: oracles of **Ino** and **Pasiphae** in Lakonia, S Greece (37 52N, 21 40E). The scant ruins of Thalamae lie about 20 km N of Areopoli, near modern Thalames. According to **Pausanias** [III.26.1], the oracle was situated to the S of Thalamae, somewhere between it and Oitylon (where he saw a sanctuary of **Sarapis**), about 13 km away. It stood by a sacred spring. Unfortunately, there is more than one venerable-looking spring in the area, so the location of the site is uncertain. Pausanias says the oracle here belonged to Ino and **incubation** was practised. His only mention of Pasiphae relates to a bronze statue of her which stood in the sanctuary. On the other hand, **Plutarch** [*Agis*, IX] says that the oracle belonged to Pasiphae, and he makes no mention of Ino. **Cicero** [I.43] also talks of an oracle of Pasiphae that practised incubation, but he locates it much nearer to **SPARTA**. There is no obvious way of satisfactorily resolving the apparent confusion.

The myths concerning Ino are many and confused. The relatively stable elements of them are that she was the daughter of **Cadmus**, wife of **Athamas**, and was transformed by **Zeus** into the goddess **Leucothea**. She had a temple dedicated to her at **LEUCOTHEA** in which the oracle of **Phrixus** was located. The myths relating to Pasiphae are also difficult to reconcile with each other. Pausanias says she was a moon goddess, but she was also the legendary mother of the minotaur. Some identify her with **Cassandra**, others with **Daphne**.

THASOS: a sanctuary of **Asclepius** in NE Greece (40 47N, 24 44E). Thasos is an island in the N Aegean, just off Kavala. Its main town, situated near its N tip, is also called Thasos, and the ruins of its ancient predecessor lie next to it.

Many buildings, including a number of temples, can be seen. However, although it is known that there was one dedicated to Asclepius, it has not been identified. An inscription dated to the fourth century BC reveals that an unnamed individual who was renting a garden had to pay a fine to the temple of Asclepius if he failed to keep the property tidy. This might mean that the cult of Asclepius had a special standing in the city, or it may just have had a special connection with the garden. The cults of **Isis** and **Sarapis** are thought to have arrived in Thasos in the third or second century BC, but their sanctuaries have not been identified either.

THEBES: two oracles of **Apollo** in Boiotia, central Greece (38 19N, 23 19E). The site of ancient Thebes is occupied by modern Thiva. Despite the city's great history, there is not very much evidence of it on the ground, although there is a good museum. Fortunately, the literary record bears a substantial witness to the place's past. Amongst other things, it formed the setting for the tragedy of Oedipus, who was king here.

It is unusual to have two separate oracles of the same god in the same city, and it is unlikely that they both operated at the same time. One is mentioned by **Herodotus** [VIII.135], the other by **Pausanias** [IX.11.5], and there is at least a five-hundred-year gap between the two writers. Herodotus talks of the oracle of Apollo Ismenios. This name derives from **Ismenos**, said to be a son of the god, after whom a local river was named. (His brother, **Teneros**, was connected with the oracle on **Mount PTOON**.) The figure of Apollo Ismenios seems to have been something of a composite of father and son. Divination took place at his cult centre by means of the inspection of sacrificed animals, the same means, Pausanias says, as that employed at **OLYMPIA**. The temple of Apollo Ismenios was known as the Ismenion, and still existed in Pausanias' time. The site of the Ismenion has been found in the SE of the city, on a small hill between the bus station and the church of **Agios** Loukas. The last temple built on the site dates from the fourth century BC, but only a few stones from it can be seen.

The temple at which the other oracle was based, that of Apollo Spodios, has not been found at all. Spodios means 'of ash', and the altar here was constructed out of the ashes left over from sacrifices, just as was the altar of **Zeus** at Olympia. According to Pausanias, the method of divination employed here was the same as that used at **SMYRNA**, which involved **omen**s in some way or other. **Teiresias** was said to have had a place from which he could observe and listen to birds here. Given the close connection in ancient Greek thought between birds and omens, it is not impossible that what happened at the oracle of Apollo Spodios also involved birds in some way. The tradition that Teiresias practised divination of some kind here while he was alive (before taking up posthumous residence at his oracle in **ORCHOMENOS**) is both strong and ancient.

THERAPNAI or **THERAPNE**: a sanctuary of **Asclepius** in Lakonia, S Greece (37 03N, 22 28E). As the location of the shrine dedicated to **Menelaus** and **Helen**, Therapnai is usually known today as Menelaion, and lies about 4 km SE of **SPARTA**, off the road to Geraki. The site stands on top of a hill and is in three parts. First there is the shrine itself, somewhat resembling a ruined pyramid. Secondly there are the excavated remains of buildings dating back to around the thirteenth century BC. Thirdly, there is a small church of much more recent construction. There is nothing obviously recognisable as an **Asclepeion**, although it would not be unusual to find a Christian church built on top of one.

THERMOS: an oracle of **Odysseus** in Aetolia, central Greece (38 40N, 21 32E). The site of Thermos lies just to the SW of modern Thermo about 35 km E of Agrinio. In ancient times the area around it was said to be occupied by the Eurytanes, a particularly aggressive people who had a reputation for preferring their meat raw. The oracle itself was said to be a dream one, which is by no means implausible. For the connection of the oracle with Odysseus to be plausible, however, some clear association of him with the place is required, and ideally it should have been where he was buried. Fortunately, there was indeed a legend that he died in Aetolia, although this story seems to have originated well after the time of **Homer**. Whether true or not, no traces of the oracle have been found, although there are substantial ruins to be seen at the site. Amongst these ruins are two temples of Apollo, one dedicated to Apollo Thermios, the other to Apollo Lyseios. The help of Apollo Lyseios was particularly sought out on matters relating to spells and curses.

THESPIAI: a sanctuary of **Asclepius** in Boiotia, central Greece (38 18N, 23 08E). The ruins of Thespiai, such as they are, lie about 16 km W of Thiva, on the road to Domvena. A few ancient stones can be spotted here and there, along with some traces of **Byzantine** wall. There is more to be seen in the National Archaeological Museum in Athens than there is at the site itself. There is also a small museum in modern Thespies, which stands on the hill above its ancient predecessor.

THIRA or **THERA**: a sanctuary of **Isis** and **Sarapis** in the Cyclades (36 24N, 25 26E). Thira, also known as Santorini, is at the S end of the group of islands.

It has a long history, punctuated by occasional outbreaks of volcanic activity. Its main town is also called Thira, as is the ancient capital some 16 km to its SE. It is there that most items of interest can be found. The settlement on this site dates back to at least the ninth century BC, but was still being developed well into **Byzantine** times. Many of the ruins date from the period between 300 and 145 BC when it was controlled by the Ptolemies of Egypt. It may have been then that the cults of Isis and Sarapis were introduced. Their sanctuary is in the S part of the site, SW of the theatre, near the ruins of a Byzantine church which had previously been a temple of **Apollo**. Unusually, it is partly cut into the rock itself. The site as a whole is an extensive one, with many substantial ruins to explore.

TITANE or **TITANI**: a sanctuary of **Asclepius** in Achaia, S Greece (37 54N, 22 38E). The remains of Titane lie in and around the modern village of Titani, about 30 km SW of Kiato. It was said to have been founded by **Alexanor**, a grandson of the god himself. According to **Pausanias** [II.11.6], it employed many local people, and its cult statue was very old. The ruins are mainly to be found in the area of the village's cemetery, which clearly resembles a small acropolis. An inscription to Asclepius was found here. It is now incorporated into the wall of the cemetery's church, which is dedicated to St Tryphon. Although usually thought of as a protector of fields, he was originally regarded as a healer, which probably explains his presence here. Titane is also the place where the earliest evidence of the cult of **Hygeia** has been found. The origins of this cult are obscure, and it is possible that Hygeia began as an **epithet** of **Athena** and only later became an independent figure. She came to be regarded as the daughter of Asclepius, although some regarded her as his wife. The Romans identified her with Salus, their own goddess (and personification) of health. Very unusually, there was a wooden image of Coronis at Titane as well. She was said to be the mother of Asclepius, although Pausanias [II.11.7] says that her statue was not kept in his temple.

TITHOREA: sanctuaries of **Asclepius** and **Isis** in Phokis, central Greece (38 36N, 22 36E). The ruins of ancient Tithorea stand near the modern village of the same name, about 10 km SE of **AMPHIKLEIA**. According to **Pausanias** [X.32.8] the sanctuary of Asclepius was about 15 km from the town, but he does not specify the direction, and it has so far escaped identification. The sanctuary of Isis lay about 8 km away from the **Asclepeion** (in a direction again unspecified). It was the most important dedicated to her in Greece, and none were allowed to enter it unless personally summoned by the goddess in dreams. Although proceedings inside the sanctuary were surrounded by a degree of secrecy, a very public festival was held outside it in the spring and autumn of each year. This involved a fair, a market, and a great deal of sacrificing. Unfortunately, the site of this sanctuary has not been found either.

TRIKKA (modern Trikala): a sanctuary of **Asclepius** in Thessaly, N Greece (39 32N, 21 47E). The sanctuary of Asclepius here claimed to be the oldest in Greece, and Trikka disputed with **EPIDAUROS** the right to be regarded as the birthplace of the god. In the event, the matter was resolved in favour of Epidauros by the oracle at **DELPHI**. The city itself dates back to at least the fifth century BC. Excavations have revealed the remains of a sanctuary a little to the E of the church of **Agios** Nikolaos. What has been found was constructed at various times from the second century BC to the fourth century AD. There appears to have been a complex of buildings centred on a square courtyard. There was a tradition that his sanctuary here was based around a cave. The excavations suggest otherwise, but it is not entirely certain that what has been found actually is the **Asclepeion**. In any event, what has been found is not only quite fragmentary, but also mostly located on private land and can only be viewed by arrangement with the local guard of antiquities. Although interesting, what can be seen is not particularly impressive.

TROIZEN or **TROEZEN**: a sanctuary of **Asclepius** in Argolis, S Greece (37 31N, 23 21E). The ruins of Troizen lie about 30 km directly SE of **EPIDAUROS**, although the journey by road is indirect and longer. They lie near the modern village of the same name, which is about 8 km NW of Galatas. The principal remains to be seen consist of walls and towers. The temple of Asclepius has not been found, but near the Episkopi church, W of the large surviving tower, there are the ruins of a square building, dating from the third century BC, which was probably where those who came to seek the god's help stayed. A passing remark made by **Pausanias** [II.32.5] suggests that there may also have been a **dream** oracle of **Pan** here. The god's sanctuary was situated somewhere below the city's acropolis, but exactly where is unclear.

HUNGARY

BRIGETIO: sanctuaries of **Asclepius** and **Apollo Grannus** in N Hungary (47 44N, 18 12E). The site lies near Szony, about 4 km E of Komárom. It was a legionary camp, although one founded over an earlier settlement. There is little to be seen there today, but there were once many sanctuaries to be found in the area. The extent to which Asclepius and Apollo Grannus were both concerned with healing here is unclear. The remains of two sanctuaries have been found, but it has not been possible to identify either of them with certainty. However, it is known that the temple of Apollo Grannus was built in the third century AD, and that it was dedicated to him jointly with **Sirona**.

IRAN

ANARIACE: a dream oracle in Media, N Iran. **Strabo** [XI.7.1] mentions the existence of this city and of the oracle there, although he makes it clear that he is not speaking from first-hand knowledge of either. The region occupied by a people called the Anariacæ lay between modern Tehran and the Caspian Sea, but it is not possible to pinpoint the location of the city. This is the most easterly of all the oracles mentioned by the classical authors.

ECBATANA: a shrine of **Asclepius** in W Iran (34 46N, 48 30E). Ecbatana has for long been known as Hamadan, and lies about 300 km SW of Tehran. Originally it was the capital of the Medes. All that is known of the shrine relates to its destruction. **Arrian** mentions, though questions, the story that **Alexander the Great** ordered it to be pulled down in his grief over the death of **Hephaestion** in 324 BC. If there was such a shrine, then it was presumably founded in the wake of Alexander's previous campaign in Persia. Alternatively, Arrian may have identified a Persian healing god with Asclepius. For centuries Hamadan had little to show of its ancient history, but excavations are now uncovering some of its buried past. The town's monuments are still mainly medieval, and include the tomb of Avicenna, the great eleventh-century philosopher.

IRAQ

BABYLON: a sanctuary of **Sarapis** in S Iraq (32 29N, 44 29E). The ruins of Babylon lie about 80 km due S of Baghdad. They are extensive but, for obvious reasons, little visited these days. The information about the temple of Sarapis here derives from supposed diaries relating to the last days of **Alexander the Great**. They claim that some of his companions spent a night in the god's temple seeking guidance on what Alexander might do to recover his health. However, it is generally believed that the cult of Sarapis did not exist at this time, but was a later innovation of **Ptolemy I**. The diaries are not regarded as sufficiently reliable to overturn this opinion. This means that the story could be a complete invention. On the other hand, it may be that such a consultation did indeed take place, but that the name of Sarapis was later substituted for that of the god really involved. Since Sarapis was sometimes identified with

Zeus, and Zeus with **Bel**, it is possible that the latter's temple was the place in question. Known as the Esagila, its ruins lie in the centre of the city, just to the S the famous ziggurat. Alexander had been to the temple himself on his first visit to the city, and ordered that the damage done to it by the Persians be repaired. Babylonian kings traditionally received their power by clasping the hand of the god's statue, and Alexander may have done the same. Such a perceived special connection between him and the god (as with **Amun** at **SIWA**) might help explain his companions' behaviour.

There may also have been an oracle of the **dead** here, depending on how one particular piece of evidence is interpreted. In one of his stories about the philosopher Menippus, 'Menippus goes to Hell', **Lucian** has him travelling to Baghdad to consult an oracle of the dead. But although Menippus was real enough, the story may be a complete fiction. On the other hand, it has been suggested that the story might nevertheless incorporate authentic details about how oracles of the dead worked. Lucian talks of a preparation period of over a month. This is insight, exaggeration or imagination according to one's point of view.

ISRAEL AND THE OCCUPIED TERRITORIES

ASCALON: a sanctuary of **Isis** in central Israel (31 39N, 34 30E). What is left of ancient Ascalon lies on the coast, about 55 km S of Tel Aviv, under and around modern Ashkelon (or Ashqelon). In fact there is not a great deal of it to be seen, although what there is is mostly to be found at the Ashkelon National Park in the SW of the town. It is not known where the sanctuary of Isis was located, or what took place there, but it is possible to see a pillar in the park bearing a relief of the goddess dating from the late centuries BC or early centuries AD. The principal associations of the area are more biblical than classical. **Samson** slaughtered thirty of its residents on a flying visit, while **Herod the Great** was said to have been born here, and in due course gone on his own more extensive killing spree.

CAESAREA PHILIPPI: an oracle of **Pan** and the **Nymphs** in N Israel (33 15N, 35 40E). The site is now known as Banyas, echoing its original ancient name of Paneas. In fact, it was often known as Caesarea Paneas, although presumably not by Philip, son of **Herod the Great**, who renamed it after himself when he made it his capital in 2 BC. The sanctuary of Pan and the Nymphs stands in the NE corner of the site, just to the N of a spring that is one of the sources of the Jordan river. A cave has been carved into the rock, and around it are three niches with dedicatory inscriptions from the second century AD. The sanctuary appears to have fallen into disuse during the fourth century AD, but when it first began to function is unknown. How it functioned is also a mystery. To the S of the river lie a variety of mainly medieval remains.

DORA: a sanctuary of **Asclepius** in N Israel (32 39N, 34 56E). The site of Dora lies at what is now known as Tel Dor (or Tantura), about 30 km S of Haifa, beside the main road. The ruins stand near the modern resort of Dor, on the small hill at the N end of the beach. Dora was an important town in **Byzantine** times, and a substantial church was built here sometime around 340. Excavations of its ruins have revealed that it was built over a sanctuary of Asclepius. Substantial portions of the fabric of the god's temple had been incorporated into the Byzantine basilica, and a large courtyard at its W end was where **incubation** would have taken place. The church itself held the tomb of two healing saints. Little is known about the history of the site when it was dedicated to Asclepius, but stories of miraculous healings have been preserved from the sixth and seventh centuries AD. They indicate that incubation was still being practised here then, but naturally with the saints, rather than the god, appearing in the dreams of those who came seeking cures. The complex was destroyed by fire at the end of the seventh century and was never rebuilt.

Excavations continue at the site and have unearthed other temples, dedicated to **Apollo**, **Zeus** and **Astarte**. Near the ruins there is a museum of marine archaeology.

JERUSALEM: a sanctuary of **Asclepius** in central Israel (31 47N, 35 14E). The sanctuary was built by the Romans at a time when the city was known as Aelia Capitolina. The place they chose lies near the N end of the Temple Mount, just to the W of the church of St Anne. Here there were two pools, constructed in earlier centuries as reservoirs, known as the Pools of Bethesda, although the one to the S was also known as the Sheep Pool. After Roman times they became filled in and forgotten, but excavations begun in 1956 have rediscovered them. The remains of a temple of Asclepius were found, although it had been largely obliterated by subsequent building. **Votive** objects, mainly of marble, were also unearthed, in the shapes of feet, ears, and other bodily parts.

ITALY

ACRAGAS (modern Agrigento): a sanctuary of **Asclepius** in SW Sicily (37 19N, 13 35E). The temple of Asclepius lies about 1 km S of the main Valley of the Temples, on a side road off the main road leading towards Gela. (Gela seems to have had its own sanctuary of Asclepius, but it has not been found.) Unlike the other temples for which Agrigento is famous, it lay outside rather than inside the city walls. It stands near the San Biagio river, by a spring that provides a supply of mineral water. The temple has been dated to the second half of the fifth century BC, making it one of the god's earliest centres outside mainland Greece. The city itself was famous as the home of the fifth-century BC philosopher **Empedocles**. It seems likely that he was associated with Pythagoreanism. As the Pythagoreans seem to have made some use of **incubation**, the preferred method of consultation at sanctuaries of Asclepius, it is possible that there was some connection between the two.

ALBA POMPEIA: a sanctuary of **Asclepius** in Piemonte, NW Italy (40 42N, 08 01E). Most of Alba Pompeia lies underneath modern Alba, about 60 km SE of Turin. The most visible ancient remains are some stretches of the old city wall. However some fragments of mosaic pavement have been unearthed near the church of **Cosmas and Damian**. These healing saints often took over earlier therapeutic centres, and it is thought that the mosaics may have originally belonged to an **Asclepeion** in the vicinity.

AMPSANCTUS: a sanctuary of Mefitis in Campania, S Italy (40 57N, 15 10E). Mefitis was one of the more unusual Roman goddesses, associated with poisonous gases, diseases and drains. However, her cult goes back to a time before the Romans dominated Italy, and it seems that originally she was regarded as a much more positive and benevolent figure. On the other hand, the location of her sanctuary at Ampsanctus is unlikely to be a mere coincidence. It was based near a small lake (now known as Lago d'Ansanto), with springs giving off noxious fumes, which can be found near the village of Rocca San Felice, about 30 km E of Avellino. What went on at the sanctuary is unclear, but a number of **votive** objects dating back as far as the fifth century BC have been found in the vicinity, suggesting that some kind of healing probably took place there. They are now on display in the Museo Irpino in Avellino. According to **Pliny the Elder** [II.208], poisonous gases emerged from an opening in the ground near the temple, perhaps a cave. **Virgil** certainly tells of 'a frightening cavern' in his *Aeneid* [VII.568], but he was sometimes susceptible to poetic licence. Nevertheless, there are obvious parallels with both **ACHARACA** and **HIERAPOLIS**, where Pluto provided oracles and healing in similarly unhealthy environments.

The sanctuary of Mefitis was taken over at an unknown date by St Felicity, and her festival is still celebrated locally on 10 July each year. She is a mysterious figure, said to have been martyred in Rome, along with her seven sons, during the reign of Antoninus Pius. However, considerable doubt has been thrown on the authenticity of this story. Perhaps here she is Mefitis in another guise, restored to her original dignity and benevolence.

ANTIUM (modern Anzio): the site of an oracle of **Fortuna** and a sanctuary of **Asclepius** in Lazio, central Italy (41 30N, 12 36E). The city was popular with early Roman emperors, especially **Nero** who was born here. Oracles were not very common in the Roman world, but the goddess Fortuna had some, and it seems they usually operated by means of the drawing of **lot**s. However, **Suetonius** ['Caligula', LVII] says that the oracle at Antium told **Caligula** to 'Beware of Cassius!', which suggests quite a different (although unfortunately unspecified) method of communication. Unfortunately for Caligula, the oracle led him to suspect and have executed the wrong Cassius, and he was duly killed by another. (Of course, it is entirely possible that there was more than one person called Cassius who was prepared to carry out the deed as Caligula was widely and deeply disliked.) The location of Fortuna's temple at Antium is no longer known, but old illustrations of it have survived. Even the appearance of the temple of Asclepius is unknown. It is thought that both buildings were situated somewhere near the harbour.

APONUS: an oracle of **Geryon** in Veneto, N Italy (45 22N, 11 49E). Aponus is now known as Albano Terme and lies 10 km SW of Padua. According to **Suetonius** ['Tiberius', XIV], the oracle here was visited by **Tiberius** before he was emperor. First he drew a **lot**. This then instructed him to throw a set of golden **dice** into the nearby fountain, and by this means he finally received his answer. Both the lot and dice methods are unremarkable, but quite why the oracle was associated with Geryon is a mystery. He was a three-headed giant, and one of the exploits of **Heracles** was the theft of his cattle. Most traditions say that Geryon lived at the W end of the Mediterranean, a long way from Aponus. Today Albano Terme is a popular spa and its celebrated hot waters have radioactive properties.

AVERNUS or **AVERNA** (**Lake**): an oracle of the **dead** in Campania, S Italy (40 52N, 14 02E). Lake Avernus (Lago d'Averno) lies near both **BAIAE** and **CUMAE**, and **AORNOS** is a Greek form of the name. The lake fills a large crater just N of Lucrino, about 15 km W of Naples. On its shore, according to **Diodorus Siculus** [IV.22], there had once been an oracle, but it had been destroyed long before his time. **Strabo** [I.2.18] is also unclear as to exactly where the oracle was located, but claims [V.4.5] that it was visited by

Odysseus and that birds flying over the lake fell into it, knocked out by its noxious vapours. This claim might be a fanciful development of the fact that 'aornos' can mean 'no birds'. He cites **Ephorus**, who also mentions the oracle, but says only that it was underground. He also gives the impression that it had already ceased to function by his time.

Near the S shore of the lake can be found a tunnel exending 200 m into the hillside, popularly known as the Cave of the **Sibyl**, while on its N shore is a so-called temple of **Apollo**. However, the cave almost certainly has nothing whatsoever to do with the Sibyl, and the 'temple' probably formed part of a large baths complex. Today there are no noxious vapours and birds swim contentedly on the lake.

BAIAE (now Baia): an oracle of the **dead** in Campania, S Italy (40 50 N, 14 3E). Baia lies in the NW corner of the Gulf of Naples. The coastline has dramatically shifted here over the centuries, and much of ancient Baiae is now covered by the sea. The ruins that remain above sea level, despite some of them being often and popularly referred to as temples, are mainly secular in nature. An underground complex of tunnels and caves has been discovered, but there is as yet no agreed interpretation of their meaning or function. One suggestion is that they contained an oracle of the dead. The fact that there are still thermal springs in the area, some of which continue to give off whiffs of sulphur, makes the presence of an oracle of the dead in the vicinity a realistic possibility. However, the site lies close to **Lake AVERNUS**, also said to have had an oracle of the dead, and it may be that there was at most one such oracle between them. Furthermore, there are several tunnels of one kind or another in the area, and most are thought to have been constructed for military rather than mystical purposes.

CLITUMNUS: an oracle of **Clitumnus** in Umbria, central Italy (42 50N, 12 47E). The site, now known as Fonti del Clitunno, lies 4 km downstream (S) from Trevi, and on it stands a fifth-century church dedicated to Christ the Saviour. However, the temple to Clitumnus used to occupy this spot and materials from it were used in the construction of its successor. Clitumnus was a local deity personifying the river. There were a number of shrines dedicated to him and other deities in the area, but this was the most important one. At some point he seems to have become associated, or even identified, with **Jupiter**. This may have been due to one of the methods of divination practised here. In addition to a simple **lot** oracle, there was another that in some way involved the interpretation of leaves. The cult of Jupiter also had connections with trees, particularly the oak. The site of the oldest temple dedicated to the god in Rome, said to have been built by **Romulus** himself, was determined by the presence of a sacred oak tree there.

According to **Pliny the Younger** [VIII.8], the temple of Clitumnus was also very old. Somewhat curiously, the cult statue of the god was dressed in the formal robe of a magistrate. The walls of the temple seem to have been covered in testimonials from grateful devotees, and at least some of the god's own oracles had also been written down and preserved.

CUMAE or **KYME**: an oracle of the **Sybil** in Campania, S Italy (40 53N, 14 02E). The ruins of Cumae (now known as Cuma) stand on and around a hill about 20 km W of Naples, overlooking the Tyrrhenian Sea. Cumae is thought to have been one of the first Greek colonies established in Italy, dating back to the eighth or ninth century BC. The Sybil of Cumae may not have been the original one, but she clearly had some claim to antiquity. The oracle at Cumae may have ceased to function during the fifth century BC. It appears to have been at best a distant memory by the time **Strabo** passed this way. The Sibyl was, moreover, not like an ordinary oracle. She (Sibyls were always female) might prophesy spontaneously, and there was no settled explanation as to the source of her inspiration. On the other hand, as with other oracles but unlike prophets, she always seemed to be identified with a particular place.

The Sibyl of Cumae owes her fame to two stories in particular. The first is that she was the Sibyl who sold the books of Sibylline Prophecies to the king of Rome in the seventh or sixth century BC. They were kept in the temple of **Jupiter** on the Capitol, and were destroyed when the temple was burnt down in 83 BC. The second is that related by **Virgil** (in book VI of his *Aeneid*) which tells of how **Aeneas** visited her, and in which she is portrayed as the inspired mouthpiece of **Apollo**. His description of the setting for this encounter presumably comes from observation rather than imagination, since for many years he owned a country estate not far away.

The Sibyl's cave was long thought to have been at nearby **Lake AVERNUS**, but the discovery at Cumae in the early twentieth century of a corridor 130 m long cut into the solid rock revived the belief that she had prophesied in the city with which she was traditionally associated. The cave itself lies at the end of the corridor, and may have been carved out in the fourth or third century BC, but there is nothing in the structure to establish a connection with the Sibyl, and it is wholly lacking in any kind of inscription.

On the way up to the acropolis from the cave the remains of a large temple of Apollo (built in the time of **Augustus**) can be seen. According to a biography of the emperor Clodius Albinus (who died in 197 after a very short reign), he received an oracle from the god here which consisted of some lines from the *Aeneid*. However, the biography is usually regarded as seriously unreliable and it is difficult to know what, if any, credibility is to be given to this assertion.

Outside the main site, nearer the shore, the remains of what are thought to be a temple of **Isis** have been found. Since trading relations between this area and Egypt may have been established as far back as the eighth century BC, it is possible that her cult arrived here at an early date.

FAESULAE: a healing sanctuary in Tuscany, N Italy (43 47N, 11 13E). Faesulae is now known as Fiesole, and lies 8 km NE of Florence. It was founded by the Etruscans before later being taken over by the Romans. Some sections of the ancient city walls are well preserved, and parts of them date back to Etruscan times. However, the city seems to have been most prosperous in the first century AD, and it was at this time that its main temple was rebuilt. This was dedicated to a healing deity, although precisely which one is still unknown. Around the temple were found the remains of a number of subsidiary buildings that would have served the needs of those who came to visit the site. The temple stands behind the modern city's cathedral, with the remains of a theatre nearby.

FREGELLAE: a sanctuary of **Asclepius** in central Italy (41 33N, 13 33E). The ruins of Fregellae lie about 1 km E of Ceprano, near the bank of the Liri river. The city was destroyed by Rome in 125 BC after leading a revolt against it. It was not rediscovered until late in the twentieth century, and excavations began there in 1987. They have revealed a temple to Asclepius set a little way outside the city's walls, standing on a small hill in the middle of a square.

GARGANUS, Mount: oracles of **Podaleirius** and **Kalchas** in Apulia, S Italy. The oracles were located on the S side of the mountain, in or near the modern town of Monte Sant'Angelo (41 43N, 15 58E). Podaleirius was a son of **Asclepius**, and brother of **Machaon** (who had his own oracle at **GERENIA**). Kalchas was linked in legend with **CLAROS** where he was said to have lost a divination duel with **Mopsus**. There were legends that placed the deaths of both of them well away from Italy. Exactly how they came to be associated with Mount Garganus is unclear. Possibly their cults arrived in the company of colonists from their original domains. It is also not known whether they shared an oracle or had one each. Details of one readily crop up in accounts of the other. (Some say that of Kalchas was at the top of the mountain and that of Podaleirius at the bottom.) What is tolerably clear is that **incubation** was involved in one or both, and that this was preceded by the slaughter of a black ram, whose skin was then slept on. (The oracle of **Amphiaraus** at **OROPOS** used a similar method.)

In Monte Sant' Angelo is a sanctuary of the Archangel Michael, who is said to have appeared there in 493. Tradition has it that he left his cloak behind when he disappeared, with instructions that the place become a Christian shrine. The way into the sanctuary is next to an impressive medieval tower. Although it looks like the entrance to an ordinary church, behind it is a flight of steps carved out of the rock that leads down into a cavern. This is thought to have been the site of the oracle (or one of the oracles). Thanks to its special visitor, Monte Sant' Angelo became a major pilgrimage site, which it remains to this day.

GELA: see **ACRAGAS**

HYBLA GELEATIS or **HYBLA GEREATIS**: a **dream** oracle in E Sicily. The site of the ancient city is probably that occupied by present-day Paterno (37 31N, 14 54E), which lies 13 km NW of Catania, on the S slopes of Mount Etna. This was certainly a place of divination, but it is unclear whether there was an actual oracle here or not. **Pausanias** [V.23.6] speaks of it as being a village in his time, but he mentions an earlier writer, **Philistos**, who described its inhabitants as interpreters of dreams and omens. (Similar stories were told of the inhabitants of **TELMESSOS**, who also seem to have been inordinately gifted in the arts of divination.) **Cicero** [I.20] mentions the same source, but talks of someone taking a dream to be interpreted, rather than undergoing **incubation** there in order to *have* a dream. Incubation may have happened, but the case is not conclusive. There is nothing to see *in situ*, although excavations have turned up a number of items and these have found their way into local museums.

Somewhere S of Paterno, perhaps in the vicinity of Lentini, was the cult centre of the Palikoi. These were twins born to the muse Thalia, their father being **Zeus**. They are said to have given oracles from time to time, but their speciality was testing oaths. These were written on tablets and cast into a sulphurous spring. If they floated, they were true; if not, not.

The Etna area in general had widespread and understandable associations with the underworld.

NEMUS (modern Nemi): a healing sanctuary of **Diana** and **Egeria** in Lazio, central Italy (41 43N, 12 43E). Nemi lies about 25 km SE of central **ROME**, and the name applies to both a village and a lake. The sanctuary of the goddess was situated in the area between the two, and the lake was known as her mirror. A celebrated healing centre in antiquity, it achieved a degree of celebrity again in the late nineteenth century when legends surrounding ancient practices there provided the stimulus (and title) for Sir James Frazer's massive work *The Golden Bough*. It was said that the priesthood of the temple (which carried with it the grand title of 'King of Nemus') could only be held by a slave, and only secured through mortal combat. Each incumbent had challenged, fought and killed his predecessor. Whatever the origins of this curious custom, it continued to be practised down to at least the first century AD when **Caligula** decided to sponsor a (successful) challenger. The origins of the sanctuary itself go back to at least the fourth century BC, and it survived until at least the fourth century AD.

The healing activities of the sanctuary seem to have been considerably less dramatic. Although Diana was its principal deity, she shared it with the water nymph Egeria, who was associated with a spring at the site. Legend had it that Egeria was the wife of **Numa**, the second king of Rome. On his death she retired to the solitude of the woods around the lake in her grief. Witnessing her copious and unceasing tears, Diana took pity on her and turned her into a spring. Both of them were approached in particular by pregnant women, since it was thought they could aid in childbirth. Excavations carried out in the late nineteenth century uncovered large numbers of figurines depicting nursing mothers. Others have been found that suggest surgery may have taken place there, and the waters of the spring were also thought to have a generally therapeutic effect. While the sanctuary was doubtless visited throughout the year, it was particularly busy at the time of the goddess' festival on 13 August when beneficiaries of her intercession walked there in procession from her temple in Rome.

There is little to be seen there now. The temple was built on a terrace, and part of that can be seen. The temple itself stood at the N corner of the terrace. However, if there are few actual remains, the site is not lacking in aesthetic appeal, and J.M.W. Turner was moved to give the place his characteristically atmospheric treatment in 1840. The painting is now owned by the British Museum.

OSTIA: sanctuaries of **Isis** and **Sarapis** in Lazio, central Italy (41 45N, 12 15E). Ostia was the port of ancient **ROME**, although changes in the coastline over the centuries mean that it now lies some 5 km inland. It is the second largest excavated site in Italy, surpassed only by **POMPEII**. It boasts temples, baths and tombs, as well as examples of domestic architecture. A sanctuary of Sarapis was constructed in the extreme W part of the city and dedicated in 127 AD. The remains of it can be found behind the House of Bacchus and Ariadne on Via Serapeo. The complex consisted of a temple, courtyard, and a number of small rooms which may have been used for **incubation**. It is known that there was a sanctuary of Isis in the city, but it has not been found. However, in the centre of Ostia, opposite its theatre, in the large square known as Piazzale Corporazioni, is a small temple thought to have been dedicated to **Ceres**. Since Isis was sometimes identified with Ceres, it is possible that her cult was celebrated here.

POMPEII: a sanctuary of **Isis** in Campania, S Italy (40 45N, 14 30E). Pompeii lies 20 km SE of Naples, at the foot of Mount Vesuvius. When the volcano erupted in 79 AD, Pompeii was buried and preserved. **Pliny the Elder** went to watch the phenomenon and died as a result of it. Before its famous end, the city had led a prosperous existence as a major port. It became a Roman possession in around 290 BC.

The temple of Isis is located in the S of the city on Via del Tempio d'Iside. It had been rebuilt fewer than twenty years before the city's destruction, and lavishly decorated. Wall paintings from the temple are now on display in Naples (where there may have been another temple dedicated to the goddess, as well as one of **Sarapis**) at the National Archaeological Museum, where there is also a model showing how the temple appeared in its heyday. The temple was discovered in 1764 and excavated over the next two years. Mozart visited the site a few years later, and it may have helped to inspire his *Magic Flute*. In 1817 Henri Beyle (aka Stendhal) came here and commemorated the fact in the time-dishonoured manner by carving his name on the temple's wall.

The sanctuary itself is of no great size and the temple standing in the middle of it is built on a very modest scale. In the SE corner of the sanctuary is a small building known as a purgatorium, used for ritual cleansing. An inner stairway leads down to a washing area. On the N side of the sanctuary is a substantial separate room whose purpose is unknown.

Just around the corner from the temple of Isis, on the way down to the city's Stabia Gate, is another small sanctuary. One theory is that this contained a temple of **Asclepius**, although some think it was dedicated to **Jupiter**.

PRAENESTE: an oracle of **Fortuna** in Lazio, central Italy (41 52N, 12 53E). Praeneste was built on the site now occupied by Palestrina, about 36 km E of **ROME**. The sanctuary was a very extensive one, occupying a number of terraces on the side of a hill. While the great temple was built on the highest level, the oracle itself lay near the bottom. Under the cathedral and seminary lies a complex of caverns, partly natural, partly excavated. What is thought to be the oracle cave itself is shaped like a clover leaf. The method used here involved a number of oaken tablets on which were written various words. When someone brought a question to the oracle, a young boy would select a piece of wood at random, and the answer would somehow be divined from it. The oracle was evidently very popular and highly regarded, and many testimonials to its reliability were left by satisfied customers. It is known to have continued functioning until at least the fourth century AD. Tombs in the vicinity date back to at least the seventh century BC, but it is questionable whether any part of the sanctuary itself predates the first century BC.

PUTEOLI: sanctuaries of **Asclepius** and **Sarapis** in Campania, S Italy (40 50N, 14 07E). Puteoli is now known as Pozzuoli, and lies about 12 km W of Naples. It was founded by colonists from **SAMOS** a little before 500 BC. After its conquest by the Romans in 318 BC it developed into a significant port and remained so until the expansion of **OSTIA** under **Trajan**. Much of what came to Italy from Egypt and the E passed through here, including foreign cults. That of Sarapis is known to have arrived in 105 BC. However, the building near the port, usually referred to as the Temple of Sarapis, is in fact nothing of the sort but rather an ancient market. There were hot springs in the area, making it a natural location for a healing sanctuary. However, although inscriptions indicate the presence of an **Asclepeion** here, none has as yet been found.

ROME: sanctuaries of **Asclepius** and **Minerva** Medica in Lazio, central Italy (41 54N, 12 28E). The cult of Asclepius was brought to Rome in 292 BC. A temple was built on an island in the Tiber, now known as the Isola Tiberina. The church of San Bartolomeo probably stands on the site of the ancient temple. The tip of the island to the E of it was carved into the shape of the prow of a boat at some point during the first century BC. Under the prow can be seen a head of Asclepius, identifiable by his accompanying traditional trademark of staff and serpent.

The temple of Minerva Medica stood to the SE of the Esquiline, near where Via Labicana meets Via Merulana. (It was *not* on the site of what is now, confusingly, called the temple of Minerva Medica, which lies at the end of Viale A. Manzoni, the continuation of Labicana. This building acquired its name because a statue of the goddess was found inside it. However, other archaeological evidence makes it clear that the temple did not stand here.) Its foundations were discovered during excavations in 1887, along with many objects evidently donated by beneficiaries of her healing powers. Some of these suggest that one of her specialities was curing baldness. It is not clear, however, whether healing was actually practised at the temple, or whether those who received cures of various kinds simply attributed them to Minerva. But some special activity in the vicinity of the temple seems very likely. Nothing remains to be seen at the site itself.

Rome also once had a sanctuary of **Isis**, but it was closed by **Tiberius** after a woman named Paulina was seduced there by a man claiming to be **Anubis**. The temple was pulled down and its priests crucified. It stood in what is now known as the Piazza Minerva, just to the SE of the Pantheon. In the centre of the square is a marble statue of an elephant. On its back is a small obelisk that was salvaged from the temple.

On the city's Capitoline Hill stood the Auguraculum, from which the flights of birds were observed for **omens**. Some scant remains just to the E of the Capitoline Museum may belong to it.

SYRACUSE: a sanctuary of **Asclepius** in SE Sicily (37 05N, 15 19E). The various remains of the ancient city are spread around modern Siracusa, and include a large theatre, the remains of a temple of **Apollo**, and a cathedral partly built out of the remains of a temple of **Athena**. Unfortunately, despite something of an embarrassment of archaeological riches, no traces of the **Asclepeion** have yet been found. Both **Isis** and **Sarapis** appear on coins from ancient Syracuse, suggesting they enjoyed considerable popularity and prestige there, but no traces of their temples have been found.

TAUROMENION: a sanctuary of **Sarapis** in NE Sicily (37 48N, 15 19E). The town is now known as Taormina. It is most famed for its theatre, the second largest in Sicily, and a major tourist attraction. The oracular connection is not so dramatic, neither is it wholly certain. However, the church of San Pancrazio, which lies outside the Porta Messina, in the N of the town, is built on top of an earlier Greek temple, part of which can still be made out. It is thought that the temple may have been one dedicated to Sarapis, in which case some kind of healing or oracular activity on this site is likely.

TIBUR (modern Tivoli): oracles of **Albunea** and **Faunus** in Lazio, central Italy (41 57N, 12 46E). The picture here is not entirely clear, but the most consistent and coherent interpretation of the sources available seems to be that Albunea was a **Sibyl** who had a sacred spring here, and that a dream oracle of Faunus was established near it. The most dramatic description of the oracle is given by **Virgil** in the *Aeneid* [VII.81-96] where Latinus comes to consult the god (who also happens to be his father). He kills a hundred sheep and sleeps on their hides. (For most enquirers a single sheep was adequate, but the principle was the same.) Tivoli lies about 28 km E of **ROME**. The so-called Temple of the Sibyl that lies in the NE of it has no obvious or known connection with Albunea whatsoever, and the location of Faunus' oracle is unknown. About 6 km SW of Tivoli are the remains of the enormous villa **Hadrian** built for himself, incorporating its own temple of **Sarapis**.

TIORA: an oracle of **Mars** in central Italy. Little is known of this oracle, but Dionysius of Halicarnassus, a writer from the time of **Augustus**, mentions it, and relates the intriguing fact that responses were delivered by a woodpecker standing on a wooden pillar. However, it seems to have fallen silent before his time. The site of Tiora itself is disputed. It was evidently in the vicinity of Rieti (ancient Reate, 42 44N, 12 51E), and probably to the E of it. About 30 km in that direction lies the village of Teora, a likely candidate. Unfortunately there is nothing to see there.

TUSCANY: an oracle of Tethys in central Italy. This oracle is something of a mystery, its existence indicated only by a remark of **Plutarch** in his life of **Romulus**. Difficulties in pinning it down are not helped by the fact that Tuscany here is to be understood in the ancient sense (meaning 'the land of the Etruscans') rather than the modern one (which designates a smaller area). Tethys was a Greek personification of the sea whose cult was subsequently adopted by the Romans. However, she is not easily identifiable with any known Etruscan goddess, nor are there any other grounds for believing her cult to have been oracular. Either Plutarch knew something we do not, or he was mistaken in some way. Whatever core of historical truth there may be in his comment resists reliable extraction.

VEII (now called Veio): a healing sanctuary of **Juno** in Lazio, central Italy (42 01N, 11 18E). The ruins of Veii lie about 18 km NW of central **ROME**. It was one of the most important cities of the Etruscans, until captured by the Romans in 396 BC. The temple of Juno stood in the highest and most fortified part of the settlement. Over time, so many thousands of offerings were made to the goddess that they could not all be stored in the temple itself. As the temple stood on solid rock, storing them underneath it was not practical either. A decision was obviously taken at some point that what could not be stored must be thrown away. A ridge nearby was chosen, and for centuries surplus offerings were routinely cast from it. In due course the resultant heap became covered over and forgotten. It was not until the seventeenth century that it began to be investigated, and extensive excavations were carried out at the end of the nineteenth. Most of the items recovered were of either terracotta or bronze. They included representations of almost every part of the body, with a large number of the terracottas depicting male and female genitalia. Exactly what took place at the temple is unknown, but it is evident that Juno enjoyed a massive reputation for healing there.

After the Roman conquest, the wooden cult statue of the goddess was removed to Rome, where a new temple was built to her on the Aventine Hill, near the present-day church of Santa Sabina. There she continued to attract devotees, mainly women. The location of her temple at Veii can still be found, but there is no longer anything of it to be seen there, although there are other attractions such as painted tombs. Many of the finds are on display in the Villa Giulia in Rome.

VELIA or **ELEA**: a sanctuary of **Apollo** in Campania, S Italy (40 11N, 15 10E). The ruins of Velia lie about 70 km SE of Salerno, a little inland, near Ascea. The cult of Apollo seems to have been very much concerned with healing here, and **incubation** was probably practised. The town was founded by Greek colonists in the sixth century BC, and soon became famous for its own school of philosophy, of which **Xenophanes** and **Parmenides** were the most famous members. The remains of a number of temples have been found during excavations, although none has been conclusively identified as that of Apollo. The earliest probably dates to the fifth century BC. Another building has been discovered which may have belonged to some kind of medical school or organisation. It incorporates a complex system of passageways whose precise purpose is unclear. The town was probably abandoned in the fifth century AD. Excavations continue at the site.

LEBANON

APHACA (now Aqfa): an oracle of **Aphrodite** in central Lebanon (34 05N, 35 52E). Aqfa lies about 40 km inland, at the source of the Nahr Ibrahim (known in antiquity as the Adonis river) which flows into the Mediterranean about 30 km north of Beirut and 7 km S of Jbail (ancient Byblos). In antiquity, it stood on the main route from Byblos to **HELIOPOLIS**. Byblos was the main centre of the cult of **Adonis**, but Aphaca was dedicated to his lover, Aphrodite. The river emerges from a cave, and between there and the modern village of Khirbet Aqfa stand the remains of the goddess' temple. Some of the stone used in its construction came from as far away as Aswan in Egypt. Temples devoted to the goddess of love were frequently viewed with some suspicion, and according to **Eusebius** [III.55] this one was ordered to be destroyed by **Constantine the Great** on account of the licentious practices that went on there. How the oracle functioned is not known, but it is still a place where people pray for the health of the sick.

BERYTUS: a sanctuary of **Asclepius** in W Lebanon (33 50N, 35 30E). Most of ancient Berytus lies under modern Beirut, and few traces of it remain. Some Roman baths have been excavated on Capuchins Street, just to the W of the main post office. Otherwise most of what is left of Berytus can be seen in museums, the National Archaeological Museum in the SE of the city, and the one at the American University of Beirut in its NW corner. In Roman times there was a famous law school here. The location of the **Asclepeion** is unknown, but it was apparently originally dedicated to the Phoenician god **Esmun**.

HELIOPOLIS: an oracle of **Jupiter** Heliopolitanus in NE Lebanon (33 57N, 36 02E). The site of Heliopolis is better known as Baalbek, which is both its ancient and its modern name. However, during the period when it is known to have been oracular, it was called Heliopolis ('City of the Sun'). The ruins lie to the W of the town, some 80 km NE of Beirut, in the Bekaa Valley. The remains of the enormous temple of Jupiter Heliopolitanus are at the W end of the surviving complex of buildings, which was begun in the first century BC but not completed before the third century AD. The cult seems to have proved a very durable one, continuing to function until 579 when it was forcibly closed down. Exactly how the oracle operated is unclear, but it seems that it involved some movement by the god's statue, which would have been kept in the innermost room of the temple.

Jupiter Heliopolitanus was a Romanised version of the Syrian god Hadad. His cult was not limited to Heliopolis, but spread to such places as **ROME** and Nemausus (modern Nîmes). In both of these he was associated with springs, and his cult may have had a healing dimension.

LIBYA

BALAGRAI or **BALANAGRAE** or **BALACRÆ**: a sanctuary of **Asclepius** in NE Libya (32 46N, 21 43E). Balagrai stood on the site of modern El Beida. The remains of the sanctuary lie at the W edge of the modern town, near the university. The cult of Asclepius probably arrived here in the fourth century BC, but what can be seen mainly dates from the second century BC. The layout of the sanctuary can clearly be seen. In the centre was a large courtyard, and the main buildings were arranged around it. To the E, opposite the main entrance, are the ruins of a modest theatre: a bust of **Sarapis** was found in its vicinity. Some columns around the courtyard have recently been re-erected. According to **Pausanias** [II.26.7] the cult of Asclepius was brought here from **EPIDAUROS**, and was taken from here, in turn, to **LEBENA**.

CYRENE: sanctuaries of **Asclepius** and **Isis** in N Libya (32 48N, 21 54E). The ruins of Cyrene lie on the outskirts of modern Shahat, and are both extensive and impressive. Cyrene was one of the first Greek colonies founded in N Africa, in about 630 BC. Those who founded it were said to have been guided by an oracle from **Apollo** at **DELPHI**. According to **Herodotus** [IV.158] the spot they settled on was known as Apollo's fountain, and both the fountain and the temple built to the god nearby can still be seen. The whereabouts of the sanctuary of Asclepius are unknown, but the remains of a temple to Isis have been identified between the **agora** and the acropolis.

SABRATA: sanctuaries of **Isis** and **Sarapis** in N Libya (32 42N, 12 20E). The ruins of Sabrata, and the modern city of the same name, lie about 64 km W of Tripoli. It was one of the original three cities (the other two being Leptis Magna and Oea) from which Tripoli derives its name. It developed in the fourth century BC as an important port, providing a convenient link between the Mediterranean and the Sahara. It is an extensive site, with the temples of Isis and Sarapis occupying two of its extremities. The temple of Sarapis is the furthest W of a group of buildings contained within the remains of the sixth-century city walls. It was probably built towards the end of the second century AD, but on the site of an earlier and smaller one, parts of which were incorporated within it. The temple of Isis is a grander affair, dating from the end of the first century AD in a location to the E of the city. It stands in the middle of an elaborate sanctuary, which may have provided facilities for **incubation**. A museum at the site contains the results of excavations there.

PORTUGAL

MIRÓBRIGA: a sanctuary of **Asclepius** in S Portugal (38 02N, 08 45W). Miróbriga lies on the outskirts of Santiago do Cacém, about 140 km S of Lisbon. Most of what can be seen there dates from between the first and fourth centuries AD. The remains of two temples, a forum and a hippodrome have been found on the higher ground occupied by the site, while the impressive remains of a baths complex stand at the bottom. Nothing has been found to definitively tie any of the buildings to the cult of Asclepius, but it is known to have been active here. Finds from excavations carried out here are on display in the museum in Santiago.

ROMANIA

ULPIA TRAIANA SARMIZIGETUSA: a sanctuary of **Asclepius** in Transylvania, W Romania (45 31N, 22 47E). Sarmizigetusa was originally the name of the royal residence of the kings of Dacia, located high in the mountains. The last king, Decebulus, was finally defeated by **Trajan** in 106 AD. Thereafter Dacia was a part of the Roman empire until **Aurelian** gave it up in 271. Ulpia Traiana was founded in 108 as a new colony on a new site, but the old name Sarmizegetusa was attached to it. The ruins of the colony lie near the modern city of Sarmizegetusa, about 17 km SW of Hateg. Colonists were brought from many parts of the empire. Among them were Greeks who seem to have brought the cult of Asclepius with them. The ruins of the city are extensive. Sections of the city walls can be seen, and the remains of many buildings both inside and outside them, including those of the **Asclepeion**. Items found in the vicinity are dispersed between the local museum, the regional one at Hunedoara, and other major collections throughout Romania.

SLOVENIA

CELEIA: a sanctuary of **Isis** in Slovenia (46 14N, 15 16E). Modern Celje lies on top of its predecessor, and little can be seen of the ancient city apart from what is in the local museum. However, just to the S of Celje, on a terraced site overlooking the city, are the remains of some ancient sanctuaries. One of these is dedicated to Isis and **Heracles**, and is quite well preserved.

SPAIN

AUGUSTA EMERITA: a sanctuary of **Sarapis** in W Spain (38 57N, 06 20W). Augusta Emerita is now known as Mérida, and lies about 60 km E of Badajoz. Although only founded in 25 BC, it rapidly became one of the most important cities in the region. The modern town is built over it, meaning that not much of Augusta Emerita remains. What can be seen mainly lies to the SE of the town centre. There, within a small area, can be found a Roman theatre and amphitheatre, the scant remains of the temple of Sarapis, and the museum of Roman art.

CARTHAGO NOVA: a sanctuary of **Asclepius** in SE Spain (37 36N, 00 58W). As its name indicates, Carthago Nova was at one time a colony of **CARTHAGE**, and it was much valued for its harbour. The Romans took it and made it a colony of their own. Like **ROME**, it was a city of hills, and on the highest of them a temple to Asclepius was built. (It is possible that, as at Carthage, there had originally been a temple of **Esmun** there.) The site is now called Castillo de la Concepción, and the city is known as Cartagena. Nothing of the temple remains today, but it evidently played an important role in the life of the city. The cult of **Hygeia** was also popular here. She may have had a temple of her own, but it is more likely that she shared one with Asclepius. Some finds from the site are in the city's museum, others in Murcia and Madrid.

EMPORION or **EMPORIAE**: sanctuaries of **Asclepius** and **Sarapis** in NE Spain (42 10N, 03 06E). The site is now known as Ampurias and lies 3 km from the village of La Escala, and 40 km NE of Gerona. Emporion began life as a trading settlement, as its name suggests, and from the fifth to the third century BC was a major port. The temple of Asclepius, which has been found in the S part of the site, was the most important one in the city. A statue of the god has also been found there. Not far away from the Asclepius temple are the remains of another, which was dedicated to Sarapis. Some of the finds from the site are on display at its own museum, others are in the archaeological museum in Barcelona.

GADEIRA or **GADES** (now Cádiz): an oracle of **Menestheus** in S Spain (36 30N, 06 17W). Menestheus was the king of Athens who took part in the war against Troy. Some legends say he died there, others that he did not. None of the legends explain why there should have been an altar to him at the other end of the Mediterranean, but it seems that there was. Nothing of it remains, and it is not known how the oracle functioned. However, it may have been based at or near Gadeira's celebrated sanctuary of **Heracles**. This was situated about 19 km to the SE of the city itself, on what is now known as the island of Sancti Petri. Here can still be seen the remains of a temple, and it is possible to walk across to the island at low tide from the hamlet of Sancti Petri on the other side of the narrow strait. The temple, which was built near a spring, was celebrated for its great wealth. When **Julius Caesar** passed this way, he received a prophecy foretelling his rise to power. Unless this was a wholly exceptional event, it clearly suggests some kind of oracular activity at the temple.

The cult here appears to have followed some unusual customs. Entry to the temple was very restricted, and its priests shaved their heads and went barefoot. There was no cult statue. It is thought that the explanation for these eccentricities is that they derive from the cult of Melqart, a god of Tyre who was brought here by Phoenicians, and who was often identified with

Heracles. It seems likely that Heracles later displaced Melqart, but that the old cult practices continued under the new management.

SUDAN

NAPATA: an oracle of **Amun** (or **Zeus**) in N Sudan (19 00N, 32 00E). **Herodotus** speaks of an oracle in Meroë [II.29] and another in Ethiopia [II.140]. However, it is clear that he never visited either, and it is almost certain that both references are to the same oracle, that at Napata, near modern Karima. Napata preceded Meroë, some 250 km to its SE, as the capital of Kush. However, while political power may have moved, or been moving, to Meroë at the time of Herodotus, Napata still retained its religious pre-eminence. It was a major centre of the cult of Amun, and the remains of his great temple can still be seen at the foot of what is now known as Gebel Barkal. The first temple here was probably built by the Egyptians around 1300 BC, but it was subsequently rebuilt and enlarged.

An inscription found at the site testifies to oracular activity here. It records how, in 593 BC, the god was consulted to decide on the choice of a new king from among the eligible candidates, and settled on Aspelta, who went on to rule for the next 25 years. **Diodorus Siculus** [III. 5.1-2] testifies to this being the normal procedure for the selection of kings in this region rather than an exception. Although Meroë came to have its own temple of Amun, it is not clear that it existed at the time of Herodotus, or that it was oracular when it did. All these facts together suggest that the oracle he refers to as being in Meroë was in fact the one at Napata.

While modern Ethiopia lies far to the SE of Napata, the name was used by the ancient Greeks to refer to a much broader and vaguer area. Herodotus mentions a Sabacos who, he says, came from Ethiopia. However, Sabacos has been identified with Shabaqo, a king of Kush who became pharaoh of Egypt in around 711 BC. Consequently there seems little reason to doubt that the 'Ethiopian' oracle that predicted a long reign for Sabacos was, again, that of Amun at Napata, which would have confirmed Shabaqo as king of Kush.

In addition to its ruined temples, the area around ancient Napata is noted for its many pyramids (all on a modest scale by Egyptian standards), and Gebel Barkal itself is very striking. It is not difficult to understand the mystique that was attached to it. The Egyptians called it the 'pure mountain', and it seems that Amun may have been believed to actually live inside it. Even today it is an atmospheric place.

SYRIA

APAMEA: an oracle of **Zeus** Belus in Syria (35 30N, 36 26E). The site of Apamea lies next to the modern village of Qalaat Mudiq, 55 km NW of Hama, and 22 km W of Khan Shaikhun. Zeus Belus was an amalgam of Zeus and the Syrian god **Bel**. It is not known when oracular activity began at this site. The city itself was founded by **Seleucus I** (and named after his wife), but the remains of the temple of Zeus Belus that can be seen today date only from the time of **Hadrian**. The temple stood near the centre of the city, behind the **agora**. This prime location suggests that the building constructed in Hadrian's time was not the first to stand here. It was eventually pulled down on the orders of the local bishop in 384. The oracle had a rather unusual speciality, which involved quoting lines from **Homer**. It is not known how this was done, but choosing a passage at random from a text is a widely recognised method of divination. Presumably it was up to the inquirer to contribute the context for the lines' interpretation.

HIEROPOLIS: an oracle of **Apollo** in N Syria (36 33N, 37 56E). There is next to nothing to be seen of Hieropolis today, but it stood near modern Manbidj, 85 km NE of Aleppo. Here was built a great temple to the local earth goddess Atargatis, sometimes identified by the Greeks with **Aphrodite**. Within the temple was a statue of Apollo, or, more correctly perhaps, of Nebo. Nebo was the god of writing and wisdom from this part of the world, but at Hieropolis he became identified at some point with Apollo. According to **Lucian** in his essay 'On the Syrian goddess', the god's statue here was clothed, which was unusual. Lucian also reveals that oracles were delivered through the statue's movements. When the god wanted to speak, he moved to indicate this. Then he was borne aloft by priests, and thereafter he gave positive responses by making them move forwards, and negative ones by making them move backwards. Unusual in the Greek world, this kind of behaviour was very typical of an Egyptian oracle.

NIKEPHORION: an oracle of **Jupiter** in NE Syria (35 57N, 39 03 E). The very meagre remains of the city lie 2 km E of Raqqa. Evidence for the existence of an oracle here comes from a life of **Hadrian**, which claims that he received a prediction of his rise to power at the shrine. Unfortunately the reliability of the evidence is a matter of some dispute.

WADI MARTHUN: an oracle or healing centre in N Syria. In the limestone hills that stretch N from **APAMEA** towards the Turkish border, an area sometimes known as the Belus Massif, lie hundreds of so-called 'dead cities'. It is thought that some of them may have had oracular shrines, but conclusive evidence is hard to come by since most of the inscriptions found in the region date only from the **Byzantine** period, and the literary record appears to be silent on the subject. One such place is Wadi Marthun in the Jebel Zawwiye hills. Its ancient name is lost. It lies 6 km SE of Bara (35 42N, 36 32E) and about 30 km NW of **APAMEA**. The scattered site has a number of interesting features including a stepped altar near its E end, and a total of 29 grottoes cut into the rocks that rise on both sides of the riverbed. Given that **incubation** is known to have been practised in this part of Syria well into Christian times, it is tempting to think that these grottoes may have been used for something similar in an earlier age. However, while this is plausible, in the absence of further evidence it remains speculative.

TUNISIA

ALTHIBUROS: a sanctuary of **Asclepius** in NW Tunisia (35 53N, 08 53E). Althiburos is now known as Medeina. It is about 11 km S of Dehmani (sometimes called Ebba Ksour). The ruins are extensive and relatively well preserved, although only the central area of the city has been properly excavated. Although the city had a long history, most of what can be seen now dates from the second to the fifth centuries AD.

What is sometimes thought to be the Asclepius 'sanctuary' here may in fact not be one at all. The building in question lies to the N of the central area, across the bed of an old stream and consists of a complex of rooms and galleries. All of the rooms had mosaics, and their themes clearly point to a connection with Asclepius. However, the complex is of unusual design and its true purpose is difficult to discern. That there was some association with the god's cult seems certain, but little more can be said with confidence. Although the layout of the rooms can be studied at the site, the mosaics (mainly of the third and fourth centuries AD) have been removed to the Bardo Museum in Tunis.

CARTHAGE: a sanctuary of **Asclepius** and an oracle of **Juno** in NE Tunisia (36 50N, 10 15E). The remains of ancient Carthage can be found to the NE of Tunis. The city was originally founded by Phoenicians, and spent much of the third and second centuries BC challenging Rome for supremacy, especially under the leadership of **Hannibal**. The Romans were ultimately victorious, and in 146 BC, after a three-year siege, they took and totally demolished Carthage. The ruins that can be seen there today are mainly from the city they later constructed on the same site (from 44 BC onwards). The **Asclepeion** was built on top of the hill known as Mount Byrsa, about 1 km NW of the Punic ports. The French erected a substantial cathedral and seminary on the same spot. In Phoenician times it had been occupied by a temple to **Esmun**. This was Carthage's richest and most important temple, and the place where councils of state were held. It was probably destroyed by the Carthaginians themselves and not by the Romans. It is said that when defeat seemed certain, the wife of a general who had surrendered set fire to it and perished in the flames along with her children.

Just inland from the commercial Punic port are the scant remains of the Tophet, sanctuary of the Phoenician goddess Tanit. It was the focal point of Flaubert's novel *Salammbo*, and he made Salammbo herself a priestess there. The Romans identified Tanit with Juno, to whom they built a temple when they refounded the city. She became its chief deity, and her cult here is said to have been oracular. Whether Juno occupied the same site as her predecessor is not known, but no traces of her temple have been found either there or anywhere else.

The cult of **Sarapis** also enjoyed some popularity both in the city and the surrounding area, but no identifiable traces of it remain.

GIGTHIS: a sanctuary of **Isis** and **Sarapis** in SE Tunisia (33 27N, 10 40E). The site of Gigthis is now known as Gighti, and is to be found on the coast 27 km NE of Medenine. In its time, Gigthis was a major port, although its harbour has long since silted up. The ruins occupy a substantial area, much of which has been excavated. It is thought that the original settlement here was Phoenician, but it only really came to prominence during Roman times. The most impressive remains here are those of the forum built during the second century AD. The temple of Isis and Sarapis is to be found near and above it.

JEBEL (or **DJEBEL**) **OUST**: a sanctuary of **Asclepius** in NE Tunisia (36 33N, 10 04E). The site lies between Tunis and Zaghouan (about 24 km to the NW of the latter). There are extensive remains of a bathing complex built around a hot spring. The buildings that can be seen are relatively late, dating from the second century AD onwards. When the cult of Asclepius arrived is not known, but statues of the god have been found, and a temple dedicated to him (perhaps jointly with other healing gods) became part of the complex. In due course it became converted into a Christian church. The ancient name of this place is unknown.

TRITONIS (Lake): an oracle of **Mopsus the Argonaut** in central Tunisia (32 10N, 20 05E). Lake Tritonis is now Chott el Djerid, the massive salt lake that stretches across the middle of the country. The Mopsus referred to here is not the one who had an oracle at **MALLUS**, but another, who was also a seer in his lifetime. He was said to have been a son of Apollo, given by his father the gift of understanding birds, the pre-eminent bearers of **omens**. He travelled on the **Argo**, but met an untimely end when the ship was temporarily stranded on the lake (which was actually a lagoon), being bitten by a snake. He seems to have had some kind of **lot** oracle after his death, but its location is wholly unclear. According to **Strabo** [XVII.3.20], there was a temple of **Aphrodite** on an island in the lake, and it is possible that Mopsus had his oracle somewhere near it. There are still some scattered remains around the lake, but all are from Roman times.

TURKEY

ABONUTEICHOS: an oracle of Glykon-Asclepius in Pontus, N Turkey (41 56N, 33 50E). The site of Abonuteichos is at modern Inebolu. This was a relatively late oracular foundation, whose origins and operations were savagely lampooned by **Lucian** in his essay 'The Bogus Oracle'. According to Lucian, the oracle was established here in the first half of the second century AD by Alexander, a worldly-wise, well-travelled, and not conspicuously honest native of the town, with the help of a large snake and a fake snake's head. Alexander claimed the beast, Glykon, was an incarnation of **Asclepius**. It proved to be his key to fame, fortune and considerable influence. Even if only half of what Lucian (the self-confessed deadliest enemy of Alexander) claims is true, it remains a remarkable story. With the aid of various accomplices, and the further assistance of considerable nerve and duplicity, Alexander seems to have plied his dubious craft for decades. One of his most notable clients was Rutilianus, who became his son-in-law and who held a number of high offices under **Antoninus Pius** and **Marcus Aurelius**. His support afforded valuable protection against the likes of Lucian. According to his arch-critic, Alexander's methods included secretly opening sealed questions, plagiarising the pronouncements of other oracles, and sometimes just scribbling down whatever came into his head. Even if these specific charges are untrue, it is difficult not to conclude that Alexander's greatest asset was his clients' willingness (if not desperation) to believe, rather than any psychic gift.

Of Abonuteichos little remains. The original Glykon has long since perished, but an enormous statue of him (4.5 m tall) was found in 1962 during excavations under an old railway station in Constanta, Romania, the site of ancient Tomis. It is now on display in Constanta's archaeological museum. Thanks to Lucian, Alexander's reputation, however dubious, lives on.

ACHARACA: a healing centre and oracle of **Pluto** and **Persephone** in Caria, W Turkey (37 55N, 28 05E). This was one of their most famous sanctuaries. It lay a little to the E of the modern village of Salavatli, and was once joined to ancient Nysa, 4 km further E, by a sacred way. (The ruins of Nysa lie just to the N of Sultanhisar.) The complex comprised a temple with attendant buildings and a nearby cave called the Charonium. The site of the temple has been identified as lying on the E side of a small ravine, at the bottom of which flows a seasonal stream. It is called the Sarisu ('Yellow Stream') on account of its high sulphur content (sulphur and Pluto often go together). From excavations carried out there in the early twentieth century, it seems to have had an unconventional design, but it is difficult to see any trace of it at all now. It is not clear when it was built, although the third or second century BC seems likely. **Incubation** was practised here with, presumably, one of the attendant buildings being set aside for this purpose. Most unusually, priests would sometimes undergo the process of incubation on behalf of others.

The site of the Charonium has proved more difficult to locate. It is known that it was a cave, and that it was located on higher ground than the temple. However, it is not known whether the cave was a natural or an artificial one. If natural, there are no obvious candidates in the area. If artificial, none of the vaulted structures visible in the vicinity today seem to be old enough. What seems most likely is that it was a natural cave that has since collapsed. On the W side of the higher part of the ravine there is a possible candidate for its location at a spot where yellow crystals encrust the grey rock. The sick would often be sent to the cave without food, sometimes for days at a time. On the other hand, those who were not sick were forbidden from entering it, and it was said to be dangerous for them to do so. The healing tradition of the area is kept alive today by a small seasonal spa in Salavatli.

The museum in Aydin, 30 km to the W, has some exhibits from the site, but it was temporarily closed in 2001.

ADADA: an oracle of **letters** in Pisidia, S Turkey (37 25N, 31 01E). The site of Adada lies about 35 km SE of Egirdir (further by road) and N of Sütçüler. It is a remote place, seldom visited, perhaps because it features on so few maps and in so few guidebooks, although it is signposted from the outskirts of Egirdir. It is relatively well preserved with some temples and towers still standing to a substantial height. One of the temples was dedicated to **Zeus**

Sarapis, and so may conceivably have been a centre of some kind of oracular activity. The **agora** is well defined, and an impressive flight of steps leads off it. Unfortunately, the precise location of the oracle is unclear. It seems that it was on an elevated site outside the city, and may have been in the vicinity of Karadiken, about 7 km to the SW of Adada. It was seen and recorded by the Wolfe expedition through this region in 1884-5, but it is possible that it has not survived to the present. It opened with the following invocation:

> Apollo, Lord and Hermes, lead the way!
> And thou, who wanders, this to thee we say:
> Be still; enjoy the oracle's excellence,
> for Phoebus Apollo has given it to us,
> this Art of Divination from our ancestors.[1]

ADRASTEIA or **ADRASTEA** or **ADRASTIA**: a sanctuary of **Apollo** Actaios and **Artemis** in Mysia, NW Turkey. The only suggestion of an oracle in this location comes from **Strabo** [XIII.1.13], who describes the sanctuary as lying in the plain of Adrasteia, between Priapus and Parion. The principal settlement in the area was also called Adrasteia (or Adrastus, 40 20N, 27 13E), but Strabo makes it quite clear that the oracle did not lie in the city itself. In any event, the temple had been destroyed well before his time, and the oracle closed. Materials from the temple had been carried off to Parion and used in the construction of a massive altar there. Consequently there was nothing to be seen when he visited the area, and there is even less to be seen there now. Even the site of the temple remains uncertain. Why and when it was dismantled and the oracle abolished, he does not say, but it may have happened as early as the fourth century BC.

Legend had it that the city of Adrasteia was founded by **Adrastus**. However, there was also a goddess by the name of Adrasteia, who may have come from this area. Whatever her precise origin, she came to be identified with **Nemesis**. A goddess connected with the operations of fate would seem to be a logical candidate for some form of association with an oracle, but this does not seem to have been the case. Strabo makes it clear that there was no temple of any kind dedicated to Adrasteia in the place that shared her name, although there was one at **CYZICUS** some 50 km or more to the east.

AIGAI (1) or **AEGAE** or **ÆGÆ** (now Nemrutkale): a sanctuary of **Apollo** Chresterios in Lydia, W Turkey (38 46N, 26 59E). The ruins of Aigai lie about

---

[1]This translation by John Opsopaus can be found at:
http://www.cs.utk.edu/~mclennan/BA/LAO.html

45 km N of Izmir. The **epithet** Chresterios means 'god of oracles', which is the main evidence for the oracular nature of the site. (He was worshipped under the same name at **CHALCEDON**.) As was often the case, the sanctuary was not located in the town itself: it lay around 6 km to the E, near a river. While the remains of the town are fairly impressive, there is little to be seen at the sanctuary. The site has not been excavated, and what the ravages of time have left standing belongs to a temple dedicated in 46 BC.

AIGAI (2) or **AEGAE** or **ÆGÆ**: a sanctuary of **Asclepius** in Cilicia, S Turkey (36 48N, 35 52E). The site of Aigai is now known as Ayas, near Yumurtalik. Most of what is known about the **Asclepeion** here relates to its destruction, which is gleefully related by **Eusebius** [III.56]. In passing, he confirms the practice of **incubation** there, but for him **Asclepius** was a deceiver and destroyer of souls, and any good his cult might have achieved was accidental and unintentional. He claims **Constantine the Great** ordered the temple to be razed to the ground, which was duly done by his soldiers with some enthusiasm. The dating of this event is uncertain, but seems to have taken place somewhere between 330 and 337. According to Eusebius, this was not the only pagan temple the emperor ordered destroyed, but the true scale of such a programme of destruction is difficult to establish.

ALEXANDRIA TROAS: a sanctuary of **Asclepius** in Mysia, W Turkey (39 45N, 26 08E). This Alexandria was not founded by **Alexander the Great** but by one of his generals, Antigonus, said by some to be Alexander's illegitimate half-brother. Its original name, not entirely unpredictably, was Antigonia. When Antigonus was defeated in 301 BC, it was renamed. What is left of it lies about 22 km W of Ezine. The most impressive feature of the site consists of ruined baths, built with a donation from **Herodes Atticus** in 135 AD. Many of the city's stones were carried off to be used in the embellishment of Istanbul, and no identifiable remains of its **Asclepeion** survive. However, it is known that the god's cult enjoyed considerable popularity in this area and probably had more than one centre. A **votive** relief to Asclepius was found in the village of Kemalli, about 8 km NE of Alexandria Troas, and may have come from there.

ANABURA or **ANABOURA**: a **dice** oracle in Phrygia, W Turkey (38 05N, 31 17E). Part of a dice oracle carved on a large stone was found at the village of Ördekçi, about 15 km N of Lake Beysehir, in 1885. The stone had evidently been incorporated into the wall of a large building. From the inscription it appears that five dice were used to consult the oracle, and most of its responses were attributed to one of many contributing divinities, as was usual. One, however (corresponding to a throw of four sixes and a four), is more enigmatically headed 'Blabe', a name with connotations of injury or mischief. It is possible that Blabe was regarded as a personification of harm, but, if so, such a usage is unknown outside the context of dice oracles. On the other hand, it would be curious for only one response to be associated with an abstraction. It may be that the oracle was compiled at a time when the distinction between personifications and abstractions was becoming increasingly blurred or unimportant. The conversation **Pausanias** had at **AIGION** concerning **Asclepius** seems to point in a similar direction. Whatever the explanation, the response in question is evidently intended to warn the enquirer off a proposed course of action owing to the harm it may occasion. The precise connection of the oracle with Anabura is unclear. The ruins of the city (now known as Enevre), including some remains of a theatre and fortifications, are near Salur, a few km to the S of Ördekçi. The stone may have been moved, but given its size (1.36 m high, 1.24 m wide) that does not seem particularly likely.

ANTIOCH: an oracle of **Zeus** Philios in S Turkey (36 11N, 36 11E). The city, founded by **Seleucus I** in 300 BC, was sometimes known as Antioch on the Orontes to distinguish it from other Antiochs. It is now known as Antakya. It lies near Turkey's border with modern Syria, and within the area known as Syria in antiquity. The oracle seems to have been of very late origin, coming into existence only in the first decade of the fourth century AD. It achieved a certain renown for its anti-Christian stance and pronouncements. Given that the tide of history was by then already flowing in the opposite direction, it may not have had a very long career. No traces of it are known to exist. There was another (and better known) oracle, of **Apollo**, at nearby **DAPHNE**. Antioch was renowned in ancient times as one of the world's most beautiful cities, but has not improved with age.

ANTIOCHEIA AD CRAGUM: a **dice** oracle in Cilicia, S Turkey (36 06N, 32 32E). The ruins of the city lie approximately halfway between Alanya and Anamur, about 19 km SE of Gazipasa. Modern Güney is built over part of it. The ancient town was founded in around 170 BC by **Antiochus IV Epiphanes**, and named after him. It survived the end of the ancient world and the ruins that can be seen today are a mixture of classical and medieval. Its unusual name reflects its location on a cliff-top site jutting into the sea. The ruins are quite spread out, but the temple on whose walls the dice oracle was carved lies in its NE part.

ATTALEIA (now Antalya): a **dice** oracle in Pamphylia, S Turkey (36 50N, 30 45E). Excavations in the late nineteenth century discovered some inscriptions that clearly belonged to a set of responses for a dice oracle. Five dice were thrown, and each possible outcome had its own interpretation. For example:

> From Pythian Apollo [i.e. Apollo of Delphi]
> Wait and do nothing, but obey the oracles of Phoebus [i.e. Apollo].
> Watch for another opportunity; for the present leave quietly.
> Shortly all your concerns will find fulfilment. (Aune 1991, p. 25)

Although Apollo is mentioned by name in this response, a number of other gods feature in others. The dice oracle's set of responses therefore seems to have been assembled from a variety of sources. Collections of oracles were not unknown in antiquity, and there were people, known as chresmologues, who put them together.

BYZANTIUM: sanctuaries of the **Dioscouri** and **Sarapis** in NW Turkey (41 01N, 28 58E). Byzantium subsequently became known as Constantinople, and more recently as Istanbul. The Dioscouri is the collective name given to Castor and Pollux. Tradition is agreed that their mother was Leda, but confused over whether their father was **Zeus** (famously assuming the form of a swan to carry out his seduction) or Leda's husband Tyndareus. One of their sisters (or half-sisters) was **Helen**, and they were members of the **Argo**'s crew. They had no associations with healing while alive, but acquired one posthumously. Unusually, **Constantine the Great** allowed a temple to be built to them in his new Christian capital, and this seems to have been constructed in the vicinity of the Hippodrome (now known as the At Meydani). In due course the healing cult of the Dioscouri was replaced by that of saints **Cosmas and Damian**, regarded by some as their Christian reincarnations. Five separate churches were dedicated to them at one time or another in Constantinople, but none have survived. However, it is thought that one of them, built in 569, was situated SW of the At Meydani, somewhere near where the mosque of Sokullu Mehmet Pasa now stands. It is not impossible that the mosque, church and temple have all been built on the same site. Cosmas and Damian are popular saints, especially in Eastern Orthodox countries, and many of their churches are doubtless constructed on the sites of earlier healing cults.

According to **Strabo** [VII.6.1], there was also a temple of **Sarapis** at Byzantium, but located some way outside the city. His description places it in the vicinity of where the fortress of Rumeli Hisar now stands, about 10 km up the Bosphorus, near the Fatih Sultan Mehmet bridge. The site seems to be an unnecessarily inconvenient one and Strabo offers no suggestions as to why it was chosen.

CASSIUS, Mount: an oracle of **Jupiter** in S Turkey (35 55N, 35 55E). Mount Cassius (or Casius), now known as Jebel Akra, lies on the border of Turkey and Syria, near the village of Yayladagi. It had a long history as a cult centre, stretching back as least as far as the time of the Hittites in the second millennium BC. Its main claim to be an oracular site comes from much later, when it is said that the emperor **Julian** went there at an appointed time (noon) and not only received a timely warning from the god, but actually saw him as well. The point that the encounter was pre-arranged points towards some kind of oracular institution, if only an occasional one. There is nothing to be seen of the temple today, but the remains of a fifth-century Christian monastery may mark the spot.

CASTABUS: a healing sanctuary of **Hemithea** in Caria, SW Turkey (36 47N, 28 08E). The site of Castabus lies 13 km SW of Marmaris, on a ridge above the village of Hisarönü at a place called Pazarlik. Hemithea had originally been called Molpadia, and was the aunt of **Anios**, who may have had his own sanctuary on **DELOS**. She was established in Castabus by **Apollo**, who saved her from being punished by her father. Hers was said to have been the only shrine in that part of the world that was neither looted nor destroyed by the Persians in their campaigns. If this is so, it must have already enjoyed considerable fame by the end of the sixth century BC. However, what remains to be seen at the site today dates from the fourth century BC. Little is left of the temple itself except for the platform on which it stood. Scant remains of a theatre from the same period lie nearby. For much of its existence, Castabus was controlled by **RHODES**, and it may have followed Rhodes into decline in the first century BC. While it still functioned, however, the sanctuary specialised in healing. The method practised there, as at many others, was **incubation**, whereby Hemithea appeared in the dreams of those who came to seek her help. **Diodorus Siculus** [V.63] claims she helped many apparently hopeless cases, and was particularly adept at midwifery. It was apparently a very popular place, and the sanctuary's great reputation for healing seems to have been the reason why it was left alone by the Persians.

A curious fact related by Diodorus is that honey and milk were used instead of wine in the rituals at Hemithea's temple, and that no one who had been in contact with a pig, or eaten any part of one, was permitted to enter. His shaky explanation of this is that she had once fallen asleep, owing to the effects of alcohol, when she was meant to be guarding her father's supply of wine. Then a pig broke in and destroyed all the jars it was kept in. (This was why her father had been seeking to punish her.) Her name, which means 'half-goddess', is also strange.

CHALCEDON: an oracle of **Apollo** in Bithynia, NW Turkey (40 59N, 29 05E). Chalcedon is now known as Kadiköy, was once known as Scutari, and is one of the Asian parts of Istanbul. It seems that as at **AIGAI (1)**, Apollo was known here by the **epithet** Chresterios, meaning 'god of oracles', and two inscriptions have been found in the area, dating from the third century BC, that suggest oracular activity. Evidence also exists of a sanctuary of **Asclepius**. However, there are no traces of any ancient institutions to be seen there today.

CHRYSE or **CHRYSA**: an oracle of **Apollo** in Mysia, NW Turkey (39 30N, 26 08E). The ruins of Chryse are just outside the village of Gülpinar, about 70 km S of **Troy**. The god was worshipped here under the unusual **epithet** of Smintheos ('god of mice'). According to legend, the hero **Teucer** had left his home on Crete because of a famine, taking his father and followers with him. A seer told them to settle where they were attacked by the natives. When they awoke one morning to find that some of their belongings had been eaten by mice during the night, they decided they had found the right place. Teucer went on to become king of Troy, and some would place the scene of this event further north, nearer to that city. It may be that there was more than one temple of Apollo Smintheos in the region. Mice were kept in the temple, and evidently treated with some reverence.

Oracular activity at Chryse is attested to by both **Ovid** and Menander (a third-century AD rhetorician, not the fourth-century BC playwright of the same name). Excavations have uncovered the platform of the temple that was built there in around 200 BC, along with various fragments and inscriptions. The remains of other buildings lie nearby. Unfortunately much of what was found when the site was rediscovered in the mid-nineteenth century has since been lost.

CLAROS: an oracle of **Apollo** in Lydia, W Turkey (37 59N, 27 11E). Claros is near the modern village of Ahmetbeyli (also known as Sahilevleri), about 20 km W of Selçuk. Since the time of the temple's construction, the water table in this area has risen considerably, with the consequence that most of its remains lie underwater for most of the year. The temple was probably begun in the fourth century BC, but seems not to have been finished until the second century AD, with **Hadrian** playing a significant role in its completion. Inscriptions there testify to his involvement. In the interim, the temple may have received some financial support from Sextus Apuleius, a nephew of **Augustus**, whose name is also recorded appreciatively.

Although there is testimony to the cult of Apollo being celebrated on this site as far back as the seventh century BC, there is no firm evidence of oracular activity until around the time work on the temple began. Tradition has it that Claros was founded by **Manto**, the daughter of the famous seer **Teiresias**, and **Mopsus**, her son (who was to have his own celebrated oracle at **MALLUS** in due course.) The name Claros was said to derive from the Greek word meaning 'to weep' because of the tears she shed here. Legend has it that a divination contest was held at Claros between Mopsus and **Kalchas** (who later had an oracle at the foot of **Mount GARGANUS**). There is more than one version of the story, but both end with the triumph of Mopsus and the broken-hearted death of Kalchas. Another legend claims that one of the **Sibyl**s made prophecies here before the time of the Trojan War. These point towards at least a generic association of the place with prophecy reaching back a very long time.

As was the case with a number of oracular sites, Claros was an isolated sanctuary, not part of any city or town. Politically it belonged to Colophon (at least from the late fourth century BC onwards), which lay about 14 km to the N of it. Ancient sources seemed to indicate that the oracle was located in a cave, which led many modern explorers to look for it in quite the wrong direction. The 'cave' turned out to be a complex of rooms and passageways under the floor of the temple. They are now clearly visible through the water. A small temple dedicated to **Artemis** lies near that of her brother.

The manner in which enquiries were dealt with at Claros was quite distinctive. Apollo communicated his prophecies through a male medium, who does not seem to have been told the questions to which answers were sought, only the names of the enquirers and the numbers they had been given. Upon receiving this information he would descend into the 'cave', take a drink of the sacred water and begin to prophesy. His utterances were taken down by an assistant, and at least sometimes rendered into verse. Consultations took place only after dark, and only on certain days. Each prophet served for one year, a relatively short period, probably connected with a belief recorded by **Pliny the Elder** [II.232] that the sacred water shortened the lives of those who drank it. In his *Annals* [II.54], **Tacitus** claimed that the prophets usually came from **MILETUS** (which had its own major oracular site at **DIDYMA**), but most regard this as unlikely.

No responses of the oracle are preserved at the site itself, although the names of many who consulted it are inscribed on the temple steps and the columns of the formal gateway to the sanctuary that lay at its SE corner. However, a number of responses are known through being found either in literature or on inscriptions discovered elsewhere. Inscriptions (mainly dated to the second century AD) mentioning Claros have been found as far apart as northern England (at Housesteads, on Hadrian's Wall) and N Africa. Most such inscriptions contain advice on religious matters, such as the appropriate gods to sacrifice to. What may be the earliest known pronouncement of the oracle appears in **Pausanias** [VII.5.1]. He assigns it to the time of **Alexander the Great**, and it is addressed to the people of **SMYRNA**, advising them to move to the new city Alexander had built for them. Tacitus recorded what he acknowledged to be a rumour that on his visit there in 18 AD, **Germanicus** was told by the oracle of his imminent death. He died within the year. Interestingly, Germanicus took a keen interest in divination and had written a book on omens.

A less complimentary view of the oracle was taken by the Cynic philosopher Oenomaus of Gadara, who lived in the second century AD. He wrote a book aimed at uncovering frauds, upon which **Eusebius** enthusiastically drew for one of his own works. Oenomaus attacked the institution of oracles on three grounds. First, an analysis of their contents revealed them as useless. Secondly, he received no help from Claros. Thirdly, prophecy was impossible anyway! In addition to his general objections against oracles, however, Oenomaus had a special problem with the one at Claros. Apparently, he and another person had asked it quite different questions but received exactly the same answer.

There are no signs of destruction at Claros, other than those attributable to the forces of nature. Its demise is as obscure as its origin. Between the two, it clearly enjoyed considerable prestige from time to time, especially in the second and third centuries AD. Its isolation and underwater remains make it a special place to visit, although few do.

CNIDUS: a sanctuary of **Asclepius** in Caria, W Turkey (36 41N, 27 24E). Cnidus stands on the long peninsula extending W from Marmaris. In fact there were two cities bearing this name. The earlier was near modern Datça, about 80 km by road W of Marmaris. The later was 30 km further W again, at the peninsula's very tip. The second city was built to replace the first one in about 360 BC, for reasons that are not entirely clear. There is little to see at the earlier site except for some remains of walls. The new city was laid out on a grid plan according to the principles of **Hippodamus**. Excavations have made it possible to appreciate the overall design of the city, as well as revealing some of its principal buildings. Unfortunately an **Asclepeion** has not yet been identified among them. Neither has the medical school that existed here, and which was one of the most important of the ancient world. It would not be surprising if the two were located close to each other. Finds from excavations at Cnidus are mainly to be found in the museums of Bodrum and Izmir.

CYANEAE: an oracle of **Apollo** in Lycia, S Turkey (36 15N, 29 48E). What is left of Cyaneae lies to the N of Yavu, about 23 km E of Kas. The ruins are spread along a ridge immediately above the village, but are overgrown and difficult to see clearly. However, according to **Pausanias** [VII.21.6] the oracle was not in the city itself, but nearby. It was located at a spring, and looking into the water was somehow supposed to provide the answers to enquirers' questions. There are a few springs in the vicinity, but none has any obvious or special claim to be the site of the oracle. The remains of the city itself are mainly from the Roman period. The most notable feature of the surroundings is the number of tombs to be found there, especially in the area near the theatre, on the other side of the ridge from Yavu. Some are free-standing, but many are cut into the rock. Apollo was known here by the **epithet** Thyrxeus, but its meaning remains a mystery.

CYME: sanctuaries of **Asclepius** and **Isis** in Lydia, W Turkey (38 46N, 26 54E). The site of Cyme lies by the sea about 45 km NNW of Izmir, near the village of Aliaga. At one time it was an important and wealthy city, although its inhabitants had a certain reputation for lacking intelligence. It was also the home town of **Ephorus**. Part of the site is now underwater, and the rest of it is very overgrown. The buildings stretched from the shore to the top of the hill, and it is there that the remains of a small temple to Isis can be found. Other ruins are more difficult to identify, and the location of the **Asclepeion** has not been found. Coins found at the site indicate that the city was occupied from at least the seventh century BC to the third century AD.

CYZICUS: a sanctuary of **Asclepius** in NW Turkey (40 22N, 27 54E). The ruins of Cyzicus are very overgrown and lie about 8 km NW of Bandirma. Remains of walls and an aqueduct can be seen, but little else is distinguishable. However, it seems that Asclepius had a temple here, but shared it with **Apollo**. This may indicate that Apollo originally functioned as a healer here in his own right. The most notable temples of the city were those dedicated to **Nemesis**, of which nothing remains, and another dedicated to the emperor **Hadrian**. Some fragments of this can be seen at the open-air museum in Erdek, a few km to the W.

DALDIS: an oracle of **Apollo** in Lydia, W Turkey (38 43N, 28 09E). By any standards, the evidence for the existence of this oracle is slight. It consists of an almost throwaway comment by **Artemidorus** [II.70], a native of the town, who claims that he was pressed to write by Apollo himself. However, he says that Apollo was called Myestes by the people of Daldis, suggesting that the cult had local peculiarities. One interpretation of these scant facts is that the Apollo of Daldis was oracular, hence his communication with Artemidorus. An alternative one is that Apollo simply appeared to Artemidorus in a dream, without any warning or prior ritual. Messages received from gods through dreams outside a formal consultation process were certainly not unknown. In the absence of any further evidence, it is impossible to know which interpretation to prefer. No evidence is likely to emerge from Daldis itself of which nothing remains to be seen. It was situated about 35 km SE of Akhisar. This stands on the site of ancient Thyatira, which had temples dedicated to **Asclepius** and one of the **Sybil**s. Not much remains of Thyatira either.

DAPHNE (now Harbiye): an oracle of **Apollo** in S Turkey (36 9N, 36 9E). Harbiye lies about 9 km to the S of **ANTAKYA**, in ancient Syria. Daphne was once a place of some note, and according to at least one version of the legend, it was here that the nymph of the same name was changed into a tree by her father in order to escape Apollo's amorous embraces. (Daphne is one of the names for the laurel tree, many of which still grow on the site.) **Seleucus I** built the first temple here in commemoration of the event, and it contained a celebrated statue of the god. Executed by the celebrated sculptor **Bryaxis**, it was said to equal in size that of **Zeus** at **OLYMPIA** (regarded as one of the Seven Wonders of the ancient world). The site was further developed and embellished by the Romans. The temple, or its replacement, was eventually destroyed by fire in 362 AD. It stood next to two springs, and the oracle worked by interpreting the sound of running water in some way.

The early history of the oracle is obscure, and it is not known if its existence preceded or succeeded that of the temple. However, some episodes of its later history are quite well known. During the caesarship of **Gallus** (351-4), the remains of St Babylas were brought here in an attempt to silence the oracle. Gallus' half brother **Julian** (who later became emperor) had the body removed. Julian was also in Daphne when the temple burnt down. Later still Babylas was brought back again, and there he stayed.

The site of the church where he was entombed (now known as the Martyrion of Qaoussié) has been found. It was built in the shape of a cross, and its mosaics have been dated to 387 AD. Given the reason why the body of Babylas was brought to Daphne in the first place, it seems likely that the church was built somewhere near the site of the ancient oracle. Stones from the temple may even have been used in its construction. Some of the mosaics from the church are on display in the museum at Antakya. Laurel trees still grow in the area, and produce one of the ingredients of the locally manufactured soap.

DIDYMA: an oracle of **Apollo** in Caria, W Turkey (37 25N, 27 15E). The site lies at modern Didim, about 4 km N of the resort of Altinkum. The oracle was often known by the name of Branchidai, meaning 'descendants of Branchos' and referring to the family who ran the place for many generations. It is located about 18 km S of ancient **MILETUS**, to which it belonged politically, and to which it was connected by a sacred way. (Some of the statuary that once lined this sacred way is in the British Museum. Other items have found their way to Berlin, Paris, Izmir and Istanbul.) Miletus also furnished a substantial proportion of the queries put to the oracle. Evidence unearthed on the site suggests that Didyma may have been a centre of oracular activity as far back as the eighth century BC, and **Pausanias** [VII.2.4] clearly believed it to be very old. According to **Herodotus** [I.46ff] it was one of the seven oracles tested by **Croesus**, and the only one he bothered with in Asia Minor. Unfortunately, it also seems to have failed the test, although Croesus did make some donations to it. The site and the temple on it (which was not the first) were destroyed and looted by the Persians in the early fifth century BC. It is said that the Branchidai were less robust in the defence of their domain than they might have been, and left with the Persian king to resettle in Sogdiana, part of central Asia. When **Alexander the Great** came upon their supposed descendants there in the next century, his treatment of them was said to be severe.

The place they had left took a long time to recover, and little is heard of it again until around 330 BC. About thirty years later, one of Alexander's successors, **Seleucus I**, began the rebuilding of the sanctuary. He may have had a special reason for doing so, as the oracle was said to have foretold his rise to power. (Curiously, a later patron of the sanctuary was **Trajan**, for exactly the same reason.) The ambitious new plans were never brought to completion, but what can be seen today is the very substantial remains from that grandiose project. The main testimony relating to the way the oracle functioned comes from a very late source, the fourth-century philosopher Iamblichus. He talks of a woman as the mouthpiece of the god, but this may have been a relatively late development, with the role originally performed by a man. Enquirers were given a written copy of the oracle's response, which was usually rendered in verse (although this may have been another late development). How often consultations were available is not known.

The location of the oracle is connected with that of a spring, the site of which was found during excavations. It lies within the confines of the temple, in a small inner enclosure. This is a feature of the curious design of Didyma. The main part of the temple is unroofed. The inner parts of the complex therefore stand open to the elements and are connected to the outer parts by steps and a pair of sloping tunnels. The exterior fabric of the building is generally quite well preserved, and the walls remain standing up to 10 m high in places. More imagination is required to reconstruct the internal plan of the building. The edifice that housed the spring also contained the cult statue, and was like a temple within a temple. However, only the foundations remain. Somewhere in the complex (there is no agreement as to where) there was an office called a *chresmographeion*. It was here that the responses of the oracle were written out (and quite likely converted into verse). Copies may also have been kept here, but if they were, few have been discovered. Some of the responses of which there is knowledge suggest that in its later years the oracle was much concerned with religious matters. **Lactantius** claimed that it even prompted **Diocletian** to persecute Christians. The sanctuary was already in decline by that time, but as one of the principal centres of the cult of Apollo (it clamed to be the place where he had been conceived), it may have continued to exist right up to 385. In that year the emperor **Theodosius the Great** forbade the consultation of oracles.

Excavations have revealed a temple of **Artemis** near to that of Apollo, and it is thought that it may have originally been dedicated to **Cybele**. While the Greeks were less fastidious about building straight roads than the Romans were, it is nonetheless noticeable that the sacred way from Miletus takes a very distinct detour when it reaches Didyma, in order to end at the sanctuary of Apollo. Without that detour it would terminate closer to the temple of Artemis. This coupled with the fact that the name Didyma implies twinship might suggest that Apollo's cult arrived here later than that of his sister. Although it must have existed long before then, the sacred way was only actually paved in 100 AD on the orders of Trajan.

ELAIUS or **ELEUS** or **ELAEUM**: an oracle of **Protesilaus** in Thrace, NW Turkey (40 4N, 26 12E). The site was said to mark the grave of the hero. By tradition, he was the first to jump ashore when the Greek fleet reached **Troy** (**Achilles** swiftly succeeded him). As a reward for his heroism, he was killed almost immediately. His body was taken across the Dardanelles to Elaius on what was then known as the Thracian Chersonese, and is now the Gelibolu (Gallipoli) peninsula. Near the very end of the peninsula, on its S side, is Morto Bay. **Schliemann** spent some time in this area and believed he had identified both Elaius and the tomb of Protesilaus, the one on the E side of the bay, the other on the W of it. The site of Elaius sustained enormous damage

Turkey

during the military engagements that took place in this area in World War One, and little remains to be seen. The possible tomb of Protesilaus is the large tumulus near the village of Seddulbahir. As an oracular institution, it attracted a certain amount of passing trade, and was popular with sailors. It had a reputation for healing, in particular. A notable visitor was **Alexander the Great** who stopped here before crossing over to Asia. According to **Arrian** (I.11), Alexander made a sacrifice here in order to ensure that he would enjoy a longer and more successful sojourn in Asia than that enjoyed by Protesilaus, which he certainly did. While Alexander's subsequent history is well known, that of the oracle is not. Little is heard of it thereafter, but it features in a dialogue called *Heroikos* ('On Heroes') which was probably written in the first half of the third century AD by **Philostratus**. One of its characters is a man who looked after the vines and gardens around the hero's tomb. He claims Protesilaus frequently communicated with him on a wide variety of subjects, including gardening. The hero is also prone to reminisce on the Trojan War, despite his extremely brief involvement with it. Protesilaus appears to lead an extremely active posthumous existence in the vicinity of his tomb, not only responding to enquiries, but also directly intervening in human affairs. How much of this is the product of Philostratus' imagination it is impossible to tell. It seems likely that the hero's sanctuary was already in serious decline by the third century AD and, despite his helpful horticultural hints, becoming overgrown.

Herodotus also mentions the cult of Protesilaus, although he makes no reference to any oracular activity in connection with it. According to him [VII.33 and IX.116], it was robbed of its considerable wealth by Artayactes, a Persian governor serving under **Xerxes**. Artayactes also seems to have used the sanctuary as a place for sexual encounters. When the tide of war turned, the Greeks took their revenge by nailing him alive to a plank.

EPHESUS: an oracle of **Apollo** in Lydia, W Turkey (37 57N, 27 21E). Ephesus is now known as Efes, and is one of Turkey's major tourist attractions, lying within day-trip range of many holiday resorts. The oracle of Apollo was a very late development here. It was established in the early years of the second century AD through the efforts of Dionysodorus, a magistrate. He set it up in the city's **prytaneion**. This seems to have been partly motivated by civic pride (or envy), as the long-established oracle at **CLAROS** was not far away. The new oracle was intended to stay and make its pronouncements in Ephesus forever. Although this turned out not to be the case, the remains of the prytaneion itself can still be seen. They are towards the S end of the site, a little way up the hill from **Trajan**'s fountain, near the upper **agora**. The sacred and inextinguishable flame of the city (long extinguished) was maintained here. Statues of **Artemis** (whose temple nearby was one of the Seven Wonders of the ancient world) were found nearby, and can now be seen in the museum in Selçuk, 3 km away. Inscriptions reveal that there was also a sanctuary of **Asclepius** at Ephesus, but its whereabouts have not been found. In an overgrown (and presently off limits) part of the site to the E are the ruins of what is thought to be a temple of **Sarapis**. The building, constructed in the second century AD, incorporates some interesting features that seem designed to facilitate a flow of water through it. Its scale is monumental and during the Christian era it was converted into a church.

ERYTHRAE or **ERYTHRAI**: an oracle of the **Sibyl** in Lydia, W Turkey (38 20N, 26 28E). The site of Erythrae is partly covered by modern Ildir, on the long peninsula extending to the W of Izmir, about 8 km NE of Çesme. If the Sibyl of **CUMAE** was the most celebrated in antiquity, then that of Erythrae could at least claim an honourable place in the order of precedence. After the Sibylline Books had been destroyed by fire in Rome in 83 BC, a deputation was sent to Erythrae to procure replacements. Known as Herophile, according to one legend she was actually born over 200 km away to the N, at Marpessus, and later buried in the sanctuary of **Apollo** at nearby Gergithium. This was fiercely disputed by the Erythraeans, and at the end of the nineteenth century it was claimed that the cave of the Sybil had been found, and that it contained inscriptions supporting their cause. But if it was found, it has since been lost again. What has been found and not lost is mainly in the Archaeological Museum in Izmir.

GRYNEION or **GRYNEUM**: an oracle of **Apollo** in Lydia, W Turkey (38 55N, 27 03E). The site of Gryneion lies about 30 km N of Izmir, close to the modern village of Yenisakran. According to **Strabo** [XIII.3.5], the temple of Apollo here was lavishly constructed of white marble, and was the most important shrine to the god in the region. There was a tradition that it was an exact replica of that at **CLAROS**. In **Virgil**'s *Aeneid* [IV.345], it is the oracle of Apollo at Gryneion that commands **Aeneas** to go to Italy (Virgil also refers to it as a **lot** oracle). The first mentions of Gryneion itself date to the fifth century BC, when it was an ally of **ATHENS**. Thereafter it seems to have enjoyed little by way of independence, and ended up being absorbed by its neighbour Myrina. It is thought that the temple of Apollo probably stood on the small headland of what is now called Temasalik Burnu. No traces of white marble have been found there, although some fragments of columns can be seen. However, if the temple has not survived, at least one of its pronouncements has.

Excavations at Caunus unearthed an inscription from the second century BC bearing part of the oracle's response to an enquiry concerning sacrifices. **Aelius Aristides** also makes reference to the oracle. Its career after that time is wholly obscure, as is the fate met by the temple.

HALICARNASSUS: see **TELMESSOS**

HERACLEIA: an oracle of the **dead** in Pontus, N Turkey (41 15N, 31 28E). The remains of Heracleia (known sometimes as Heracleia Pontica, or ad Pontus, to distinguish it from several others with the same name) are located near modern Eregli, on the SW shore of the Black Sea. The modern city is heavily industrial, and famous for its steel works. What remains of Heracleia lies to the E of it. As the name of the ancient city suggests, **Heracles** was its legendary founder. The river that reaches the sea here was known as the Acheron (one of the rivers of Hades) in antiquity, as was the one that flowed past the oracle of the dead at **EPHYRA**. The headland now called Baba Burnu (which extends W from Heracleia) once had the name of Acherousia (also attached to the lake near Ephyra). It was through a cave on the headland that Heracles was said to have made his own descent into the underworld. A place known locally as Cehennemagzi ('the entrance to hell') lies to the NE of Eregli, near the village of Kavakderesi. This may have been the location of the oracle, or it could have lain somewhere further W, on the headland. Unfortunately a substantial part of this area is now inaccessible owing to it being a military zone. Some materials from the ancient city have been reused in the buildings of Eregli. There is little to be seen *in situ*.

HIERACOME: an oracle of **Apollo** in Caria, W Turkey. Hieracome stood near to ancient Tralles (37 45N, 27 53E), the site of which is adjacent to modern Aydin. It is said that the oracles here were delivered in verse, but exactly where 'here' was is unknown. The name Hieracome means 'sacred village', and might have been applied by Greek colonists to an oracle they found already established when they arrived. The museum at Aydin contains a variety of finds from around the region, but was closed in 2001. The ruins of Tralles stand to the N of the town. There is very little to be seen there, but it could once boast its own temple of **Asclepius**.

HIERAPOLIS: oracles of **Pluto** and **Apollo** in Phrygia, W Turkey (37 55N, 29 18E). Hierapolis is one of the most popular archaeological sites in Turkey, but it is better known as Pamukkale. Its most impressive features are its chalk terraces, which are what most come to explore. There are also many well-preserved tombs to be seen. The remains of the oracles that once functioned here may be less impressive, but they exist and are easily found a little to the E of the Pamukkale Motel. The connection between the two oracles is not easy to fathom. The excavated ruins of the temple of Apollo date from a third-century AD construction. **Strabo** [XIII.4.14] visited the place (probably in the first century BC) and makes no mention of it. He does refer to a temple in the vicinity, but it seems to have been dedicated to **Cybele**. Inscriptions found on the site point to oracular activity going back as far as the second century BC, and some of the materials used in the construction of Apollo's temple have clearly been reused from an earlier building. These materials indicate that at least two different kinds of oracle functioned here at one time or another. First, there are the remnants of a **letter** oracle. Secondly, there are parts of an oracular response in verse which has clearly been prompted by a specific enquiry. This probably dates to the second century AD. Apollo is referred to in this response by the **epithet** Careius. The temple itself survived until at least the fifth century, but it is most unlikely that Apollo was still being consulted by this time.

The other oracle on the site was under the temple. It comprised an opening in the ground which extended some way into the hill. Deadly vapours emerged from this chasm, and even to go near it could be fatal. Entrance to it is still barred today, although nothing particularly noxious seems to emanate from it. Exactly how this place functioned as an oracle is unclear, although there are obvious similarities with the institution not too far away at **ACHARACA**. When Strabo visited the place, the chasm was cordoned off by a handrail beyond which it was dangerous to pass. According to him, only the eunuch priests of Cybele, who were known as Galli, could enter the chasm without suffering harm. As with **HIERACOME**, the name Hierapolis may indicate a pre-Greek origin for the oracle. The city itself does not seem to have been particularly ancient, probably dating to no earlier than the late fourth century BC.

Fragments of a statue of **Asclepius** have been found at the site (and are in the museum there), but no sanctuary of the god has been found. However, excavations continue and may yet reveal one.

KASTABOS: see **CASTABUS**
KLAROS: see **CLAROS**
KNIDOS: see **CNIDUS**
KYANEAI: see **CYANEAE**
KYME: see **CYME**
KYZIKOS: see **CYZICUS**

LABRANDA or **LABRAYNDA** or **LABRAUNDA**: an oracle of **Zeus** in Caria, SW Turkey (37 25N, 27 45E). As with the sites of many oracles, Labranda was a sanctuary rather than a town. It is situated 13 km NW of Milas (ancient Mylasa), which usually enjoyed control over the sanctuary, and to which it was joined by a sacred way. Some parts of this can still be traced. The site is an ancient and impressive one, although most of what is visible there now dates from the fourth century BC. During that time two of its benefactors were **Mausolus** and his brother. The site is also a steep one, and buildings are perched on it at different levels. The temple of Zeus itself is at the N (higher) end. More interesting from an oracular point of view, however, are the ruins that lie about 200 m to the SE of it, and almost 100 m below. This was a two-storey building, much of which is still standing, set right on the perimeter of the sanctuary precinct. It is known that special bejewelled fish were kept at the sanctuary, and it is thought that this building might have been their home. It is also thought that they may have functioned as some kind of oracle here. (There were certainly other fish oracles, for example at **SURA** and **LIMYRA**.) But how the oracle functioned is not known, and some would dispute that there ever was one here at all.

LIMYRA: an oracle of **Apollo** and an oracle of **letters** in Lycia, S Turkey (36 20N, 30 12E). The ruins of Limyra lie 4 km E of modern Turunçova, which is 6 km N of Finike on the S Turkish coast. The site is quite an extensive one. On the higher side of the modern road are the theatre and the acropolis above it, on the lower, the remains of a **Byzantine** monastery and a large structure whose identification is uncertain. Somewhat bizarrely, a later wall was built right through the middle of it. The oracle of Apollo here made use of fish, with responses being indicated by the way in which the creatures reacted to the food given to them, whether they ate it or rejected it. The oracle at Limyra evidently enjoyed some celebrity, and there was a time when it was advertised on local coinage. It is said that the oracle moved around, but it is not clear exactly how this happened. However, there are a number of springs in the lower part of the site, and it is possible that there were several sacred pools inhabited by the fish, with different ones being used at different times. Or perhaps there were linked pools, with the fish moving from one to another.

An oracle of letters was found here in the nineteenth century, but its precise location is unclear. Such oracles were frequently carved onto the walls of tombs, and there are hundreds of tombs in the area, especially on the hill of the acropolis. A number of them are highly decorated, and many bear inscriptions. A full investigation of them all would be a lengthy task. Near the top of the hill, but outside the acropolis proper, are the remains of a Byzantine church. It may stand on the site of an earlier temple of **Sarapis**.

MAGNESIA ON THE MAEANDER: an oracle of **Apollo** in Lydia, W Turkey (37 40N, 27 32E). What is left of Magnesia lies about 14 km NE of Söke, and 25 km directly inland from the resort of Kusadasi. The most obvious features of the site are the city's **Byzantine** walls. It was famous in antiquity for its magnificent temple of **Artemis**, and the ruins of this can also be seen. Excavations have been going on here since 1984, and a number of further buildings have been brought to light. The oracle seems to have been located in a cave somewhere outside the city, but exactly where is unknown. The problem of finding it is complicated by the fact that the city itself was relocated in around 400 BC, and its previous site has not been found. However, it is evident from what **Pausanias** says [X.32.4] that the cult of Apollo in and around Magnesia had some very unusual features. It seems to have had a distinctly shamanistic dimension, with some devotees apparently acquiring almost superhuman physical powers. The area near the city boasts a large number of burial mounds. It may be that one of these was the 'cave' in question, and that the oracle was originally associated with shamanism and the **dead**, only later becoming attached to Apollo.

MALLUS or **MALLOS**: oracles of **Amphilochus** and **Mopsus** in Cilicia, S Turkey (36 40N, 35 22E). The site of ancient Mallus is near modern Kiziltahta, about 15 km NE of Karatas, the site of Mallus' former port. However, the river Ceyhan (known to the ancients as the Pyramos) has changed its course and now enters the gulf of Alexandria a few km to the E of Karatas. Unfortunately, Kiziltahta seems to have been substantially built from the materials of Mallus, so there is nothing left to see. In its time, however, Mallus was a place of considerable significance. **Alexander the Great** made a point of visiting it, and according to **Pausanias** [I.34.2], who was certainly a connoisseur of these matters, the shrine of Amphilochus there was the most reliable oracle of his day. **Amphiaraus**, the father of Amphilochus, also had an oracle, at **OROPOS**, while there was another oracle of Amphilochus in **AKARNANIA**, but this may have belonged to another with the same name. At Mallus, questions were put to Amphilochus in writing, and his charges were very reasonable.

Mopsus was said to be the grandson of **Teiresias**, and either the nephew or half-brother of Amphilochus. He came to be associated in some way with **CLAROS**, but had much stronger connections with the area around Mallus. About 30 km to the NE of Mallus are the remains of Mopsuestia, which means 'the hearth of Mopsus'. An eighth-century BC inscription (written in Hittite and Phoenician) found further NE at Karatepe has a king identifying himself as a descendant of Mopsus. This would suggest that Amphilochus was a comparative newcomer, and one legend certainly treats him as something of an intruder. According to **Plutarch**, there was a story that Mopsus was once able to answer a question before it had even been put.

Amphilochus and Mopsus set up a dream oracle at Mallus, but at some point they fell out, and may even have killed each other. In any event, their tombs were respectfully positioned so that one could not be seen from the other. In his account of Alexander's visit, **Arrian** [II.6] makes no mention of Mopsus, and **Pausanias** shows no knowledge of any oracle at Mallus apart from that of Amphilochus. It may be that the newcomer's oracle lasted the longer of the two. Or perhaps the two underwent a posthumous reconciliation and operated as a joint venture.

MELAENAE or MELAINAI: a sanctuary of **Asclepius** in Lysia, W Turkey. The site of Melaenae is unknown, but it seems to have lain to the N of Edremit, ancient Adramyttium (39 34N, 26 58E). It is mentioned by **Strabo** [XIII.1.44] who describes the place itself as a village but notes that it has an **Asclepeion** founded by Lysimachus. He was one of **Alexander the Great**'s generals, who carved out a kingdom for himself based around Thrace when Alexander died. He himself died in battle in 281 BC at the age of eighty. Somewhere near the village of Zeybekçayiri, 30 km due N of Edremit, is a possible location, but Strabo's directions are very imprecise.

MILETUS: a sanctuary of **Sarapis** in Caria, W Turkey (37 31N, 27 15E). Miletus (now known as Milet) lies near the village of Balat, about 18 km N of **DIDYMA**, to which it was connected by a sacred way. The sanctuary of Didyma was always under the control of the city of Miletus. The temple of Sarapis lies in the SW of the site, just to the W of the S **agora**. It seems to have been a very late construction, perhaps dating to the third century AD. The museum at the site contains some striking sculptures of the god taken from it. It is thought that there may also have been a sanctuary of **Asclepius** at Miletus, but so far it has eluded discovery. Miletus was famous in antiquity for producing some of the earliest figures in the history of western philosophy. **Thales** is usually regarded as the very first philosopher, and he was a native of the city.

NEOCAESAREA: an oracle of Men in Pontus, NE Turkey (40 35N, 36 59E). Neocaesarea was also known as Cabeira, but is now known as Niksar and lies about 55 km NE of Tokat. The origins of the cult of Men, a moon god with a special interest in healing, are unclear, but it appears to have been introduced to Neocaesarea in the early second century BC. The city was also the home of Gregory Thaumaturgus ('the miracle worker'), the third-century AD saint and theologian. According to his biographer, oracles were still on offer at the temple during Gregory's time. He paid a visit there, worked one of his miracles, and converted Men's prophet to Christianity. Nothing remains of the temple, but there is a medieval castle in Niksar that incorporates earlier elements.

NIKOMEDIA: a sanctuary of **Asclepius** and another of **Isis** in Bithynia, NW Turkey (40 48N, 30 05E). **Pausanias** [III.3.8] makes the most fleeting of references to this place. The site of Nikomedia is now occupied by Izmit, and is at the far E end of the Sea of Marmara. The only ruins to be seen *in situ* are medieval. All else is in the local museum. For over 500 years, from its foundation in the third century BC, it was a flourishing and important city. Its decline was mainly due to a combination of earthquakes and the foundation of Constantinople nearby.

OLYMPUS: oracles of **letters** in Lycia, S Turkey (36 19N, 30 32E). What is left of Olympus lies about 30 km E of Kumluca. Once remote and difficult to reach, the area around the ruins is now becoming a popular, if still modest, resort. The site lies on either side of a seasonal stream, where it meets the sea. Because it is overgrown, exploration and identification of buildings can be difficult. The oracles lie away from the centre of the ruins, to the SW where there are hundreds of tombs on the hillside. Two of them have letter oracles carved into their stonework. Exactly how a letter was chosen is not clear. Presumably the presence of these oracles on tombs indicates that the descendants of the occupants came to seek posthumous advice from their ancestors. While some of the responses are the same on each tomb, some are different. Most of the responses, however, amount to the advice either to go ahead with what is planned, or to refrain from doing so. The easier tomb to find is the vaulted structure on top of the outcrop of rock that stands across the stream from the ticket booth at the entrance to the site. The oracle is inscribed on the short pillar to the left-hand side of the opening to the tomb itself, and much of it is legible. Three examples of its helpful advice as translated by John Opsopaus are:

> Z (zeta, sixth letter): 'Flee the very great storm, lest you be disabled in some way.'

H (eta, seventh letter): 'Bright Helios [Sun], who watches everything, watches you.'

Θ (theta, eighth letter): 'You have the helping gods of this path.'[2]

Interestingly, the responses of this letter oracle are identical with those at **LIMYRA**, and about a third of them are identical with those at **ADADA**. This suggests that such oracles drew on a limited and oft-repeated repertoire.

PANAMARA: an oracle of **Zeus** in Caria, W Turkey (37 15N, 28 10E). The remains of Panamara lie on a hilltop site about 12 km SE of Eskihisar, and 15 km W of Mugla. The site is rarely visited and remains unexcavated. What can be seen mainly comprises stretches of wall and a ruined building. Although Zeus was the principal god of this sanctuary, others were worshipped at it too, including **Sarapis**. Little is known of the early history of the place, although its origins are thought to be very old. The sanctuary was a possession of **STRATONICEIA**, to which it was linked by a paved road, and it is there that clear evidence of the oracle's existence has been found. An inscription, probably from the third century AD, records the reply of Zeus of Panamara to an inquiry put to him by the people of Stratoniceia. How and how often the god replied to inquirers is not known. What is known is that there was an annual ten-day festival dedicated to the god during which his cult statue was carried from Panamara to Stratoniceia on the back of a bull. It is possible that consultations only took place at this time of the year.

PATARA: an oracle of **Apollo** in Lycia, S Turkey (36 12N, 29 21E). Ancient Patara lies on the Mediterranean coast, about 50 km SE of Fethiye. The nearby modern village of Gelemis is also sometimes known as Patara. The site lies between the village and the beach. Like **DELOS** and **TEGYRA**, Patara claimed to be the birthplace of Apollo. It was also said that when the oracle at **DELPHI** closed during the winter it was because the god had gone to Patara. It therefore seems likely that the oracle here only functioned at this time, although quite how long its season lasted is not clear. **Herodotus** [I.182] says that the priestess was shut up in the temple at night when the oracle was open for business. This might mean that her dreams were the god's medium. (On the other hand, the same god's oracle at **CLAROS** also functioned after dark, and dreams had no role to play there.) While it evidently enjoyed a high

---

[2]The full translation, along with an introduction and annotations, can be found at: http://www.cs.utk.edu/~mclennan/BA/LAO.html. The translation was actually made from the text copied from Limyra, but it has been found to be in perfect agreement with the Olympus inscription, so far as the latter is decipherable.

reputation for a very long time, no actual oracular pronouncements have been recorded.

As is often the case, the origins of the oracle here are obscure. It does, however, seem clear that it went into a serious decline during the late centuries BC, and perhaps closed down altogether at the end of the first century BC. Nevertheless, it was revived, at least in part due to the benevolence of **Opramoas of Rhodiapolis**, and was certainly active in the second century AD. Thereafter its precise fate is uncertain, but it presumably shared that of all such institutions at the end of the fourth century AD, if it survived until then. The city itself survived into the Christian era, and St Nicholas (aka Santa Claus) was born here.

To date, three possible candidates have been put forward as the site of the oracle. The first is the small hill to the W of the monumental triple-arched gateway through which the site is entered. Parts of a giant statue of Apollo were found there, but the area has not been properly excavated. The second is a curious 'cistern' on top of the hill behind the theatre. This suggestion seems to be based on little more than its very unusual design, indicating it may have had a special purpose. How it might have functioned as an oracle, however, is not at all apparent, and it is difficult to reconcile a location here with the testimony of Herodotus. The third is the small temple (dated to the second century AD) that lies about halfway between the gateway and the theatre. As the only temple so far discovered at the site, the temptation to identify it with that of Apollo is obvious. However, ancient Patara had more than one temple, and no description of that dedicated to Apollo has survived. There is consequently no particular reason to suppose that this temple belonged to him as opposed to another god. Indeed, given the importance of his cult here, something on a rather grander scale would be expected. Consequently, none of the three candidates has a decisive claim. Whether continuing excavations at the site will change that or turn up a better one remains to be seen.

PERGAMON: sanctuaries of **Asclepius** and **Sarapis** in Mysia, W Turkey (39 03N, 27 13E). Pergamon (modern Bergama) was one of the great centres of the cult of Asclepius, rivalled only by **EPIDAUROS** and **KOS** on the Greek mainland and islands respectively. Pergamon led a relatively independent existence until its last king bequeathed it to Rome on his deathbed in 133 BC. A sanctuary of Asclepius was established here in the fourth century BC. The site on which it was built had previously been the sanctuary of another god, whose identity is not known, but who may also have been a healer. Most of what can be seen at the site today dates from a second-century AD rebuilding programme, when it was reconstructed and embellished on a grand scale. The principal ruins of Pergamon itself stand to the NE of the modern town, but the **Asclepeion** is to the W of it. The sanctuary was linked to the other parts of the city by a sacred way, sections of which can still be seen. Unusually, the temple here is round, its design based on that of the Pantheon in Rome. It was built in 150 AD at the personal expense of Cuspius Pactumeius Rufinus, a prominent politician, and stands on the E side of a large courtyard. There is a second, two-storeyed, round building next to it that seems to have played some role in the healing process, but exactly what role is a matter of dispute. Some have claimed it to be the temple of **Telesphorus**. A tunnel connects it to the centre of the courtyard. At the NW corner of the complex is a well-preserved theatre. The courtyard is surrounded by the remains of **stoas**, and within it are the sparse ruins of a variety of buildings, most of them now difficult to identify. One or more of them must have served as an **abaton**, and there were also small temples to **Apollo** and **Hygeia**, among others. Water evidently played an important role in the functioning of the sanctuary. What may be the original sacred spring (opinions differ) is near its NW corner, with places for bathing in and taking the waters nearby.

Aelius Aristides spent some time here and left a literary record of his experiences. (According to Aelius, this was in accordance with the wishes of none other than the god himself.) From what he says, it is evident that a wide range of healing activities were practised, with the ritual of **incubation** being merely one among many means available. Special diets, bathing, strenuous exercise and bloodletting are some of the treatments he describes. It is evident that some people might stay at the sanctuary for a considerable period of time, perhaps months, and that medically trained assistance was at hand as well as divine intervention. One of the greatest medical experts of antiquity, **Galen**, was born in Pergamon and worked at the sanctuary before moving to **ROME**. However, divine guidance, when it was sought, was not limited to medical matters. Aelius reveals that Asclepius could also provide some coaching for a boxer during incubation. He also indicates that Asclepius was helped in his work by Telesphorus, who had his own temple and priests somewhere within the complex.

For most practical purposes the history of the Asclepeion of Pergamon ended with an earthquake at the end of the third century. The sanctuary sustained very substantial damage, and only managed to limp along for a few more decades after that.

In the middle of modern Bergama there is a building known as Kizil Avlu ('Red Courtyard') because of the colour of its brickwork. It is situated astride a small river and still stands to an impressive height. It is thought that this was a temple to Sarapis and other Egyptian gods. It dates to the second century AD, and is the largest structure surviving from ancient Pergamon. At its E end there is a large plinth which was presumably designed to support the cult statue. Some think that the statue was hollow and that a cavity found beneath the plinth was used by priests to deliver oracles through its mouth, although it is not entirely clear how this could have been done.

Also in modern Bergama is a modest museum of local finds. These include a selection of **votive** objects unearthed at the Asclepeion.

POEMANENOS or **POIMANENON**: a sanctuary of **Asclepius** in Mysia, NW Turkey (40 01N, 28 00E). The scant unexcavated remains of Poemanenos can be found near the village of Eski Manyas, about 45 km by road S of Bandirma. Its main claim to fame is that **Aelius Aristides**, something of a connoisseur in these matters, made special mention of the place as having 'a temple of Asclepius both holy and renowned' (Edelstein 1975, I, p. 417). Little is known about the history of the place, although it enjoyed sufficient status to have its own bishop by 450.

PRIENE: a sanctuary of **Isis** and **Sarapis** in Caria, W Turkey (37 37N, 27 19E). Priene is now known as Prien, and lies on the high ground above the small town of Güllübahçe, about 14 km SW of Söke. It is notable for being an early and fine example of a planned city, and is laid out in the form of a grid, following the principles of **Hippodamus**. It was built from scratch to replace an earlier city, whose site has not been found. The new city was under construction when **Alexander the Great** passed through the area in 334 BC, and he made a personal contribution to the costs of the project.

The site is a dramatic one, and attracts large numbers of visitors. However, the sanctuary of the Egyptian Gods, as it is known, is not one of Priene's major attractions. Lying in the NE part of the city, it consists of an open space with scant remains of a monumental gateway and surrounding buildings. Within it can be found the substantial ruins of the sanctuary's altar. A stone was found here (no longer *in situ*) that gave details of how rituals were to be conducted, and of what would happen if they were performed incorrectly. Some have interpreted this to mean that the cult followed practices unfamiliar to the Greeks, hence their need to be reminded of them in this way.

SARPEDON: an oracle of **Artemis** in Cilicia, S Turkey. Sarpedon was the name given to a promontory near Liman Kalesi, about 10 km SW of Silifke (36 22N, 33 59E). It took its name from that of the legendary king (and son of **Zeus**), who was said to have conquered this area and in which he enjoyed a posthumous hero cult. **Strabo** [XIV.5.19] talks of an oracle of Sarpedonian Artemis, but does not specifically locate it on Sarpedon itself. Since there was a temple of Sarpedonian **Apollo** in **SELEUCIA**, it is entirely possible that there was an oracle of Sarpedonian Artemis that was not on Sarpedon either. As he mentions the oracle directly after referring to the area to the E and S of **AIGAI (2)**, it may be that it was situated somewhere in that region. In any event, there is nothing to be seen at Liman Kalesi from ancient times, although there are the remains of a fourteenth-century Turkish fortress there.

SELEUCIA: an oracle of **Apollo** in Cilicia, S. Turkey (36 22N, 33 59E). Seleucia ad Calycadnum, to give it its full name, occupied the site of modern Silifke, and there are some remains of it to be seen in the modern town. The ancient city was probably founded in the early third century BC, and the earliest literary mention of an oracle there dates from the first century BC. However, the only temple that has survived and been identified is one dedicated to **Zeus** built in the second century AD. It is handily located near the bus station.

SIDYMA: an oracle of **Apollo** in Lycia, S Turkey (36 25N, 29 10E). The ruins of Sidyma lie in and around the modern village of Dodurga, about 20 km due S of Fethiye. Little is known of the city's history. It is thought to have been a place of some antiquity, but what can be seen today is mainly of Roman construction. Some stretches of wall remain, along with some tombs and a ruined theatre. A temple dedicated to the emperors was found here, but is now barely discernible. There is no indication of a temple to Apollo, and some dispute the existence of an oracle here at all.

SINOPE: an oracle of **Autolycus** in Paphlagonia, N Turkey (42 01N, 35 11E). Sinope lay on the Black Sea, and its modern successor Sinop stands on top of it. One of the ancient city's claims to fame was as the birthplace of **Diogenes**, the celebrated Cynic philosopher. Autolycus was said to be the son of **Hermes**, the grandfather of **Odysseus**, and one of the **Argonauts**. Indeed, he is said to have joined the **Argo** at Sinope. Although there is therefore a clear connection between him and the city, it is not known how he came to have an oracle here, or, indeed, an oracle at all. The legends surrounding him suggest that he had a reputation as a cunning thief rather than as a seer. Nevertheless, the existence of his oracle at Sinope is clearly indicated (in the past tense) by **Strabo** [XII.3.11]. It is thought that **incubation** was the method used at Autolycus' shrine. No trace of it has been found, but the remains of a second-century BC temple of **Sarapis** can be seen near the middle of the modern town. The cult seems to have had a significant following in Sinope.

Tacitus even believed it originated here, but this is generally regarded as incorrect. However, since incubation was also practised in many sanctuaries of Sarapis, and given that it was by no means unknown for an oracle to change affiliations, it is entirely possible that the temple of Sarapis was built on the site of the earlier shrine of Autolycus. A museum with a display of local finds is near the temple.

SMYRNA (modern Izmir): an oracle of **omens** and a sanctuary of **Asclepius** in Lydia, W Turkey (38 25N, 27 08E). According to **Pausanias** [IX.11.5] the sanctuary of omens was outside and above the city. Unfortunately, there is very little left of the city of his time, and so it is by no means easy to be sure where it ended. However, it is known that the city had previously been relocated in the fourth century BC. Its first site was in the modern city's suburb of Bayrakli, which lies at the NE corner of the Bay of Izmir. There, on a small hill called Tepekule, is what has been found of Old Smyrna. It is possible to see, among other things, the remains of a temple of **Athena** dating to the seventh century BC, built atop an impressive terrace. This is the oldest Greek temple found in Asia so far. Oracles tended not to move, so if the sanctuary of omens was an ancient one, it may have been on or around Tepekule, which could be construed as being both above and outside the later city. How it operated is not clear, but it may have resembled the oracle of **Hermes** at **PHARAI (1)** where the first words heard by an enquirer after leaving the sanctuary constituted the required omen. In the case of Smyrna, however, Pausanias does not mention the name of any hero or deity connected with the oracle, which is unusual.

The whereabouts of the sanctuary of Asclepius is also problematic. The topographical indications given by Pausanias [VII.5.3] have so far eluded satisfactory interpretation. A possible candidate is the place known as the Baths of Agamemnon, about 11 km W of Izmir, about 1 km S of the road to Çesme. Here there are some hot mineral springs, and **Aelius Aristides** says that Asclepius began to prophesy here. It would be a logical choice of location for one of his sanctuaries, but there is no evidence to prove that it was. What little can be seen at the site is too recent to be of any assistance in identification.

There is literary evidence, also from Aelius Aristides, that there was a temple of **Isis** in the city, and he claims to have witnessed a ceremony there. Unfortunately, there are no clues as to its whereabouts.

The museum in Izmir has a very extensive display of items found both locally and further afield, with useful general information about many of the archaeological sites in the region.

SOLI: a sanctuary of **Asclepius** in Cilicia, S Turkey (36 46N, 34 35E). The site of Soli lies at Viransehir, about 12 km SW of Mersin (which is also known as Içel). Its Turkish name means 'ruined city', which is entirely appropriate. A row of columns is its most conspicuous landmark, although there are many other unexcavated remains lying around and about. The only thing known about the sanctuary of Asclepius is that, according to **Arrian** [II.5], **Alexander the Great** sacrificed to the god on his passage through here in 333 BC. Traditionally, the inhabitants of the city spoke very ungrammatical Greek, and their shortcomings have been perpetuated in the word 'solecism'. After some unhappy years, the city was refounded in 67 BC by **Pompey** and its grateful citizens celebrated this fact by renaming it Pompeiopolis.

STRATONICEIA: a sanctuary of **Sarapis** in Caria, W Turkey (37 20N, 28 03E). The remains of Stratoniceia lie under and around the village of Eskihisar, about 30 km E of Milas. The city was founded around 270 BC by **Antiochus I** of Syria and named in honour of his wife Stratonice. She had previously been his stepmother, but he was fortunate in having a very understanding father. The remains are quite substantial, although they are threatened by mining activities in the area and access can be problematic. Eskihisar itself is almost a ghost town. The most striking building here is the one known as the temple of Sarapis, which is in the centre of the site (although some believe that it housed the city council rather than a god, an interesting and unusual confusion). It was built around 200 AD, and still stands to a reasonable height. Inscriptions on its N wall commemorate thanks offered by the people of Stratoniceia to **Helios-Zeus**-Sarapis for his protection. An oracle delivered by Zeus of **PANAMARA** is also recorded here. The sanctuary of Zeus at Panamara, to the SE of the city, belonged to Stratoniceia, and was linked to it by a paved road.

SURA: an oracle of **Apollo** in Lycia, S Turkey (36 16N, 29 40E). Sura lies about 4 km W of Kale (which is also known as Demre). Its small acropolis stands near the side of the road, with a few unimpressive ruins on its summit. At its foot are inscriptions carved into the rock recording the names of numerous priests who served at Apollo's temple here. The temple itself lies at the foot of the cliff behind the acropolis, about 100 m and a difficult descent below. It stands on marshy ground, and is usually waterlogged. It is modest in size, but its rear wall still stands to its full height. Inside it there are more inscriptions, although, curiously, not all are to Apollo. The oracle here was a very celebrated one, involving fish. Exactly how the oracle worked is not known. However, for once the problem is too much rather than too little information, as ancient sources conflict. Some claim that it was the behaviour of fish as they ate the food given to them that was observed, others that it was the species of fish that came for the food that was the deciding factor. Whichever it was it seems that the observations took place somewhere in front of the temple, where there was a small whirlpool. Once sea, this area is now marshland. A short distance away from the temple to the NE is a spring that may have contributed in some way to this phenomenon. Its abundant waters, smelling faintly of sulphur, still swirl around the temple's foundations. Nearby are the remains of a **Byzantine** church of uncertain date. Indeed, little is known of the history of either the city or the oracle.

SYRNA: a sanctuary of **Asclepius** in Caria, SW Turkey (36 42N, 28 10E). The site of Syrna lies at Bayir, about 15 km SW of Marmaris as the crow flies, but rather further should the crow choose to walk. There is next to nothing to see there now, but it enjoyed an important status in antiquity. According to legend, the city was founded by none other than **Podaleirius**, the son of Asclepius himself; hence the sanctuary here had a special connection with the god. Syrna was the name of his wife. It is said that he first met her when she had fallen off a roof. After nursing her back to health, he married her. In Bayir's mosque there is a carved marble slab which clearly came from the sanctuary. The inscription on it has been dated to around 200 BC and it records the contributions made to some building work that was carried out at the sanctuary. Sadly, but scarcely surprisingly, the work itself has not survived.

TARSUS: an oracle of **Apollo** in Cilicia, S Turkey (36 54N, 34 58E). Ancient Tarsus is mainly to be found (or rather not found) under the modern city of the same name. Famous as the place where **Antony** met **Cleopatra**, and the home town of **St Paul**, there is little of its history visible. The small local museum displays some of the results of excavations. It is not certain that the cult of Apollo was oracular here, but whether it was or not it has left no traces of its existence.

TEFENNI: a **dice** oracle in Phrygia, W Turkey (37 18N, 29 45E). Tefenni lies about 70 km SW of Burdur. Its ancient name is unknown, and there is no evidence that there was ever any significant settlement here in antiquity. The nearest of any size were Olbasa to the E and Saraganda to the S. Unless the oracle came from either of them, why it should have turned up in Tefenni is a complete mystery. It was found and recorded in 1884, inscribed on a large stone being used as the base for a wooden column. Five dice were used to consult it, and twenty responses could be seen, although there must have been more. Its present whereabouts are unclear. Most of Tefenni's few visitors today come to see the nearby rock reliefs.

TELMESSOS or **TELMISSUS**: an oracle of **Apollo** in Caria, SW Turkey. Telmessos lay about 11 km from ancient Halicarnassus, modern Bodrum. It is thought to have been situated on a hill just to the N of the modern village of Gürice (37 04N, 27 20E), W of Bodrum, on the road to Turgutreis. Some walls, some tombs, and the lower levels of a tower can be found there, but nothing resembling a temple. Telmessos not only had an oracle of Apollo, but the inhabitants of the place were said to be particularly talented in the divinatory arts. **Herodotus** [I.78-84] says that **Croesus** sent a messenger there to interpret an **omen** he had witnessed. Unfortunately, by the time the messenger returned Croesus had become a prisoner of the Persians. The town itself seems to have declined after the founding of Halicarnassus, but the oracle probably continued to function for some time after this. This Telmessos is not to be confused with the other city of the same name, which lay on the site of modern Fethiye, and which boasts some impressive tombs of its own. Halicarnassus itself had a temple of **Isis**, but nothing remains of it.

TERMESSOS: a **dice** oracle in Pisidia, S Turkey (36 50N, 30 15E). The ruins of ancient Termessos lie about 25 km NW of Antalya, in the Güllükdagi National Park. Although the city was probably of considerable antiquity, the first mention of it in historical sources is in connection with the campaign of **Alexander the Great** in the area in 333 BC. The ruins are extensive. However, because they lie in a national park, the vegetation around them is allowed to grow relatively unconstrained. Temples, tombs and a theatre can all be found within the city's walls, which are themselves well-preserved in places. The walls do not seem to have existed in Alexander's time, and were perhaps built in the second century BC. Where the main road from the NE entered the city there was a substantial gateway, and the dice oracle was located on the inner side of this. The modern path from the car park up to the ruins follows the same route. The gateway has totally collapsed, but some of its stones remain where they fell, and some inscriptions can still just about be made out on a few of them. This dice oracle required seven dice to be thrown, producing 120 possible outcomes, with each outcome having a verse corresponding to it inscribed on the wall. Only a few verses have been found. Most oracles of this kind tend to be comprised of many different variations on 'do it' and 'don't do it'. One of the surviving examples at Termessos reads:

Cronos the Child-Eater
Three fours and two sixes. This is the god's advice:
Stay at home and go not elsewhere,
Lest the destructive Beast and avenging Fury come upon you;
For I see that the business is neither safe nor secure. (Bean 1989d, p. 99)

The oracle may be significantly later than the wall itself, perhaps dating from the second century AD when such institutions were apparently very popular and when the road seems to have been constructed.

THERMAI PHAZOMENITON: a sanctuary of **Asclepius** in Pontus, N Turkey (40 58N, 35 38E). The site of Thermai Phazomeniton is now known as Havza, and lies about 80 km SW of Samsun. In ancient times it was famous for its springs. Inscriptions have been found there that clearly indicate that it was a centre of the cult of Asclepius. Unfortunately there are no ruins of the sanctuary, or of any other buildings from antiquity, to be seen.

THYATIRA: see **DALDIS**

THYMBRA: an oracle of **Apollo** in Mysia, NW Turkey. The precise location of Thymbra is uncertain. It seems to have lain a little to the N of **Troy** (39 54N, 26 15E), and according to one legend it was the place where **Achilles** died. Nowhere seems to quite fit all the clues to its location. Since a tumulus to the NW of Troy, near the coast, is said to be that of Achilles, and the remains of a town named after him lie a little to the N of it, somewhere in this area seems likely.

THYMBRIA: an oracle of **Pluto** in Caria, W Turkey (37 35N, 27 26E). The evidence for an oracle here is somewhat slight, but its existence is clearly suggested by some comments of **Strabo** [XIV.1.10]. He mentions a town called Myus, the remains of which can be found 15 km E of **MILETUS**. He then goes on to say that about 1 km outside it, to the N, there is a place called Aornum, with a sacred cave called the Charonium which emitted deadly vapours. The combination of names and factors makes it difficult to doubt that here, as at **ACHARACA**, there was at some time an oracular cult of Pluto, perhaps specialising in healing. Strabo makes no mention of this fact, which may mean that it had already ceased to function.

TRALLES: see **HIERACOME**

ZELEIA: an oracle of **Apollo** in Mysia, NW Turkey. Zeleia seems to have been at or near the site of modern Sariköy (40 16N, 27 36E), about 45 km W of Bandirma. The existence of an oracle here at some time is clearly attested by **Strabo** [XIII.1.13]. Unfortunately all he reveals about it is that it had ceased to function before his time. Today there is nothing to be seen of Zeleia either. **Alexander the Great** passed this way and registered a notable victory over the Persians not far from the city.

UKRAINE

LEUCE: a healing sanctuary of **Achilles** in S Ukraine (44 15N, 30 08E). Here the hero of the Trojan War was consulted through the medium of dreams. Quite how the temperamental warrior became transformed into a healer after his death is unclear. However, there was a tradition that Achilles had been brought up by **Chiron**, a notable practitioner of the medical arts, so there is some connection between his two careers, however tenuous. There is also a theory that the sanctuary here might have been originally dedicated to **Jason**, but that he was subsequently supplanted by Achilles.

The location of Leuce is a matter of dispute. It is agreed by all that it was an island in the Black Sea. However, while some would place it opposite the delta of the Danube, others claim it lay further to the N and E, near the estuaries of the Dniester or Dnieper. The Danubian candidate is today known as Ostrov Zmeiny ('Serpent's Island'), and lies about 30 km E of the delta. (Although presently in the possession of Ukraine, its ownership is disputed by Romania.) The presence of a large military base on the island means that access to it is tightly controlled. However, those who explored the island in the early nineteenth century observed the ruins of a very substantial temple there, as well as those of other buildings. According to tradition, the sanctuary of Achilles was very extensive, and the ruins on Ostrov Zmeiny are apparently on the same scale and of the same complexity. Although not conclusive, the evidence for identifying Ostrov Zmeiny with Leuce has some strength. The alternative claim to its location is suggested partly by a different reading of surviving texts, but also partly by indications of the cult of Achilles being particularly strong in the area around the Dnieper estuary.

Wherever the precise location of the healing sanctuary, it is evident that Achilles was venerated around the NW part of the Black Sea, and games in his honour were held in the region.

UNITED KINGDOM

AQUAE SULIS: a healing sanctuary of **Sulis Minerva** in W England (51 24N, 02 20W). Now known as Bath, this was a major healing centre of Roman Britain, although its origins are clearly earlier. Before Minerva arrived it was the domain of the Celtic goddess Sulis, and the two names are often found joined together here. The Roman complex took shape in the first century AD and was in use until at least the fifth. At the heart of it, both physically and religiously, was the sacred spring. Around this a reservoir was built, which in turn was surrounded by a number of buildings, including a large temple. One of the curious features of this particular site is the evidence indicating that some who came seeking the goddess' intercession had things other than health on their minds. A lead tablet was found there on which there is an inscription written backwards. It calls for a curse to be put on the unknown person guilty of a particular crime, which appears to have been some kind of abduction. It is also known that the complex supported a school of haruspices, people who practised the ancient art of divination through examining the entrails of sacrificed animals.

NODENS: a healing sanctuary of **Mars** Nodens in W England (51 43N, 02 31W). The site of this temple is now known as Lydney, 15 km NE of Chepstow. One of the features of the cult of Nodens, the Celtic god sometimes associated with Mars as he was here, is that he was never depicted in human form. Many images of dogs have been found at Lydney, possibly reflecting a perceived association between these animals and healing in antiquity. The sanctuary at Nodens was both large and wealthy. Most of what has been found there dates from the third and fourth centuries AD, and includes a mosaic floor dedicated by one Titus Flavius Senilis, who was a priest there. However, the money that paid for it was not his own, but came from those who visited the sanctuary. It was evidently designed to cope with a substantial number of visitors, and one of the buildings may have been set aside for the practice of **incubation**.

Glossary

Many of the earlier dates given below are matters of keen dispute. I have given those that are most commonly accepted, but it is possible that some may be significantly wide of the mark. Dates are AD unless indicated otherwise.

Abas: a legendary king of **ARGOS**.

abaton: technically this could mean any forbidden area, but in the context of oracles it usually meant a special building set aside for the purposes of incubation.

Achilles: the greatest Greek warrior in the campaign against Troy. Although nearly invulnerable, he was nevertheless killed before the city fell.

Adonis: a legendary Greek hero famed for his physical beauty.

Adrastus: a legendary king of **ARGOS**.

Aelian: first/second-century writer, mainly about celebrities and animals.

Aelius Aristides (d. 189): writer and hypochondriac, a pupil of Herodes Atticus.

Aeneas: according to legend, a prince of Troy who became the founder of Rome. He is the hero of Virgil's epic poem the *Aeneid*.

Agios: a Greek term equivalent to both 'saint' and 'holy'. The feminine form is **Agia**, and the plural form **Agioi**.

agora: an open space used for meetings and markets.

Ahmose I: ruled Egypt 1570-1546 BC, the husband of Ahmose Nefertari and father of Amenhotep I.

Ahmose Nefertari (*c*. 1570-1505 BC): daughter of one pharaoh, wife of another, and mother of a third, she was one of Egypt's more notable queens.

Albunea: a nymph, a prophetess, and perhaps one of the Sibyls.

Alexander the Great: king of Macedonia (and eventually much more) 336-323 BC.

Alexanor: according to legend he was the son of Machaon, grandson of Asclepius and brother of Polemocrates.

Amenhotep I: son of Ahmose Nefertari, he ruled Egypt 1570-1546 BC. He was a successful military leader abroad and keen builder at home.

Ammianus Marcellinus: fourth-century historian.

Amphiaraus: a legendary king of **ARGOS**, he was also a celebrated warrior and prophet. His great-grandfather was another prophet, Melampus.

Amphilochus: two related characters in Greek legend bore this name. One was a son of Amphiaraus, the other a grandson. Confusingly, both went to the Trojan War and both were prophets.

Amun (or **Ammon**): one of the greatest of the Egyptian gods, who came to be identified with both Zeus and Jupiter.

Anios: a legendary king of **DELOS**. A prophet, he predicted the Trojan War would last ten years, which it did.

Antiochus I: king of Syria 280-261 BC.

Antiochus IV Epiphanes: king of Syria 175-163 BC.

Antoninus Pius: Roman emperor 137-61.

Antony [Marcus Antonius]: ally of Julius Caesar, lover of Cleopatra, first friend then enemy of Augustus. He committed suicide in Egypt in 30 BC.

Anubis: an Egyptian god of the dead, usually portrayed with the head of a jackal.

Anyte: a writer of the third century BC, mainly noted for her poems.

Aphrodite: the Greek goddess of love.

Apis: Egyptian bull god, associated with Ptah.

Apollo: the pre-eminent Greek god of oracles, adopted by both the Romans and the Gauls. He was the son of Zeus and Leto, brother of Artemis, and father of Asclepius, Ismenos, and Teneros, among others.

Apollonius of Rhodes: third-century BC author of *The Voyage of Argo*, the most complete surviving version of the story.

Apuleius: second-century author of *Metamorphoses* (also known as *The Golden Ass*) which contains valuable information about the cult of Isis.

Argo: the legendary ship in which Jason and his companions went in search of the golden fleece.

Argonaut: a companion of Jason on his voyage to find the golden fleece.

Aristomachus: the name of a number of minor characters from Greek legend and history. Among them were a famous beekeeper and an authority on wine-making.

Aristophanes: an Athenian writer of comic dramas of the fifth/fourth century BC.

Arkamani: king of Meroë, ruled 218-200 BC. The kingdom of Meroë was located in what is now northern Sudan.

Arrian: second-century AD author who wrote, among other things, a biography of Alexander the Great.

Artemidorus: second-century author of a book on dreams.

Artemis: Greek goddess of the hunt, sister of Apollo, daughter of Zeus and Leto. The Romans identified her with Diana.

Asclepeion: a sanctuary dedicated to Asclepius.

Asclepius: the greatest Greek god of healing. The son of Apollo and a mortal mother, he was also the father of Machaon, Podaleirius and Hygeia. He was taught medicine by the centaur Chiron and became so successful that he could return the dead to life. For this he was killed by Zeus, but subsequently made into a god. The Romans called him Aesculapius.

Astarte: a Phoenician fertility goddess. Her association with love led her to be often identified with Aphrodite.

astralagomancy: a technical term for divination by means of dice. The Greek word for knucklebones, which were used as dice, is *astralagoi*.

Athamas: legendary king of Greek **THEBES**. He was the husband of Ino, and father of Phrixus by an earlier marriage.

Athena: the Greek goddess of wisdom, and principal deity of Athens.

Augustus: founder of the Roman empire and emperor 27 BC – 14 AD.

Aurelian: Roman emperor 270-5.

Autolycus: a son of Hermes, Argonaut, and grandfather of Odysseus. He taught Heracles to wrestle, and was renowned for his cunning.

Bel: a Babylonian god. Technically, Bel was a title (meaning 'lord') rather than a name. It was applied by the Babylonians to their great god Marduk, who was sometimes identified with Zeus.

Glossary

Bes: Egyptian dwarf god especially connected with childbirth, sometimes identified with Priapus.

binary (oracle): any kind of oracle that involves a choice between two alternatives.

Blemmyes: a warlike people inhabiting the Libyan desert. They were a major force to be reckoned with in S Egypt from *c.* 200 until they suffered a decisive defeat in 535.

Borvo (or **Bormo**): a Gaulish god of healing, usually associated with springs. French placenames beginning with 'Bourbonne' often indicate an ancient connection with his cult.

Bryaxis: a fourth-century BC Athenian sculptor. He worked on the original mausoleum, the tomb of Mausolus.

Byzantine: relating to the later Christian Roman empire based around Constantinople, the city founded by Constantine the Great in 330 and captured by the Ottoman Turks in 1453.

Cadmus: according to legend he was both the founder of Greek **THEBES**, and the person who introduced the knowledge of writing into the Greek world.

Caligula: Roman emperor 37-41. A son of Germanicus, he took even excess to excess.

Caracalla: Roman emperor 211-17.

Cassandra: a prophetess, daughter of Priam of Troy. According to one legend, she resisted Apollo's advances. He put a curse on her ensuring that she would always speak the truth but never be believed.

Ceres: Roman goddess of cereal crops and, more broadly, of nature.

Charon: the mythical ferryman who transported the dead to the underworld.

Chiron: a centaur (half man, half horse) famed for his wisdom and medical knowledge.

Cicero: a Roman politician, lawyer, writer and philosopher of the first century BC.

Claudius: Roman emperor 41-54.

Cleopatra (VII): queen of Egypt 48-30 BC, she was the lover first of Julius Caesar and then of Mark Antony.

Clitumnus: a Roman river god.

Constantine the Great: joint Roman emperor 306-23, sole emperor 324-37. He moved the empire's capital to his new city of Constantinople, and was the first Roman emperor to become a Christian.

Constantius II: joint Roman emperor 337-50, sole emperor 350-61, a son of Constantine the Great.

Cosmas and Damian: Christian healing saints. Nothing is known about their lives, but they first attained popularity in the fifth century.

Croesus: sixth-century BC king of Lydia. His wealth was legendary. He also took a keen interest in oracles and, according to Herodotus [1.46ff] sent the same challenging question to seven different ones by way of a test.

Cybele: an earth goddess, originally from Phrygia, Asia Minor, whose cult spread throughout the Greek and Roman worlds.

Damona: a Gaulish goddess of fertility and healing. Although her name means 'great cow', she was portrayed in human form, sometimes with a snake.

Daphne: lusted after by Apollo, she escaped his clutches by being turned into a laurel tree.

dead (oracle of the): a place where it was believed the dead could be consulted. Such places were often located around caves or other openings in the ground.

Demeter: a Greek earth goddess particularly associated with fertility in agriculture. Her daughter was Persephone.

Democritus: fifth-century BC Greek philosopher, one of the first to propose a theory of atoms.

Diana: the Roman goddess of hunting and woods, often identified with Artemis.

dice (oracle): an oracle where dice were thrown to select one of a pre-determined set of responses.

Diocletian: Roman emperor 284-305. Unusually, he voluntarily retired from his high office and did not die until 316.

Diodorus Siculus: first-century BC historian from Sicily who wrote at length about the history of the world from the earliest times to his own.

Diogenes of Sinope: a celebrated philosopher of the fourth century BC who took great delight in shocking his contemporaries with his unconventional behaviour.

Dionysus: Greek god of wine who was associated with intoxication and other states of possession.

Dioscouri: the collective name for Castor and Pollux, sons of Leda. The name means 'sons of Zeus'.

Djoser: ruled Egypt 2668-2649 BC.

dreams (oracle of): a place where responses to inquiries were received in sleep.

Egeria: according to legend she had been the wife of the early Roman king Numa, and later became a water nymph.

Empedocles: philosopher of the fifth century BC who supposedly died by throwing himself into the crater of Mount Etna on his native Sicily.

Ephorus: a Greek historian of the fourth century BC.

epithet: a second name added to that of a god. Sometimes it was connected with a specific location or feature of it, e.g. Apollo Kyparissos, 'of the cypress tree', and Apollo Chresterios, 'of oracles'. Sometimes it indicated that the cults of two different gods had been joined together, e.g. Apollo Grannus.

Esmun: a Phoenician god of healing. His cult became merged with that of Asclepius.

Eusebius (265-340): a bishop of Caesarea in Palestine, he wrote the first history of the Christian church, a biography of Constantine the Great, and an overview of Greek thought.

Faunus: a Roman god of the countryside, especially forests. He was sometimes identified with Pan.

Fortuna: originally a Roman fertility goddess, she later came to be more closely associated with fate.

Galen: a famous second-century physician who produced many medical writings.

Gallus: a nephew of Constantine the Great, he was given responsibility for Syria and surrounding territories by Constantius II, who had him executed in 354.

Ge (or **Gaia**): Greek earth goddess, and mother of most of the early gods.

Germanicus: brother of Claudius and father of Caligula, he died in 19 at the early age of 34, possibly poisoned.

Gorgasus: a son of Machaon, and an Argonaut.

Grannus: a Gaulish god of healing springs whose cult became merged with that of Apollo.

Hadrian: Roman emperor 117-38.

Hannibal (247-182 BC): Carthaginian leader who made a famous crossing of the Alps with his elephants.

Harpocrates: the Greek name for the son of Isis and Osiris, known to the Egyptians as Horus, and usually depicted as a child.

Harsaphes: an Egyptian ram-headed god, sometimes identified with Heracles.

Hathor: Egyptian goddess usually depicted with the head of a cow. She was associated with love, sexuality and maternity.

Hatshepsut: queen of Egypt 1498-1483 BC. Widow of Tuthmosis II, she kept his appointed successor, her stepson, off the throne and ruled in her own right.

Helen: possessor of the legendary face that launched a thousand ships. Her switch in emotional allegiance from her husband Menelaus to Paris led to the Trojan War.

Helenus: a prince of Troy, son of Priam and twin brother of Cassandra. Like her, he had the gift of prophecy.

Helios: Greek god of the sun, grandson of Gaia, usually portrayed as a radiant youth.

Hephaestion: friend, companion, and probably lover of Alexander the Great.

Hera: Greek goddess, the often-betrayed consort of Zeus.

Heracles: the greatest of Greek heroes. He performed great numbers of impressive feats before finally being made into a god.

Heraclides of Pontus: fourth-century BC Greek philosopher.

Hermes: Greek god, son of Zeus and father of Autolycus. He often served as a messenger for the gods, but was also responsible for protecting travellers.

Herod the Great: king of Judaea 31-4 BC.

Herodes Atticus: wealthy second-century orator, educator and politician.

Herodotus: fifth-century BC writer, the first Greek historian.

Herophile: the Sibyl of Erythrae.

Hippocrates: a fourth-century BC physician, often regarded as the father of medicine.

Hippodamus of Miletus: fifth-century BC politician who first proposed building cities on a grid plan.

Homer: the legendary author of the *Iliad* and the *Odyssey*, the first great works of ancient Greek literature, both probably composed before 700 BC, and perhaps a lot earlier.

Horace: first-century BC Latin poet.

Horus: a complex Egyptian god, usually portrayed with the head, and sometimes also with the body, of a falcon.

Hygeia: Greek goddess and personification of health. She was usually regarded as the daughter of Asclepius.

Imhotep: holder of high offices under Djoser. He designed the first pyramid and wrote many books. He came to have a reputation as a healer, and the Greeks identified him with Asclepius.

incubation: the practice of sleeping in order to receive a message through a dream.

Ino: daughter of Cadmus and wife of Athamas, she was later transformed into the goddess Leucothea.

Isis: popular Egyptian goddess, wife of Osiris and mother of Horus. From the fourth century BC onwards she was often associated with Sarapis.

Ismenos: a son of Apollo.

Jason: brought up by Chiron, he led the Argo expedition. Curiously, although his name derives from a Greek word for healing, no healing cult seems to have been attached to him.

Julian II: Roman emperor 361-3. Often referred to as 'the Apostate', he tried to revive paganism but an early death scuppered his plans.

Julius Caesar: Roman politician, general and author. After his defeat of Pompey in 49 BC he ruled Rome until his assassination on the Ides of March in 44 BC.

Juno: Roman goddess, wife of Jupiter and mother of Mars. She was identified by the Greeks with Hera.

Jupiter: the supreme Roman god, who came to be identified with both Zeus and Amun. He was originally a sky god and always remained associated with lightning.

Kalchas: grandson of Apollo, given by his grandfather the gift of prophecy. The wooden horse of Troy was said by some to have been his idea.

katagogion: a hostel or lodging house, often for the use of pilgrims.

Khnum: Egyptian earth god, sometimes portrayed with the head of a ram.

Khonsu: Egyptian moon god, sometimes depicted with a falcon's head.

Lactantius: second/third-century author. A tutor to one of Constantine the Great's sons, he wrote on the early history of Christianity.

Leda: mother of the Dioscouri and Helen.

Lenus: an important Gaulish healing god, sometimes identified with Mars.

Leto: the mother of the twin deities Apollo and Artemis (whose father was Zeus). She came to be identified with the Egyptian cobra goddess Wadjet.

letters (oracle of): an oracle where dice were probably thrown to select one of a pre-determined set of responses. It differed from a dice oracle in that the number of responses available was limited to 24, the number of letters in the Greek alphabet. Each response began with a different letter.

Leucippus: sixth/fifth-century BC Greek philosopher, perhaps the first to advance the theory that everything is made up of atoms.

Leucothea: the white goddess. Born as Ino, the daughter of Cadmus, she was elevated to divine status after being driven mad by Hera and throwing herself into the sea.

lot (oracle): an oracle where one of a number of pre-determined answers was selected through some random means. One method was to pick one of a number of pieces of inscribed wood.

Lucian: second-century writer, best known for his many satirical works.

Machaon: according to legend he was the son of Asclepius. He and his brother Podaleirius went to the Trojan War as healers. His children included Alexanor, Gorgasus, Nicomachus and Polemocrates.

Maleatas: a hero or god connected with healing and hunting. He became associated with **Apollo** at **EPIDAUROS** and possibly elsewhere.

Mandulis: a sun god brought to Egypt from neighbouring Nubia.

Manto: there was more than one Manto in Greek legend, but the most famous was the daughter of Teiresias and mother of Mopsus. However, the name Manto is so similar to the Greek word *manteuo* ('to prophesy') that she may well be a pure invention.

Marcus Aurelius: Roman emperor 161-80.

Mardonius: a Persian general who fought against the Greeks and died in 479 BC.

Mars: Roman god, son of Juno. He was originally a benevolent protector of fields and boundaries, but later acquired war-like characteristics. Amongst the Celtic peoples of Europe he was often regarded as a healer.

Mausolus: ruler of Caria 377-353 BC. His capital, **HALICARNASSUS**, is covered by modern Bodrum. His widow erected the first mausoleum in his honour.

Melampus: according to legend, he was the first Greek to receive the gift of prophecy. He was said to be able to understand the language of birds (the pre-eminent bearers of omens) because his ears had once been licked by snakes.

Menelaus: legendary king of Sparta. The abduction of his wife, Helen, led to the Trojan War.

Menestheus: legendary king of Athens who took part in the Trojan War, and was one of those smuggled into Troy in the famous wooden horse.

Min: an Egyptian fertility god who was also regarded as a special protector of mines.

Minerva: Roman goddess of crafts. Originally Etruscan, Numa is said to have introduced her cult to Rome. She was sometimes identified with Athena.

Montu: an Egyptian god usually depicted with the head of a hawk. He was often equated with Horus.

Mopsus the Argonaut: a legendary prophet who received his gift from Apollo.

Mopsus: a legendary prophet, the son of Manto. According to some legends, Apollo was his father.

Mullo: a Gaulish god whose cult became merged with that of Mars. His name suggests a possible association with horses.

Mut: an Egyptian goddess originally represented as a griffin vulture. She later became regarded as the wife of Amun.

Mys: an otherwise unknown individual chosen by Mardonius to carry out a survey of Greek oracles.

necromanteion (or **nekyomanteion**): a place where there was an oracle of the dead.

Neith: Egyptian creator goddess, sometimes identified with Athena. **SAIS** was the centre of her cult.

Nemesis: Greek goddess, daughter of Nyx. She was associated with the punishment of both crime and pride.

Nero: Roman emperor 54-68.

Nicomachus: a son of Machaon and an Argonaut.

Nodens: a British god, often associated with Mars.

Numa: the legendary second king of Rome, regarded as the founder of its religious institutions.

Nymphs: a large and varied class of minor female deities in Greek mythology. They were usually associated with features of the landscape such as rivers, trees and mountains. They rarely had temples.

Nyx: the Greek goddess (and personification) of night. She was the mother of Nemesis.

Odysseus: legendary Greek leader renowned for his cunning. He fought in the Trojan War, and the tale of his long and eventful journey home is related in Homer's *Odyssey*.

omen: something that happened (as opposed to something that was done) that was interpreted as bearing some message about the future. In principle, this could be almost anything, but in practice certain phenomena received particular attention. These included the movements of birds, sneezes, and chance things overheard.

Opramoas of Rhodiapolis: a second-century philanthropist who financed many building projects in Lycia.

Orpheus: legendary musician, an Argonaut, and one of the few humans to descend into the Underworld and return.

Osiris: legendary king of Egypt who became a god of the Underworld. Husband of Isis and father of Horus, he was sometimes identified with Pluto.

Ovid (43 BC-18 AD): a Latin poet, best known for his *Metamorphoses*.

Pan: Greek god of the countryside whose form was half human and half goat. He was particularly associated with shepherds and their flocks, and was renowned for his sexual energy.

Paris: a prince of Troy, son of Priam and seducer of Helen.

Parmenides: a Greek philosopher of the fifth century BC who wrote a famous poem on metaphysics.

Pasiphae: a complex legendary character, said (among other things) to have been the wife of king Minos of Crete and mother of the minotaur. She also seems to have been regarded as a moon goddess.

Paul, St (*c.* 1-64): early Christian missionary, theologian and letter writer.

Pausanias: an inveterate traveller who wrote one of the world's first travel books, a guide to Greece, in the second century. He was particularly interested in oracles.

Pelops: grandson of Zeus, grandfather of Menelaus, and legendary founder of the Olympic Games. The Peloponnese ('Island of Pelops') is named after him.

Persephone: the niece of Pluto, she was abducted by him and became his wife, thereafter spending half of each year in the Underworld and the other half in the world above. She was the daughter of Demeter.

Pharnaces: first-century BC king of Pontus, defeated by Julius Caesar.

Philip II: king of Macedonia 359-336 BC, father of Alexander the Great.

Philistos: fifth/fourth-century BC author of a history of his native Sicily.

Philostratus: first/second-century writer. Exactly what he did or did not write is a matter of some dispute, and there may have been more than one author with the same name.

Phrixus: son of Athamas, he was saved from death by Zeus who sent a ram with a golden fleece to rescue him.

Pliny the Elder: first-century Roman writer who compiled an enormous collection of reliable and unreliable facts in his *Natural History*. He died during the eruption of Vesuvius that buried Pompeii in 79. He was the uncle of Pliny the Younger.

Pliny the Younger (61-113): nephew of Pliny the Elder, by whom he was adopted. A man of letters who also held public office.

Plutarch: first/second-century writer, mainly of essays and biographies. He also served for some time as a priest at **DELPHI**.

Pluto (or **Hades**): Greek god of the Underworld.

Podaleirius: son of Asclepius and brother of Machaon, he went to the Trojan War as a healer. Later he married Syrna.

Polemocrates: a son of Machaon and brother of Alexanor.

Pompey: Roman general, first an ally then an enemy of Julius Caesar, who ultimately defeated him. He was murdered in Egypt in 48 BC.

Poseidon: Greek god primarily associated with the sea, but also with earthquakes and horses. His symbol is the trident.

Priam: legendary king of Troy at the time of the Trojan War.

Priapus: Greek god of fertility. He is often portrayed with massively exaggerated genitals, and sometimes identified with the Egyptian god Bes.

Glossary

Protagoras: fifth-century BC Greek philosopher, most famous for his observation, 'Man is the measure of all things.'

Protesilaus: legendary Greek hero; the first casualty of the Trojan War.

prytaneion: something like a town hall, but with more religious overtones.

Ptah: an Egyptian creator god. He was often associated with Apis.

Ptolemaic: the period of Egyptian history from 323-30 BC.

Ptolemy I: one of Alexander the Great's generals who created an empire for himself in Egypt after Alexander died. He formally ruled 305-282 BC.

Ptolemy II: son and successor of Ptolemy I, he ruled Egypt at first jointly and then alone 285-46 BC.

Ptolemy III: son and successor of Ptolemy II, he ruled Egypt 246-222 BC.

Ptolemy IV: son and successor of Ptolemy III, he ruled Egypt 222-205 BC.

Ptolemy V: son and successor of Ptolemy IV, he ruled Egypt 205-180 BC.

Ptolemy VI: son and successor of Ptolemy V, he ruled Egypt 180-145 BC.

Pythagoras: a somewhat mysterious Greek philosopher of the sixth century BC.

Pythia: the title of Apollo's priestess at Delphi.

Ramesses II: one of the greatest of the pharaohs of Egypt, who ruled 1279-1212 BC.

Romulus: the legendary founder of Rome.

Samson: celebrated Old Testament strongman.

Sarapis (or **Serapis**): an Egyptian god of the sky, the underworld and healing, usually associated with Isis. His cult seems to have been initiated by Ptolemy I in an attempt to improve the religious unity (and his control) of the country: Sarapis was an amalgam of Osiris and Apis.

Schliemann, Heinrich: nineteenth-century archaeologist who most famously excavated the site of Troy.

Seferis, George: twentieth-century Greek poet and diplomat, winner of the Nobel Prize for Literature in 1963.

Seleucus I: one of Alexander the Great's generals who carved out an empire for himself based around Persia when Alexander died. He was assassinated in 280 BC.

Sequana: a Gaulish healing goddess, the personification of the River Seine.

Serapeum: a temple of Sarapis.

Seth: a complex Egyptian god particularly associated with the desert. He was often regarded as a malevolent figure and was widely feared.

Seti I: ruled Egypt 1291-1278 BC, father of Ramesses II.

Sibyl: originally the name of a prophetess, it became the title of a number of them. There may have eventually been as many as ten Sibyls. Most of what is known about them, including their often extraordinary lifespans, is clearly legendary. Books of Sibylline prophecies were kept in a temple in Rome.

Sirona: a healing goddess from Gaul, particularly associated with hot springs.

Sobek: the principal crocodile god of Egypt and son of Neith. The Greeks called him Suchos, and he also appeared in a number of local forms in the Faiyum area.

Sophocles: a fifth-century BC writer of Greek tragedies.

Stephanus Byzantius: fifth-century writer based at Constantinople who composed a major reference work of geography.

stoa: a hall, open with columns on one side.

Strabo: first-century BC/first-century AD author of a geographical survey of the Roman empire.

Suetonius: first/second-century Roman writer, best known for his brief biographies of the early Roman emperors.

Sulis: British water and healing goddess, sometimes identified with Minerva.

Syrna: daughter of king Damaethus of Caria, she married Podaleirius.

Tacitus: first/second-century Roman historian.

Taweret: an Egyptian goddess of childbirth, sometimes depicted with the head of a hippopotamus.

Teiresias: a legendary prophet from Greek **THEBES**. He was blinded when young, and also spent part of his life as a woman. When finally despatched to the underworld he was permitted to retain his full senses.

Telesphorus: a minor healing deity, usually found in association with Asclepius. He was usually portrayed as a youth.

Teneros: a son of Apollo and brother of Ismenos.

Teucer: the legendary ancestor of the royal family of Troy.

Thales: sixth-century BC philosopher.

Themis: Greek goddess of law. According to one tradition, she taught Apollo how to prophesy.

Themistius: fourth-century writer who spent most of his life in Constantinople.

Theodosius the Great: Roman emperor 379-92, although for most of that time he only ruled the eastern part of the empire.

Thoth: Egyptian god of wisdom, sometimes depicted with the head of an ibis. The Egyptians regarded him as the inventor of writing.

Tiberius: Roman emperor 14-37.

Trajan: Roman emperor 98-117.

Trophonius: see under **LEBADEIA**

Troy: a city of Asia Minor (now NW Turkey). The Trojan War of legend, which lasted ten years, may be based on historical events around 1200 BC.

Tuthmosis III: Egyptian pharaoh who ruled 1504-1450 BC.

Tutu: also known as Tithoes, he was a popular deity in Roman Egypt, believed to be especially effective in warding off demons.

Varro: a Roman scholar and encylopaedist of the first century BC. He was put in charge of the public library founded in Rome by Julius Caesar.

Vercingetorix: a leader of the Gauls, he was one of Julius Caesar's most troublesome enemies.

Vespasian: Roman emperor 69-79.

Virgil: first-century BC Latin poet, best known for his *Aeneid*, an epic about the origins of Rome, but also for some shorter works.

votive: literally something in furtherance of a vow. Votive objects were often offered to divinities in thanks for cures or other favours received.

Wadjet: Egyptian goddess, usually depicted in the form of a cobra.

Xenophanes: sixth/fifth-century BC Greek philosopher who was especially interested in religious matters.

Xerxes: king of Persia 486-465 BC.

Zeus: greatest of the gods of Greece, father of many others. He became identified with Amun and Jupiter.

Zoodochos Pigi: literally 'life-receiving spring'. A number of Orthodox churches have this dedication.

Bibliography

Ancient sources in translation

'Aelius Spartianus' et al., *Lives of the Later Caesars* [The Augustan History], trans. Anthony Birley. Harmondsworth: Penguin (1976)

Ammianus Marcellinus, *The Later Roman Empire (AD 354-378)*, trans. Walter Hamilton. Harmondsworth: Penguin (1986)

Apollodorus, *Gods and Heroes of the Greeks: the Library of Apollodorus*, trans. Michael Simpson. Amherst: University of Massachusetts Press (1976)

Apollonius of Rhodes, *The Voyage of Argo*, trans. E.V. Rieu. Harmondsworth: Penguin (1959)

Aristophanes, *Plays: 1*, trans. Patric Dickinson. Oxford: Oxford University Press (1970)

Arrian, *The Life of Alexander the Great*, trans. A. de Selincourt. Harmondsworth: Penguin (1958)

Artemidorus, *The Interpretation of Dreams*, trans. Robert J. White. Park Ridge: Noyes Press (1975)

Cicero, 'De Divinatione' in Cicero, *De Senectute, De Amicitia, De Divinatione*, trans. W. A. Falconer. Cambridge, MA: Harvard University Press (1923) Loeb Classical Library

Diodorus Siculus, *The Library of History* (12 vols), trans. C.H. Oldfather. Cambridge, MA: Harvard University Press (1936-1967) Loeb Classical Library

Eusebius, 'Life of Constantine' in *A Select Library of Nicene and Post-Nicene Fathers of the Christian Church*, vol. V. Oxford: Parker (1890) pp. 405-560

Herodotus, *The Histories*, trans. A. de Selincourt. Harmondsworth: Penguin (1965)

Homer, *The Iliad*, trans. E.V. Rieu. Harmondsworth: Penguin (1950)

Homer, *The Odyssey*, trans. E.V. Rieu. Harmondsworth: Penguin (1946)

Lactantius, *The Minor Works*, trans. Mary Francis McDonald. Washington: Catholic University of America Press (1965)

Lucian, *Lucian* vol. 8, trans. A.M. Harmon. London: Heinemann (1925) Loeb Classical Library

Lucian, *Satirical Sketches*, trans. Paul Turner. Harmondsworth: Penguin (1961)

Ovid, *Metamorphoses*, trans. Mary M. Innes. Harmondsworth: Penguin (1955)

Pausanias, *Guide to Greece* vol. 1, trans. Peter Levi. Harmondsworth: Penguin (1971a)

Pausanias, *Guide to Greece* vol. 2, trans. Peter Levi. Harmondsworth: Penguin (1971b)

Pausanias, *Pausanias's Description of Greece* (6 vols), trans. J.G. Frazer. New York: Biblo and Tannen (1965)

Philostratus, *Heroikos*, trans., intr. and ed. Jennifer K. Berenson Maclean and Ellen Bradshaw Aitken (*Writings from the Graeco-Roman World I*). Atlanta: Society of Bible Literature (2001)

Plato, *Phaedrus*, ed. Hackforth. Indianapolis: Bobbs-Merrill (nd)

Pliny the Elder, *Natural History: a selection*, trans. John F. Healy. Harmondsworth: Penguin (1991)

Pliny the Younger, *The Letters of the Younger Pliny*, trans. Betty Radice. Harmondsworth: Penguin (1969)
Plutarch, *Lives*, vols II & X, trans. Bernadotte Perrin. London: Heinemann (1959) Loeb Classical Library
Plutarch, *Moralia*, vol. V, trans. Frank Cole Babbitt. London: Heinemann (1962) Loeb Classical Library
Strabo, *Geography*, trans. H.L. Jones (8 vols). London: Heinemann (1917-1935) Loeb Classical Library
Suetonius, *The Twelve Caesars*, trans. Robert Graves. Harmondsworth: Penguin (1957)
Tacitus, *The Annals of Imperial Rome*, trans. Michael Grant. Harmondsworth: Penguin (1977)
Tacitus, 'The History' in *Tacitus: Historical Works* vol. 2, trans. Arthur Murphy. London: Dent (nd)
Vergil, *The Aeneid*, trans. W.F. Jackson Knight. Harmondsworth: Penguin (1958)

Modern books and articles

Athens and Attica – a Phaidon Cultural Guide (1986) New York: Prentice Hall
Atlas of Ancient and Classical Geography (nd) London: Dent
Baedeker's Italy, 4th ed. (1999) Basingstoke: AA
Cure and Cult in Ancient Corinth: a guide to the Asklepeion (1977) Princeton: American School of Classical Studies at Athens
Greece – a Phaidon Cultural Guide (1985) Oxford: Phaidon
Italy – a Phaidon Cultural Guide (1985) Oxford: Phaidon

Adams, William Y. (1977) *Nubia: Corridor to Africa*. London: Allen Lane
Adkins, Lesley and Adkins, Roy A. (1996) *Dictionary of Roman Religion*. New York: Facts on File
Akurgal, Ekrem (2001) *Ancient Civilizations and Ruins of Turkey*, 2nd ed. Istanbul: NET
Anderson, Brian and Anderson, Eileen (1994) *Landscapes of Turkey (around Antalya)*, revised ed. London: Sunflower Books
Anderson, Brian and Anderson, Eileen (1998) *Landscapes of Turkey (Bodrum and Marmaris)*, 2nd ed. London: Sunflower Books
Anderson, Graham (1994) *Saint, Sage and Sophist: holy men and their associates in the Early Roman Empire*. London: Routledge
Athanassiadi, Polymnia (1992) *Julian: an intellectual biography*. London: Routledge
Aune, David E. (1991) *Prophecy in Early Christianity and the Ancient Mediterranean World*. Grand Rapids: Eerdmans
Azema, James (2000) *Libya Handbook*. Bath: Footprint Handbooks
Baines, John and Malek, Jaromir (1991) *Atlas of Ancient Egypt*. Amsterdam: Time-Life
Bean, George E. (1989a) *Aegean Turkey*. London: John Murray
Bean, George E. (1989b) *Lycian Turkey*. London: John Murray
Bean, George E. (1989c) *Turkey beyond the Maeander*. London: John Murray
Bean, George E. (1989d) *Turkey's Southern Shore*. London: John Murray
Bell, H. Idris (1975) *Cults and Creeds in Graeco-Roman Egypt*. Chicago: Ares
Bertaux, Jean-Paul (1991) 'Le Sanctuaire de l'Eau' in *Les Dossiers d'Archéologie* no. 162. Dijon, pp. 38-41

Bibliography

Borgeaud, Philippe (1998) *The Cult of Pan in Ancient Greece,* trans. Kathleen Atlass and James Redfield. Chicago: Chicago University Press

Bousfield, Jonathan and Richardson, Dan (1993) *Bulgaria.* London: Rough Guides

Bowman, Alan K. (1986) *Egypt after the Pharaohs.* London: British Museum Publications

Buck, Robert J. (1979) *A History of Boeotia.* Edmonton: University of Calgary Press

Bunson, Matthew (1994) *Encyclopedia of the Roman Empire.* New York: Facts on File

Burford, Tim and Richardson, Dan (1998) *Romania.* London: Rough Guides

Burkert, Walter (1985) *Greek Religion: Archaic and Classical,* trans. John Raffen. Cambridge MA: Harvard University Press

Burns, Ross (1999) *Monuments of Syria: an historical guide,* revised ed. London: I.B. Tauris

Casson, Stanley (1968) *Macedonia, Thrace and Illyria.* Groningen: Bouma's Boekhuis

Chandler, Richard (1775) *Travels in Asia Minor.* Dublin: Society of Dilettanti

Claridge, Amanda (1998) *Rome: an Oxford archaeological guide.* Oxford: Oxford University Press

Cook, J. M. (1973) *The Troad.* Oxford: Clarendon Press

Curnow, T (1999) *Wisdom, Intuition and Ethics.* Aldershot: Ashgate

Dakaris, Sotirios I. (nd) *The Antiquity of Epirus: the Acheron Necromantieon, Ephyra, Pandosia, Cassope.* Athens: Apollo

Dakaris, Sotiriou (1996) *Dodona,* 2nd ed. Athens: Ministry of Culture Archaeological Receipts Fund

de Boer, J.Z. and Hale, J.R. (2000) 'The geological origins of the oracle at Delphi, Greece' in W.G. McGuire, D.R. Griffiths, P.L Hancock and I. S. Stewart (eds) (2000) *The Archaeology of Geological Catastrophes.* London: Geological Society, pp. 399-412

Demand, Nancy H. (1982) *Thebes in the Fifth Century.* London: RKP

Dillon, Matthew (1997) *Pilgrims and Pilgrimage in Ancient Greece.* London: Routledge

Dubin, Marc (1993) *Cyprus: the Rough Guide.* London: Rough Guides

Dunn, Joseph (2000) 'Shrine of the times' in *The Sunday Times Magazine,* 20/8/2000, pp. 36-39

Dyer, Louis (1891) *Studies of the Gods in Greece at certain Sanctuaries recently excavated.* London: Macmillan

Edelstein, Emma J. and Edelstein, Ludwig (1975) *Asclepius: a collection and interpretation of the testimonies.* New York: Arno Press

Etienne, Roland and Françoise (1992) *The Search for Ancient Greece,* trans. Anthony Zielonka. London: Thames and Hudson

Evans, Penelope (2000a) 'La dolce vita on the delta' in *The Sunday Times Magazine,* 20/8/2000, pp. 41-43

Evans, Penelope (2000b) 'The land that time drowned', in *The Sunday Times Magazine,* 20/8/2000, pp. 28-33

Fakhry, Ahmed (1990) *Siwa Oasis.* Cairo: American University in Cairo Press

Farnell, Lewis Richard (1907a) *The Cults of the Greek States,* vol. III. Oxford: Clarendon Press

Farnell, Lewis Richard (1907b) *The Cults of the Greek States,* vol. IV. Oxford: Clarendon Press

Farnell, Lewis Richard (1921) *Greek Hero Cults and Ideas of Immortality.* Oxford: Clarendon Press

Fontenrose, Joseph (1978) *The Delphic Oracle: its responses and operations*. Berkeley: University of California Press

Fox, Robin Lane (1973) *Alexander the Great*. London: Allen Lane

Fox, Robin Lane (1986) *Pagans and Christians*. Harmondsworth: Penguin

Frankfurter, David (1998) *Religion in Roman Egypt: assimilation and resistance*. Princeton: Princeton University Press

Frazer, J.G. (1922) *The Golden Bough* (abridged ed.). London: Macmillan

Freely, John (1988) *The Western Shores of Turkey*. London: John Murray

Freely, John (1991) *Classical Turkey*. Harmondsworth: Penguin

Gallazzi, Claudio (1999) 'Further Surprises from Tebtunis' in *Egyptian Archaeology* no. 14. London: Egypt Exploration Society, pp. 16-17

Giubelli, Giorgio (1997) *Phlegrean Fields*. Naples: Carcavallo

Glover, T.R. (1917) *The Conflict of Religions in the Early Roman Empire*, 6th ed. London: Methuen

Goldman, Hetty (1931) *Excavations at Eutresis in Boeotia*. Cambridge MA: Harvard University Press

Gonen, Rivka (1987) *Biblical Holy Places: an illustrated guide*. London: A & C Black

Grant, Michael (1971) *Roman Myths*. London: Weidenfeld and Nicolson

Graves, Robert (1960a) *The Greek Myths* vol. 1, revised ed. Harmondsworth: Penguin

Graves, Robert (1960b) *The Greek Myths* vol. 2, revised ed. Harmondsworth: Penguin

Green, Miranda J. (1983) *The Gods of Roman Britain*. Princes Risborough: Shire

Green, Miranda J. (1992) *Dictionary of Celtic Myth and Legend*. London: Thames and Hudson

Green, Miranda (1997) *The Gods of the Celts*. Stroud: Sutton

Greenhalgh, Peter and Eliopoulos, Edward (1985) *Deep into Mani*. London: Faber and Faber

Grimal, Pierre (1991) *Penguin Dictionary of Classical Mythology*, trans. A.R. Maxwell-Hyslop. Harmondsworth: Penguin

Haag, Michael (1995) *Cadogan Guide to Syria and Lebanon*. London: Cadogan

Hadzi-Vallianou, Despina (1989) *Lebena: the ancient city and the shrine of Asclepius*. Athens: Ministry of Culture Archaeological Receipts Fund

Halliday, W.R. (1913) *Greek Divination*. London: Macmillan

Harvey, Paul (1984) *The Oxford Companion to Classical Literature*. Oxford: Oxford University Press

Hastings, James (ed.) (1958) *Encyclopaedia of Religion and Ethics*. Edinburgh: T & T Clark

Hazlitt, William (1995) *The Classical Gazetteer*. London: Senate

Hellander, Paul, Humphreys, Andrew and Tilbury, Neil (1999) *Israel and the Palestinian Territories*, 4th ed. Melbourne: Lonely Planet

Hope, Colin (1994) 'Excavations at Ismant el-Kharab in the Dakhleh Oasis', in *Egyptian Archaeology* no. 5. London: Egypt Exploration Society, pp. 17-18

Hornblower, Simon and Spawforth, Anthony (eds) (1998) *The Oxford Companion to Classical Civilization*. Oxford: Oxford University Press

Jacobs, Michael (1990) *A Guide to Andalusia*. London: Viking

Janin, R. (1969) *La Géographie Ecclésiastique de l'Empire Byzantin*, part 1, vol. 3, *Les Églises et les Monastères*, 2nd ed. Paris: L'Institut Français d'Études Byzantines

Jayne, Walter Addison (1962) *The Healing Gods of Ancient Civilisations*. New Hyde Park, NY: University Books

Bibliography

Jones, Cheslyn, Wainwright, Geoffrey, Yarnold, Edward and Bradshaw, Paul (eds) (1992) *The Study of Liturgy*, revised ed. London: SPCK

Jordan, Michael (1992) *Encyclopaedia of Gods*. London: Kyle Cathie

Kasas, Savas and Struckmann, Reinhard (1990) *Important Medical Centres in the Antiquity: Epidaurus and Corinth*. Athens: Editions Kasas

Kingsley, Peter (1995) *Ancient Philosophy, Mystery and Magic*. Oxford: Clarendon Press

Kingsley, Peter (1999) *In the Dark Places of Wisdom*. Shaftesbury: Element

Kininmonth, Christopher (1981) *The Traveller's Guide to Sicily*, 3rd ed. London: Jonathan Cape

Kirk, G. S. (1990) *The Nature of Greek Myths*. Harmondsworth: Penguin

Klauck, Hans-Josef (2000) *The Religious Context of Early Christianity*, trans. Brian McNeil. Edinburgh: T & T Clark

Lanciani, Rodolfo (1892) *Pagan and Christian Rome*. Boston/New York: Houghton, Mifflin and Co.

Lang, Mabel (1977) *Cure and Cult in Ancient Corinth*. Princeton: American School of Classical Studies at Athens

Lempriere, J. (1984) *Lempriere's Classical Dictionary*. London: Bracken

Levi, Peter (1991) *Atlas of the Greek World*. Time-Life

Lewis, Neville (1987) *Delphi and the Sacred Way*. London: Michael Haag

Lindsay, Jack (1965) *The Clashing Rocks: early Greek religion and culture and the origins of drama*. London: Chapman and Hall

Loewe, Michael and Blacker, Carmen, eds (1981) *Divination and Oracles*. London: George Allen and Unwin

Macadam, Alta (1988) *Blue Guide Sicily*, 3rd ed. London: A & C Black

Manley, Bill (1996) *The Penguin Historical Atlas of Ancient Egypt*. Harmondsworth: Penguin

Matthews, John, ed. (1992) *The World Atlas of Divination*. London: Headline

McDonagh, Bernard (1995) *Blue Guide Turkey*, 2nd ed. London: A & C Black

McGuinness, Justin (1999) *Tunisia Handbook*, 2nd ed. Bath: Footprint Handbooks

McLachlan, Anne and McLachlan, Keith (eds) (1995) *Morocco and Tunisia Handbook*. Bath: Trade and Travel Handbooks

Mee, Christopher and Spawforth, Antony (2001) *Greece: an Oxford archaeological guide*. Oxford: Oxford University Press

Meinardus, Otto F.A. (1974) *St John of Patmos and the Seven Churches of the Apocalypse*. Athens: Lycabettus Press

Melas, Evi (ed.) (1973) *Temples and Sanctuaries of Ancient Greece: a companion guide*. London: Thames and Hudson

Morkot, Robert G. (2000) *The Black Pharaohs: Egypt's Nubian rulers*. London: Rubicon

Morris, Peter and Jacobs, Daniel (1995) *Tunisia*, 4th ed. London: Rough Guides

Moynihan, Brian (2000) 'The Lost Jewels of the Nile', in *The Sunday Times Magazine*, 20/8/2000, pp. 16-25

Murnane, William J. (1983) *The Penguin Guide to Ancient Egypt*. Harmondsworth: Penguin

Murphy-O'Conner, Jerome (1998) *The Holy Land: an Oxford archaeological guide*. Oxford: Oxford University Press

Nataf, André (1994) *The Wordsworth Dictionary of the Occult*. Ware: Wordsworth

Ogden, Daniel (2002) *Magic, Witchcraft, and Ghosts in the Greek and Roman Worlds: a sourcebook*. New York: Oxford University Press

Oswalt, Sabine G. (1969) *Concise Encyclopaedia of Greek and Roman Mythology*. Glasgow: Collins

Parke, H.W. (1939) *A History of the Delphic Oracle*. Oxford: Blackwell

Parke, H.W. (1967a) *Greek Oracles*. London: Hutchinson

Parke, H.W. (1967b) *The Oracles of Zeus: Dodona, Olympia, Ammon*. Oxford: Basil Blackwell

Parke, H.W. (1985) *The Oracles of Apollo in Asia Minor*. London: Croom Helm

Parke, H.W. (1988) *Sibyls and Sibylline Prophecy in Classical Antiquity*. London: Routledge

Parker, Richard A. (1962) *A Saite Oracle Papyrus from Thebes*. Providence: Brown University Press

Pemberton, Delia (1992) *Ancient Egypt*. San Francisco: Chronicle Books

Peña, Ignacio (1993) 'Dos santuarios oracularios en Siria: Wadi Marthun y Banasra', in *Liber Annus 1993*. Jerusalem: Studii Biblici Franciscani, pp. 295-302

Pettifer, James (1994) *Blue Guide Albania*. London: A & C Black

Pillement, George (1975) *Unknown Greece: the islands of the Aegean Sea, Rhodes, Crete*, trans. Barbara Whelpton. London: Johnson

Pollard, John (1965) *Seers, Shrines and Sirens*. London: George Allen & Unwin

Quirke, Stephen (1992) *Ancient Egyptian Religion*. London: British Museum Press

Radice, Betty (1973) *Who's Who in the Ancient World*, revised ed. Harmondsworth: Penguin

Raven, Susan (1993) *Rome in Africa*, 3rd ed. London: Routledge

Rice, Michael (1999) *Who's Who in Ancient Egypt*. London: Routledge

Rohde, Erwin (1925) *Psyche*. London: Kegan Paul, Trench, Trubner

Rosen, Roger (1991) *An Introduction to the Georgian Republic*. Hong Kong: Twin Age

Rossiter, Stuart (1981) *Blue Guide Greece*, 4th ed. London: Ernest Benn

Salway, Peter (1993) *The Oxford Illustrated History of Roman Britain*. Oxford: Oxford University Press

Schneider, Dux (1975) *Travellers' Guide: Turkey*. London: Jonathan Cape

Seton-Williams, Veronica and Stocks, Peter (1993) *Blue Guide Egypt*, 3rd ed. London: A & C Black

Siliotti, Alberto (1996) *Guide to the Valley of the Kings*. London: Weidenfeld and Nicolson

Siliotti, Alberto (2000) *Abu Simbel and the Nubian Temples*. Cairo: American University in Cairo Press

Smith, William, ed. (1848) *A Dictionary of Greek and Roman Antiquities*, 2nd ed. London: John Murray

Smith, William, ed. (1873) *A Dictionary of Greek and Roman Geography*. London: John Murray

Soprintendenza archeologica di Pompei (2001) *Brief Guide to Pompeii*. Ministero per i Beni e le Attivita Culturali

Speake, Graham (2002) *Mount Athos; renewal in paradise*. New Haven: Yale University Press

Sterrett, R. J. Sitlington (1888a) *An Epigraphical Journey in Asia Minor* (*Papers of the American School of Classical Studies at Athens*, vol. II). Boston: Damrell & Upham

Sterrett, R.J. Sitlington (1888b) *An Epigraphical Journey in Asia Minor* (*Papers of the American School of Classical Studies at Athens*, vol. III). Boston: Damrell & Upham

Stilwell, Richard, MacDonald, William and McAllister, Marian Holland (eds) (1976) *The Princeton Encyclopaedia of Classical Sites*. Princeton: Princeton University Press

Strudwick, Nigel and Strudwick, Helen (1999) *Thebes in Egypt: a guide to the tombs and temples of ancient Luxor*. Ithaca: Cornell University Press

Talbert, Richard J.A. (ed.) (2000) *Barrington Atlas of the Greek and Roman World*. Princeton: Princeton University Press

Taylor, John H. (1991) *Egypt and Nubia*. London: British Museum

Thevenot, Émile (1968) *Divinités et Sanctuaires de la Gaule*. Paris: Fayard

Tomlinson, R.A. (1983) *Epidauros*. St Albans: Granada

Turcan, Robert (1996) *The Cults of the Roman Empire*, trans. Antonia Nevill. Oxford: Blackwell

van der Heyden, A.A.M. and Scullard, H.H. (eds) (1959) *Atlas of the Classical World*. London: Nelson

Wallace, Paul W. (1979) *Strabo's Description of Boiotia: a commentary*. Heidelberg: Carl Winter Universitätsverlag

Watterson, Barbara (1996) *Gods of Ancient Egypt*. Godalming: Bramley

Welsby, Derek A. (1996) *The Kingdom of Kush: the Napatan and Meroitic empires*. London: British Museum Press

Whiting, Dominic (2001) *Turkey Handbook*. Bath: Footprint Handbooks

Wightman, Edith Mary (1970) *Roman Trier and the Treveri*. London: Rupert Hart-Davis

Wilkinson, Richard H. (2000) *The Complete Temples of Ancient Egypt*. London: Thames and Hudson

Wilkinson, Richard H. (2003) *The Complete Gods and Goddesses of Ancient Egypt*. London: Thames and Hudson

Wiseman, James (1998) 'Rethinking the "Halls of Hades" ' in *Archaeology* vol. 51 no. 3, pp. 12-18

Witt, R.E. (1971) *Isis in the Graeco-Roman World*. London: Thames and Hudson

Wood, Michael (1997) *In the Footsteps of Alexander the Great: a journey from Greece to Asia*. London: BBC Books

Zaidman, Louise Bruit and Pantel, Pauline Schmitt (1992) *Religion in the Ancient Greek City*. Cambridge: Cambridge University Press

Websites

In the course of researching this book I have looked at literally hundreds of websites, and it would be impractical to list them all. Most of them can be tracked down through the good offices of Google [www.google.com]. A few, however, are worthy of special mention. The works of Homer, Virgil, Herodotus and many others can be found on the *Internet Classics Archive* [http://classics.mit.edu/Browse/]. Pausanias and Strabo can be found via *Perseus* [http://www.perseus.tufts.edu/cache/perscoll_Greco-Roman.html], which also offers many secondary resources including the excellent *Princeton Encyclopedia of Classical Sites*. Two useful gateways to a wide range of materials are the *Ancient World Web* [http://www.julen.net/ancient/] and the *World Atlas of Archaeology on the Web* [http://archaeology.about.com/cs/archaeologyatlas/]. The *Hellenic Ministry of Culture* [http://www.culture.gr/2/21/

171

toc/arc_sites.html] provides an extensive guide to Greek archaeological sites, while *Discover Turkey* [http://www.bodrumpages.com/turkey/ancient_sites/] provides a more limited resource for Turkish ones It should be noted, however, that websites have an annoying habit of migrating or disappearing, so while these are recommendations, they are not guarantees.

Concordance of Oracles and Sites

Oracles appear in bold type with sites in ordinary type. Refer to the Index of Sites for the page numbers of this book.

Achilles: Leuce
Ahmose: Abydos
Ahmose Nefertari: Thebes (Egypt)
Albunea: Tibur
Amenhotep I: Thebes (Egypt)
Amphiaraus: Knopia, Oropos
Amphilochus: Akarnania, Mallus
Amun: Napata, Siwa, Thebes (Egypt)
Amynos: Athens
Anios: Delos
Aphrodite: Aphaca, Paphos
Apis: Memphis
Apollo: Abai, Abdera, Adrasteia, Aigai (1), Albaece Reiorum Apollinarium, Alesia, Argos, Athos, Brigetio, Chalcedon, Chios, Chryse, Claros, Cumae, Cyaneae, Daldis, Daphne, Delos, Delphi, Didyma, Ephesus, Epirus, Essarois, Eutresis, Gortyna, Grand, Hierapolis, Hieropolis, Hochscheid, Hysiai, Ichnae, Korope, Lesbos, Limyra, Magnesia on the Maeander, Orobia, Pagasai, Patara, Ptoon, Seleucia, Sidyma, Sura, Tarsus, Tegyra, Telmessos, Thebes (Greece), Thymbra, Velia, Zeleia
Aristomachus: Marathon, Rhamnous
Artemis: Adrasteia, Lousoi, Sarpedon
Asclepius: Abia, Achladokampos, Acragas, Aegina, Aegira, Aigai (2), Aigion, Alba Pompeia, Albaece Reiorum Apollinarium, Alexandria Troas, Alipheira, Althiburos, Anaphe, Antium, Apollonia, Argos, Asine, Asopos, Astypalaia, Athens, Balagrai, Berytus, Boiai, Brasiai, Brigetio, Buthrotum, Carthage, Carthago Nova, Chalcedon, Cnidus, Corinth, Cyme, Cyrene, Cyzicus, Delos, Dimitrias, Dion, Dora, Ecbatana, Emporion, Ephesus, Epidauros, Epidauros Limera, Eretria, Fregellae, Gela, Gerenia, Githio, Gonnos, Gortyna, Gortys, Halieis, Hierapolis, Hyettos, Hyperteleaton, Hypsoi, Jebel Oust, Jerusalem, Kaous, Kassopi, Kenchreai, Kleitor, Korone, Kos, Krannon, Kyllene, Kyphanta, Lambaesis, Larisa, Las, Lebena, Leuktra, Lissos, Mantineia, Megalopolis, Melaenae, Memphis, Messene, Miletus, Milos, Mirobriga, Mytilene, Naupaktos, Nikomedia, Nikopolis, Olous, Omolion, Onkios, Orchomenos, Panopeus, Paros, Patrai, Pautalia, Pellana, Pellene, Pergamon, Phalanna, Pharai (1), Pharsalos, Pheneos, Pherai, Phigalia, Philippopolis, Phlious, Piraeus, Poemanenos, Pompeii, Puteoli, Rhamnous, Rhodes, Rome, Samos, Sikyon, Smyrna, Soli, Sparta, Syracuse, Syrna, Thasos, Therapnai, Thermai Phazomeniton, Thespiai, Thyatira, Titane, Tithorea, Tralles, Trikka, Troizen, Ulpia Traiana Sarmezigetusa

173

Autolycus: Sinope
Bes: Abydos
Borvo: Aquae
Clitumnus: Clitumnus
Damona: Alesia
The Dead: Aornos, Avernus, Babylon, Baiae, Ephyra, Heracleia, Hermione, Koronia, Phigalia, Tainaron
Demeter: Patrai
Diana: Aquae Mattiacae, Nemus
Dice: Anabura, Antiocheia ad Cragum, Aponus, Attaleia, Delphi, Tefenni, Termessos
Dionysus: Amphikleia, Pangæum
Dioscouri: Byzantium
Dreams: Anariace, Hybla Geleatis
Earth: Aegira, Delphi, Olympia
Egeria: Nemus
Faunus: Tibur
Fortuna: Antium, Praeneste
Ge: Aegira, Delphi
Glanis: Glanum
Glaucus: Delos
Glykon-Asclepius: Abonuteichos
Gorgasus: Pharai (2)
Harsaphes: Heracleopolis Magna
Hathor: Tentyra
Hatshepsut: Thebes (Egypt)
Hemen: Hefat
Hemithea: Castabus
Hera: Perachora
Heracles: Bura, Hyettos
Hermes: Pharai (1)
Horus: Ombos
Ino: Epidauros Limera, Thalamae
Isis: Ascalon, Carantanus, Celeia, Cherchell, Corinth, Cumae, Cyme, Cyrene, Delos, Dion, Epidauros, Eretria, Gigthis, Gortyna, Halicarnassus, Kenchreai, Koptos, Krannon, Kysis, Lambaesis, Maharraqa, Menouthis, Nikomedia, Ostia, Philae, Philippi, Piraeus, Pompeii, Priene, Rome, Sabrata, Soknopaiou Nesos, Smyrna, Soloi, Syene, Syracuse, Thasos, Thira, Tithorea
Juno: Carthage, Veii
Jupiter: Cassius, Heliopolis, Lambaesis, Nikephorion
Kalchas: Garganus
Khnum: Elephantine
Khonsu: Thebes (Egypt)
Leto: Buto
Letters: Adada, Hierapolis, Limyra, Olympus
Lot: Aponus, Attaleia, Canopus, Clitumnus, Delphi, Gryneion, Lambaesis, Menouthis, Tritonis
Machaon: Gerenia

Mandulis: Talmis
Maponos: Chamalières
Mars: Allonnes, Augusta Treverorum, Nodens, Pommern, Tiora
Mefitis: Ampsanctus
Men: Neocaesarea
Menestheus: Gadeira
Min: Koptos
Minerva: Aquae Sulis, Rome
Montu: Thebes (Egypt)
Mopsus: Mallus
Mopsus the Argonaut: Tritonis
Mut: Thebes (Egypt)
Neith: Sais
Nicomachus: Pharai (2)
Nymphs: Apollonia, Caesarea Philippi, Delphi, Kithaeron
Nyx: Megara
Odysseus: Thermos
Omens: Smyrna
Orpheus: Antissa
Pan: Akakesion, Caesarea Philippi, Delphi, Lykaion, Troizen
Pasiphae: Sparta, Thalamae
Persephone: Acharaca
Phrixus: Leucothea
Pluto: Acharaca, Aiani, Canopus, Hierapolis, Thymbria
Podaleirius: Garganus
Polemocrates: Eua
Poseidon: Delphi, Onchestos
Protesilaus: Elaius
Ptah: Memphis
Ramesses II: Abu Simbel
Sarapis: Abydos, Adada, Alexandria, Augusta Emerita, Babylon, Berenice, Byzantium, Canopus, Carthage, Corinth, Delos, Emporion, Ephesus, Gigthis, Gortyna, Lambaesis, Limyra, Krannon, Kysis, Maharraqa, Miletus, Oitylon, Ostia, Oxyrhynchus, Pergamon, Priene, Puteoli, Sinope, Sabrata, Sparta, Stratoniceia, Syracuse, Tauromenion, Tibur, Thasos, Thira
Sequana: Fontes Sequanae
Seth: Kellis
Sobek: Bacchias, Dionysias, Karanis, Soknopaiou Nesos, Tebtunis, Theadelphia
Sybil: Cumae, Erythrae, Tibur, Thyatira
Taweret: Oxyrhynchus
Teiresias: Orchomenos
Tethys: Tuscany
Thoth: Pselchis
Trophonius: Lebadeia
Tutu: Shenhur
Zeus: Antioch, Apamea, Dodona, Labranda, Napata, Olympia, Panamara, Siwa, Skotussa

Index of Sites